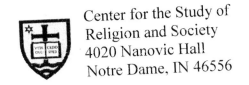

The Christian Story and the Christian School

The
CHRISTIAN
Story
and the
CHRISTIAN
School

John Bolt

 Christian Schools International
Grand Rapids, Michigan

CHRISTIAN SCHOOLS INTERNATIONAL
3350 East Paris Ave., S.E.
Grand Rapids, Michigan 49512

© 1993 by CHRISTIAN SCHOOLS INTERNATIONAL
Printed in the United States of America
All rights reserved

ISBN 0-87463-142-4

To those many visionary pioneers
—parents, teachers, and students—
who believed that the Christian story
also had to be told in school.

The Christian Story and the
christian School

Contents

Preface

This volume joins a growing list of books about Christian education today. My reasons for adding to this list are fourfold. I write from within a decidedly Reformed theological and confessional tradition, a tradition that has in the past century in North America enjoyed a successful and even impressive track record in Christian education from the elementary to the college and university level. Yet the context within which education takes place today is quite different from that of a hundred, fifty, or even twenty-five years ago. Those of us who are involved in Christian education and those who support it need to reflect on this changed context if the education we offer is to be relevant, true to the vision that gave rise to Christian schools, and faithful to our Lord. Furthermore, in this changed cultural and social context significant questions are also being raised by the supporting constituency of Christian education. Some people even question the very enterprise itself. An apology in the classic sense of the word is called for. Believing strongly as I do that Christian education is needed now more than ever, I have written this book as a defense of the project of separate and distinct Christian schools. Because such a defense must be particular to its own time and because it is essential for Christian educators and supporters to understand the context of Christian education today, the first half of this volume is devoted to exploring the cultural and social forces of our age in terms of their impact on education.

In the second place, I believe that it is necessary to address the matter of Reformed identity. Because there has been a growth explosion in Christian schools in recent years, it is essential to reflect on what is distinctive about Reformed Christian education. Not all visions of Christian education are the same. A Reformed vision differs from a Roman Catholic or fundamentalist one. It is not necessary or particularly helpful to become defensive or polemical about this, but it is important to be honest about the kind of education offered by schools in the Reformed tradition. Parents ought not to have mistaken expectations, and staffs cannot teach or administer in situations where there are uncertain or dramatically conflicting goals. If parents expect the school to shelter their children by isolating them from contemporary culture while teachers see their mission as equipping students to confront and engage that same culture, we have a guaranteed recipe for disaster.

My third reason for writing arises out of personal conviction about and professional scholarly interest in the notion of narrative. What is distinctive about this account of Christian education is that it is built on the foundation of a narrative understanding of the Christian faith and provides a narrative interpretation of Christian education. As I indicate in Chapter 5, narrative is a popular topic today. There is a resurgence of interest in story particularly in the fields of education, developmental psychology, and moral philosophy. It would be easy to dismiss this phenomenon as simply the latest in a long series of educational fads that have bedeviled North American education in the twentieth century, but this time I am convinced that something significant—and even promising—is afoot.

My final reason for writing arises from concerns about the current crisis in North American education, a crisis that reflects broader uncertainties about Western civilization itself. Faced with a growing diversity of populations and religious-cultural visions, North America is becoming increasingly pluralistic. Accompanying this pluralism is a growing hostility toward the legacy of Western civilization informed and shaped by Christianity. Whereas the public school system of education was originally designed to enfold and incorporate immigrants into the American melting pot, multicultural education today rejects the melting pot notion in favor of a pluralistic mosaic. On the face of it, pluralism promises a more just vision of society. In practice, however, multiculturalism tends to be critical of and hostile to the Christian religion and to the Christian character of Western civilization. However, the structures of Western religious, political, cultural, and economic freedom have been shaped by Christianity and are in some sense dependent upon it, so the suppression of the Christian story may ultimately jeopardize the possibility of pluralism itself. Thus, Christian schools where the Christian story is told and the Christian tradition is celebrated serve a public, national, social good. The Christian school is not just for the Christian community. Throughout this volume I have tried to keep the public role of the Christian school before the reader.

The customary practice of authors to acknowledge their indebtedness to others is more than a polite convention. Although writing is sometimes a lonely task, no writer is able to complete a manuscript in total isolation. We writers run up large personal as well as intellectual debts. I am particularly aware of that with the completion of this book since work on it was dramatically—and, thankfully, temporarily—interrupted in May 1992 when I suffered a stroke. Finishing this manuscript has had and will continue to have an additional spiritual significance for me. I am profoundly grateful to God for my spared life and recovery. I am also thankful for well-equipped hospitals, sophisticated medical technology and tests, and competent, caring medical professionals and therapists. The loving support of my family, especially my wife, Ruth, and the prayers and encouragement of many Christian brothers and sisters across North America sustained me in need and gave me hope. My gratitude for life itself and its numerous personal and communal joys cannot be adequately expressed in these few words, but at the very least these few words must be said.

Providentially, I was scheduled for a sabbatical leave from my teaching obligations at Calvin Theological Seminary in the winter and spring quarters of the 1992-93 school year, a leave that made it possible to finish this book. Herewith are my sincere thanks to the Board of Trustees of Calvin Seminary for the sabbatical, to the seminary administration for its active support of faculty scholarship and writing, and to my colleagues in the Theological Division for constructive critical feedback on parts of the manuscript. I am truly grateful for the outstanding administrative and collegial support that Calvin Seminary provides.

I am delighted that this volume is being published by Christian Schools International. During the last decade I have been involved in several CSI projects, and I continue to be impressed with the quality of its visionary leadership in Christian school education. Sheri Haan, CSI's executive director, has been unfailingly supportive and encouraging, for which I am truly grateful.

Finally, I am keenly aware that my love for and commitment to Christian education has been nurtured by dedicated parents, stimulating teachers in my own Christian education, and supportive colleagues in institutions I have been privileged to serve as a teacher. Having been an active participant in two pioneering ventures in Christian education—as a second-grade student when the one-room, one-teacher Ladner (Delta), British Columbia, Christian school was opened in 1954 and as a charter faculty member of Redeemer College in Hamilton, Ontario, in 1982—I am awed by the numerous visionary pioneers who courageously ventured forth in faith, often in the face of ridicule and opposition. It is to them that this book is appreciatively and gratefully dedicated.

Critical Questions About Contemporary Education

Introduction

This book is about North American Christian school education. More specifically it is a reconsideration of the foundations on which Christian schools are built. It will suggest a direct answer to the question, Why should we have Christian schools and for what purpose? This first chapter, however, will focus attention on contemporary public school education. This is both necessary and risky.

It is necessary because Christian education does not operate in a vacuum. Parents, teachers, administrators, and board members are directly influenced by what happens in public school education. Deep-seated concerns about public schools have sometimes served as negative reasons for building and supporting Christian schools. In such instances Christian education tends to function in a predominantly reactionary mode. On the other hand, new trends and directions in educational psychology, teaching methods, and curricula often find their way, for good or for ill, into Christian schools only a step or two behind such changes in public education. In the former instance, Christian schools become preoccupied with being different from public schools; in the latter, they fear being left behind the cutting edge. In a recent article exploring the distinctive character of schools in the Reformed tradition and affiliated with Christian Schools International, Steven Vryhof traces a movement from the former to the latter mode: "Historically, Reformed Christian schools have tended to isolate and protect. . . . To maintain doctrinal and ethnic purity, they segregated Dutch immigrant children from the rest of society." However, as the Dutch Reformed community became Americanized, "[e]ducationally, an oh-if-we-could-only-be-like-the-public-schools mindset developed."[1] When these two attitudes, both present still today, clash in a particular Christian school community, serious conflict often arises. All who are involved in Christian education need, therefore, to be aware of what is happening in public schools. Christian schools are affected by developments, both negative and positive, in public school education.

It will be argued in this volume that the availability of alternative Christian education in North America is essential to the future of public education itself. In fact, the very idea of a monopolistic system of government education is under question today. The crisis in public education, results to a large degree from assumptions that are no longer warranted. To see how this has come about, we need to examine the present situation in public education.

Although it is necessary for us to reflect on the current state of public education, such reflection poses a significant risk. In recent years the number of independent Christian schools has grown dramatically as evangelical Christians have become increasingly dissatisfied with public school education. While this dissatisfaction includes concerns about a decline in academic standards, the chief reason for flight is the changed moral dimension of public schools. Among other things, the exclusion of prayer and Scripture, the deliberately valueless approach to sex education, and a general orientation that is aggressively secular and humanistic, have led many Christian parents to choose Christian schools or even home schooling for their children. Such profound dissatisfaction is viewed by some as a great opportunity for Christian schools to grow, but it also entails risks.

In the first place, a negative attitude toward public education is not a sufficient or good foundation for building solid Christian schools. When Christian education is born out of reaction and cultivated in fear, it will likely become isolationistic and indifferent to the needs of the broader world. It loses all sense of mission. It is even possible that other negative and quite unchristian motives such as racism, classism, and anti-intellectualism will then play a role in encouraging parents to establish separate schools. When the primary reason for Christian education is, to use the title of Susan Rose's book on evangelical schooling in America, to keep children out of the hands of Satan,[2] it is difficult to equip children positively for a life of joyful discipleship in God's world. A climate of fear and separatism overwhelms.

Second, if the failure of the public school is the primary rationale for establishing Christian schools, Christian parents and Christian school officials have a vested interest in the failings of the public school. Real problems in public school education may even be exaggerated or distorted to confirm the validity of opting out. Global judgments about all public schools are made, which fail to discriminate among quite diverse schools. The relationship between Christian schools and public schools is then seen as a competitive game. The Christian school thrives when, and perhaps only when, the public school fails.

It cannot be stated too strongly that this is a profoundly

unchristian posture. Christians, if they are to reflect the Lord's love for the world, must be concerned about the health of public education. Christians are called to love their neighbor and to pray for the welfare of the city in which they reside (Jeremiah 29:7). Christian love does not delight in evil, and Christians cannot be indifferent to the well-being of their society and its public institutions. Good public schools are essential to the common good. Supporting Christian education does not imply studied indifference or open hostility to public education.

A Crisis?

Today the word *crisis* appears with monotonous regularity in tandem with *education*. A spate of books and articles along with countless speeches describe the crises in public education: a crisis of declining academic standards, a literacy crisis, a cultural literacy crisis, a crisis in behavior and discipline, a moral value crisis, a racial crisis, a funding crisis, and a teacher crisis. On each of these points, it is not hard to find substantiating horror stories.[3] But it should be noted that, as in the story of the boy who cried wolf, overuse of the word *crisis* is counterproductive. Three important observations concerning the current crisis will help us keep a balanced perspective.

First, education is the predominant cultural institution in our society. If it is perceived to be in crisis, it is likely that culture as a whole is being questioned critically. If there is confusion about the purpose of education, it is likely that this confusion reflects society's uncertainty about its values and goals. (Since many astute observers have concluded that our culture is indeed in such a crisis, we shall devote the next chapter to an examination of that broader issue.) The crisis in education is primarily, and perhaps with reason, a crisis in confidence. As educator Daniel E. Griffiths observes, "The crisis in American education is, first, the same crisis faced by all American institutions—a lack of confidence on the part of the public."[4]

Second, some historical distance is needed to provide a balanced assessment of the current crisis. This can be neatly illustrated by the following citation from an article on education addressed to teachers:

> By this late date it must be obvious to everyone engaged in teaching that a strong groundswell is running against us. Entire issues of popular magazines have been devoted to critical examinations of public education, each year more books are published which attack educational practices, and in meetings of boards of education more and more voices are being raised demanding changes in the schools.

This telling observation first appeared in 1952. The author reflected on its significance in an essay written in 1978.

> Although this might well be the lead for an article published in 1978, actually it is the opening paragraph of my "Open Letter to Teachers," in the July 1952 issue of *Harper's*. Then, as now, there were charges that the quality of education had deteriorated, that discipline was being neglected, that children were not learning to read, and that there were too many "frills" in the schools. Then, as now, the proposed remedy was a return to "basic education." And then, as now, the criticism could not wisely be ignored by educators, because the schools had some serious defects.[5]

When a paragraph with such specificity, originally published in 1952, sounds so contemporary in 1978, 1985, and 1993, it is clear that if there is a crisis in education today, it is a "continuing crisis."[6] At the very least, it is a recurring crisis. This suggests an appropriate caveat against excessive alarm about the present and also supplies some hope that lessons can be learned from the past. In "School Criticism in the 1950s and 1970s," Paul Woodring says:

> Since it now seems clear that criticism of the schools comes
> in waves and that the wave of the late seventies closely
> resembles that of the early fifties, we ought to be able to learn
> something from the past. Unfortunately, most of the critics
> seem unaware of the history of educational criticism, while
> the current defenders of the schools seem reluctant to learn
> from the past.[7]

A final caution on the other side. It may be true that as
Columbia University education professor Diane Ravitch
points out, "from the early nineteenth century on, it has
been commonplace to find a fairly consistent recitation of
complaints about the low state of learning, the poor training of teachers, the insufficient funding of education, the
inadequacies of school buildings and the apathy of the
public."[8] The "historic gap between aspiration and reality"
and the resultant dissatisfaction may be a permanent feature of the American educational landscape. While this
cautions us against excessive alarm about the schools, the
other danger is that complacency about real problems may
set in and any significant differences between past and present educational problems may be overlooked. According
to Ravitch there are fundamental differences between the
past and the present that must not be ignored in the midst
of many recurring problems in education. The key difference, in her judgment, is that "many present complaints
are reactions to hard-won reforms of the past." Her observations on this point are worth citing at some length:

> One important difference [in today's crisis] is that so much of
> the past agenda of educational reformers has been largely ful-
> filled. In one sense, the educational enterprise is the victim of
> its own successes, since new problems have arisen from the
> long-sought solutions to earlier problems. Idealistic reform-
> ers, eager to improve the schools and to extend their promise

to all children, sought the appropriate level of change. If only teachers had college degrees and pedagogical training; if only teachers would band together to form a powerful teachers' union; if only there were federal aid to schools; if only all children were admitted to school regardless of race or national origin; if only all students of high ability were admitted to college; if only colleges could accommodate everyone who wanted to attend; if only students had more choices and fewer requirements in their course work; if only schools were open to educational experimentations; if only there were a federal department of education. . . . The "if only" list could be extended, but the point should be clear by now. All these "if onlies" have been put into effect, some entirely and others at least partially, and rarely have the results been equal to the hopes invested.

Ravitch concludes:

Paradoxically, the achievements of the recent past seem to have exhausted the usually ready stock of prescriptions for school reform and to have raised once again the most basic questions of educational purpose.[9]

If this analysis is correct, part of the current crisis in education arises from the implementation of previously advocated reforms. Perhaps all the options for educational reform have been exhausted because they have been tried and found wanting. Perhaps expectations for what reform could accomplish were unrealistic and destined to disappoint. Perhaps contradictory reform proposals have made the situation worse. What about reform in American education? Is reform itself a culprit? What did it attempt and achieve? Is there hope for schools today?

Educational Reform

Talk about crisis or crises and calls for educational reform have dominated American public discussion for the last half-century.[10] In Diane Ravitch's words, "since [the 1930s],

American schools have lurched from crisis to crisis, and their internal confusions and aimlessness remain intact."[11] The field of education has been a battleground for competing educational philosophies broadly described as "progressive" and "traditional." A pendular swing between these two opposing approaches to educational philosophy and policy can be observed.

> From the mid-1940s until the mid-1950s, the "good school" followed progressive practices; from the mid-1950s until the mid-1960s, the "good school" emphasized the study of science, mathematics, and foreign languages and insisted on high academic standards; from the mid-1960s until the mid 1970s, the "good school" installed open classrooms, eliminated course requirements, and experimented with minicourses and electives; since the mid-1970s, the "good school" has been eliminating frivolous courses, reinstating curriculum requirements, and restoring academic standards.[12]

The debate about education in the last half-century is extensive and complex. Reducing this complexity to a couple of catch-all terms—"traditional" and "progressive"—is of course an oversimplification akin to the common practice of labeling political convictions as either "liberal" or "conservative." Yet, as in the political arena, such a broad characterization of key differences in educational policy is not without some value. A traditionalist approach focuses on subject content and mastery of basic knowledge and skills and insists on clearly defined and rigorous standards of excellence. Progressivism is primarily concerned with active, experientially based learning, creativity, originality, critical thinking, and cooperative learning for "the whole child." Much of the current debate oscillates between these two general poles.

The progressive "life adjustment education" of the late 1940s and early 1950s, with its emphasis on student needs, on practical, vocational, and how-to courses, along with "socio-personal adjustment" (health and guidance), went out of favor for two reasons. Not only did hostile traditional critics fault it for debasing academic standards, but the Sputnik crisis of 1957 in particular gave rise to a high level of public indignation about the failure of American schools to train students for world-class performance in math, science, and engineering. Insisting upon American leadership in these areas, the public demanded excellence and academic rigor. Undoubtedly the political climate of the Cold War played a significant role here, as did the public image of John F. Kennedy's presidency. The youthful, vigorous "best and the brightest" who surrounded Kennedy served as models for the promise of educational excellence.

By the mid-1960s, however, much of the hope and optimism disappeared. Increasingly complaints were raised about the competitiveness and the joylessness of American schools.[13] Commentators such as John Holt, Paul Goodman, A. S. Neil, Ivan Illich, and Charles Silberman criticized American schools for their preoccupation with standards, rules, efficiency, order, and control. Countercultural turmoil on university campuses, protest against the establishment, and middle-class values of success and achievement dominated public attention. The civil rights struggle, the escalating war in Vietnam, a growing ecological awareness, and the sexual revolution all contributed to the cultural uncertainty and unrest of the late 1960s and early 1970s. Concerns about peace and justice along with greater participation in the political process directly affected education. The school was seen by many as an instrument to achieve broader social reform. At the very best, the school itself could become a therapeutic community. The proposed reform: open or informal education. Again, Diane Ravitch's summary is clear and to the point:

The informal approach was typified by individualized learning activities, rather than group instruction; by emphasis on play, experience, and concrete activities, rather than reading and listening; by an informal relationship between the teacher and the student; by student participation in selecting the day's activities; and by informal arrangement of classroom time, space, and materials to encourage student choice. Behind such practices was the belief that children develop and learn at different rates; that the best way to learn is through activity and experience, motivated by interest; and that children are by nature eager to learn. Some advocates went so far as to insist that the child had to be free to decide what to learn, when to learn, and how to learn, with the goal being not to "educate" the child in the traditional sense of filling him up with knowledge, but to free him from his dependence on teachers, schools, and books.

The open education philosophy answered perfectly the need for a set of educational values to fit the countercultural mood of the late 1960s; it stimulated participatory democracy; it justified the equal sharing of power between the authority figure (the teacher) and the students; it made a positive virtue of nonassertive leadership; and it implied that children should study only what they wanted. At the high school level, this philosophy led to dropping of requirements, adoption of minicourses, creation of schools-without-walls, and alternative schools.

Once again, however, the results of these reforms have been judged by many to be less than satisfactory. In particular, public concerns about educational mediocrity have focused on such markers of eroding academic achievement as declining SAT scores. Fears are expressed about America's ability to complete in the international arena of commerce if the skills of American workers are inferior to those of Europeans and Asians. There are, once again, cries for "a return to basics." The wheel has thus come full circle again. Says Ravitch, "In recent decades, American educational policy has been pulled from extreme to extreme every ten years or so, in response to charges in the social and political climate."[14] This brings us to the current crisis. Exactly where are we right now in "the great school debate"?[15]

Symptoms and Solutions

Among the waves of proposed reform lapping the shores of education in the 1990s, perhaps the largest one is labeled "choice." The diagnosis of what ails public education focuses here on the stagnation and unresponsiveness of the system because it enjoys the luxury of being a self-protecting monopoly. The real problem with public education, it is suggested, is an institutional one. Political control and a bloated bureaucracy dedicated to its own self-perpetuation are the reasons why public education is failing to meet the needs of the present.

The very idea of public education, common schools financed and controlled by government, is now being called into question. In a recent and much-discussed publication of the Brookings Institution,[16] authors John Chubb and Terry Moe "argue that government has not solved the education problem because government is the problem. They contend that the political institutions that govern America's schools function naturally and routinely, despite everyone's best intentions, to burden the schools with excessive bureaucracy, to inhibit effective organization, and to stifle student achievement."[17] Chubb and Moe contend that such basic questioning of institutional issues has thus far not taken place in discussions about educational reform because it is blocked by vested interests in the present system. "[T]eacher's unions and myriad associations of principals, school boards, superintendents, administrators, and professionals—not to mention education schools, book publishers, testing services, and many other beneficiaries of the institutional status quo. . . are opposed to institutional change, or at least any change that is truly fundamental."[18] The authors indicate their mild surprise at the relatively light, concerted opposition to the educational establishment. "Despite all the grumbling, no powerful political groups with a stake in public education—business groups, civil rights groups, civic groups, religious groups—have dedicated themselves to reforming the institutions of educational governance."[19] Bruce MacLaury claims that "The nation's education problem, then, is an institutional problem. To overcome it, the authors recommend a new system of public education based on fundamentally new institutions. They propose a shift away from a system of schools controlled directly by government—through politics and bureaucracy—to a system of indirect control that relies on markets and choice."[20]

Apparently this diagnosis and prescription had the endorsement of President George Bush and his Secretary of Education, Lamar Alexander. Bearing a strong resemblance to the 1988 Education Reform Act of former British Prime Minister Margaret Thatcher[21] and in keeping with the 1980s push toward government deregulation in numerous sectors of society, the theory is that parental choice will force schools to improve. In President Bush's words: "It's time parents were free to choose the schools that their children attend. This approach will create the competitive climate that stimulates excellence in our private and parochial schools as well."[22]

A wide variety of specific proposals can be included under the broad umbrella of school choice. The most elementary of these is simply permitting parents to opt out of sending their children to neighborhood schools and allowing children to attend other schools in the same district or even outside their own district. Such open enrollment gives parents the right to walk away from bad schools and thus provides an incentive to such schools to upgrade or go out of business. Taking the choice option a step further would be some version of a voucher plan, which would permit parents to send their children to private or parochial schools as well. One of the most interesting experiments involving school choice is presently underway in Milwaukee, Wisconsin, where low-income, inner-city parents are offered $2,500 vouchers to enroll their children in private schools. Perhaps the ultimate model of combining choice with market mechanisms is the attempt to operate schools themselves as for-profit business enterprises. Some such experiments, funded by large corporations, are already underway.[23]

School choice had enthusiastic backers in the Bush White House and in the federal Department of Education during his administration, but critics were also numerous and vocal. Any school choice plan that would include religiously based private schools would face the overwhelming legal hurdle of the U.S. Constitution First Amendment's stricture against "establishment of religion."[24] Many opponents are especially fearful that open enrollment and voucher plans will close off opportunities especially for blacks and Hispanics by turning back the progress in desegregating schools. They predict that parental choice will further separate children along racial and class lines. Proponents, of course, disagree, arguing that school choice truly empowers the poor and disadvantaged, giving them options that are presently available only to the well-to-do. Clearly the debate about school choice will continue for some time.

How does this issue affect Christian education? At first glance, the push toward genuine school choice is one that proponents of Christian education would applaud. After all, the very *raison d'être* of Christian education is the choice for an alternative, a positive choice for an education that is consistent with the Christian commitment of the home. Furthermore, school choice, it can be argued, is in keeping with one of the fundamentals of a Christian socio-political philosophy, namely, that education is first of all a parental matter rather than a state matter. Already in the 1920s and 1930s, Gresham Machen and other Christian leaders warned against what they considered to be the growing intrusion of government, particularly the federal government, into the "sphere" of the family's responsibility for education.[25] A compulsory, monopolistic government system of secular education is thus seen as a violation of basic Christian liberty. A similar concern about "who owns the children"[26] fuels much of the movement toward separate, independent Christian schools as well as the growth in home schooling. Quite rightly, parents are deeply committed to maintaining a high degree of control in the content of their children's education and thus make their own difficult and often costly choices. And finally, school choice is at the heart of a sophisticated Christian social-philosophical argument recently made by some Reformed scholars for greater structural and confessional pluralism in public education.[27] Thus, the movement toward greater school choice appears to be a step in the right direction as far as many supporters of Christian education are concerned.

Nonetheless, there are some aspects of the present debate that should be disquieting for Christians who support alternative education. Is the model of a marketplace where "schools compete for support and clients are free to go where they want"[28] really an appropriate model for education? Should the school be run as a for-profit business? And is the school's primary task one of equipping today's students with marketable skills for the demands of a high-tech, intensely competitive global economy? Should the needs of the changing world economy dictate the goals of contemporary education? Is an emphasis on excellence really a semantic disguise for what some would call a "conservative vision of a school as a small white-collar factory"?[29]

Since this present debate was to a large extent fueled and shaped by the 1983 report of the National Commission on Excellence in Education entitled "A Nation at Risk," it is worth recalling its basic concern. The report begins as follows:

> Our Nation is at risk. Our once unchallenged preeminence in commerce, industry, science, and technological innovation is being overtaken by competitors throughout the world. This report is concerned with only one of the many causes and dimensions of the problem, but it is the one that undergirds American prosperity, security and civility. We report to the American people that while we can take justifiable pride in what our schools and colleges have historically accomplished and contributed to the United States and the well-being of its people, the educational foundations of our society are presently being eroded by a rising tide of mediocrity that threatens our very future as a Nation and a people. What was unimaginable a generation ago has begun to occur—others are matching and surpassing our educational attainments.
>
> If an unfriendly foreign power had attempted to impose on America the mediocre educational performance that exists today, we might well have viewed it as an act of war. As it stands, we have allowed this to happen to ourselves. We have even squandered the gains in student achievement made in the wake of the Sputnik challenge. Moreover, we have dismantled essential support systems which helped make those gains possible. We have, in effect, been committing an act of unthinking, unilateral education disarmament.[30]

America's loss of competitive economic and technological advantage thus becomes the focal point of concern about education in general and educational excellence in particular. It is perhaps worth noting that a report commissioned by the Ontario, Canada, Ministry of Education, and released to the public on February 15, 1988, sounds a similar note:

> While the education system has not changed all that dramatically in recent years, what has changed is the degree to which we must rely on it for our very survival as an economically competitive society.
>
> Education has long been recognized as an important contributor to economic growth, of course—but now it has become the paramount ingredient for competitive success in the world economy.[31]

Of course, the importance of a relevant education that produces versatile and teachable workers in a high-tech world is not to be scorned altogether. Christian citizens of North America cannot be indifferent to the erosion of excellence and loss of entrepreneurial creativity that is alleged to be taking place. Prosperity is a social good, not merely a personal good. Furthermore, developing such skills is especially important for economically disadvantaged people. It is a luxury of privileged and well-to-do people to disparage marketable skills. And, finally, it is appropriate to consider proposals for excellence, which usually include re-introducing a core curriculum with heavy emphasis on English, history, math and science and eliminating most electives; raising academic standards; insisting on discipline and order; eliminating streaming and returning to a one-track curriculum; raising standards for teaching along with incentives for upgrading; and shifting away from process to content and outcome. The debate is valuable in raising important questions.

Yet, is marketability of skills the most important goal of education? Is there nothing to be learned from the countercultural protest of the 1960s and 1970s? It is instructive to listen once again to a typical countercultural blast from Christian educator Arnold De Graaf:

> In the face of social upheaval and massive criticism, public education has responded with a reaffirmation of its trust in science, technology, and efficiency. Young people are indoctrinated in the belief that the good life consists of the production and consumption of more and more material goods, and that the road to greater economic progress is charted by science and technology in the service of business and industry. The schools support a hedonistic, materialistic way of life that fosters injustice, global poverty, inequality and a deep sense of alienation.[32]

It is possible to state this point in somewhat more temperate terms and present an alternative vision that focuses on wisdom as the goal for Christian education. John Van Dyk writes that

> Wisdom is not merely collecting and amassing theoretical or factual knowledge; nor is it simply gaining technical skills. Wisdom is knowledge and understanding deepened into spiritual insight and expressed in loving servcie (James 3:13). Wisdom originates in the fear of the Lord and is enhanced by faith, hope, love, knowledge, spiritual insight, and active discipleship. . . .
>
> Thus a Christian school is a place where Christian educators refuse to be satisfied with providing only factual knowledge and marketable skills. Rather, teachers in a Christian school seek to transform all activities and studies into an expression of biblical wisdom, training the students to walk as disciples of Jesus Christ.[33]

Much of the current emphasis on excellence and the marketplace, therefore, falls short of Christian expectation for educational reform. The working assumption of much current thinking on education seems to be something like this: When market pressures make our schools competitive and efficient, standards will improve, SAT scores will rebound, our graduates will be literate and employable, American supremacy in the international economic order will return, and life—particularly the pursuit of happiness, wealth and success—can go on as usual. What's really wrong with the system is that it isn't working at peak levels of maximum efficiency. There is little acknowledgment in this diagnosis that beyond the crisis of efficiency and excellence there may be a crisis of the soul. Christians should realize that we need to dig deeper to matters of the heart.

What's Really Wrong with Public Education?[34]

To the degree that the current debate about education is fixated on economic needs, Christians must judge that both the analysis and prescription are not radical enough. They do not get to the root of the problem. On this issue Christians should find themselves aligned with some of the more radical critics of public education. They share with them dissatisfaction with the parameters of a discussion in which, as Stanley Oronowitz and Henry Giroux claim, "Schools become important only to the degree that they can provide the forms of knowledge, skills, and social practices necessary to produce the labor force for an increasingly complex, technological economy." Furthermore, suggestions for quick-fix reforms that are "strongly shaped by the technocratic and instrumental logic that informs this model of economic reason" and that include such "largely technical" solutions as "extending the school day, raising teachers salaries and enforcing school discipline" are seen to be as inadequate as the "procedural demands for more stringent modes of competency testing and evaluation."[35] According to Oronowitz and Giroux, the more basic issue is "a crisis in public philosophy." A public philosophy that is defined narrowly in terms of technical reason, economic needs, and consumer desires must be replaced, they say, by one that justifies "linking schools to a mission that promotes a civic consciousness, one that encourages the development of an active citizenry and public participation on the basis of moral and ethical principles, as opposed to forms of participation tied merely to economic self-efficiency and self-interest."[36]

These authors are calling for a renewed commitment to education that promotes civic community. Their conviction is that our true identity as free human beings is found in community with others and not in meeting individual economic needs or satisfying individual consumer tastes. The decision made in the summer of 1991 by the Maryland Board of Education requiring seventy-five hours of community service as a high school graduation requirement is in keeping with at least a version of this goal.[37]

From a Christian point of view, there is something salutary about such a shift of emphasis. As human beings we are not merely *homo economicus*. Christians affirm that our true humanity is not exhausted by our work, important and valuable as it is. Instead, we aspire to a life of service in community with our neighbors and in fellowship with God. But here we encounter a knotty problem for public education: sharply conflicting visions of the community values and practices that should be inculcated in students as well as radically opposing strategies by which such goals can be met.

This can readily be seen when we compare two diametrically opposed approaches to the question of preparation for community, which can be summarized under the umbrella terms "critical literacy" and "cultural literacy."[38] Advocates of critical literacy begin with the assumption that public schools as they exist right now play an integral role in maintaining an unjust and oppressive socio-political order. They argue that Western civilization in general and American civilization in particular are built on a foundation of exploitation and oppression. The dominant culture, which the public school is called to preserve and transmit, is the culture of the powerful victors; it opens no space for marginalized persons: blacks, other ethnic minorities, and women. In this scenario intellectuals should be adversaries of the dominant culture and teaching should be a socially and politically subversive activity. As a much-read book of the 1970s by Neil Postman and Charles Weingartner put it: "We believe that the schools must serve as the principal medium for developing in youth the attitudes and skills of social, political, and cultural criticism."[39] It seems odd initially to consider the goal of turning students into counter-cultural rebels as a strategy for creating community awareness, civic-mindedness, and a commitment to service. It is not odd, however, once the utopian character of the community ideals is recognized. In this view, socializing children for life in community does not mean socializing them to become useful citizens in the present society but rather helping them to become useful instruments of social criticism and social transformation until a time when a truly free, participatory democracy is achieved. The two key virtues of educated citizens are then "critical literacy" and "civic courage,"[40] the former a codeword for skills of protest and revolt and the latter for a willingness to protest and revolt. The orientation is open-ended and futuristic; the key ideals are empowerment, emancipation, and equality. The assumption is clear: the present order of things is so beset by unjust structures and arrangements (sexism, racism, class exploitation, and militarism, to name a few of the major ones) that society needs radical transformation and structural change. Furthermore, up to now public education has impeded transformation by serving as an instrument of social control over marginalized groups.[41] Rather than promoting social and economic mobility and improving life in society, public schools have impeded social progress for all but the narrowly privileged.

How must schools change to equip students to become agents of social transformation? One clear example of curricular change that springs from the radical vision is the attempts at peace education that proliferated in the 1980s.[42] In 1983 the National Education Association (NEA) published a teaching unit for junior high students entitled *Choices: A Unit on Conflict on Nuclear War.* Prepared by a political action group, the Union of Concerned Scientists, the unit is introduced by Harvard psychiatry professor John Mach:

> Young, and even very young, children are telling their parents and teachers that they are afraid of dying in a nuclear war. In the past we have been poorly informed and ill-equipped to respond to these fears and have offered little to young people outside of unconvincing reassurances. This history of silence and ignorance in too many American classrooms is now being overcome, as pioneering curricula on the subject of nuclear war are being introduced in high schools and junior high schools throughout the country.[43]

In a nutshell, the unit seeks to evoke terror of a nuclear holocaust through photographs and fear-inducing exercises, attributes the world nuclear arms buildup to American paranoia about what was formerly the Soviet Union ("whether our opponents are perceived as a friend, enemy, or stranger may produce very different resolutions to the conflict"), and attempts to create guilt by pointing out repeatedly that the United States invented the bomb and dropped it on Hiroshima and still spends money for bombs rather than helping economically disadvantaged people.

The message is clear: U.S. defense spending is irresponsible and exploitative, and the American establishment is paranoid. To reinforce such ideas, children are encouraged to change tug-of-war games into tug-of-peace games (becoming vulnerable and letting the other side win), to organize peace marches, to make buttons for peace, to draw portraits of "peacemakers" such as Joan Baez and Ghandi, and to sing peace songs.

Education for critical literacy has both severe critics as well as passionate defenders. Critics fear the psychological harm done by "terrorizing our children" but also profoundly disagree with the radicals' assessment of American society. While it is absurd to contend that the United States has perfect social and political institutions, the opponents of critical literacy contend that on balance the country is a force for good and its institutions protect a relatively free and open society. Furthermore, while acknowledging the need for critical assessment and self-correction in American society, these educators insist that the foundations of American liberal democracy remain valid for all citizens and need to be revived and restored if a free American society is to survive. In the words of Sidney Hook:

> In our pluralistic, multi-ethnic, uncoordinated society, no institutional changes of themselves will develop that bond of community we need to sustain our nation in times of crisis without a prolonged schooling in the history of our free society, its martyrology, and its national tradition. In the decades of mass immigration in the 19th and 20th centuries that bond was largely forged by the American public school. What I propose is that our schools, reinforced by our colleges and universities, do the same job today in a more intelligent, critical, and sophisticated way.[44]

Here we have a significantly different vision of American society and of the task of its schools. Here "cultural literacy"—preserving, transmitting, learning, and assimilating our traditions and gaining an appreciation for our institutions—is seen as essential to maintaining our free society. The assumption is that the story of the United States is large enough to embrace those who have been marginalized, that it is precisely the greatness of the American story that discrimination against any group of citizens is an affront to the story itself. There is, however, an American mainstream culture and for children and adults to thrive, they need to become literate in that culture. E. D. Hirsch, the foremost proponent of cultural literacy, insists that the concept is neither reactionary nor closed. He observes: "Conservatives who wish to preserve traditional values will find that these are necessarily inculcated by traditional education, which can in fact be subversive of the status quo."[45] A good example of this would be the powerful way in which civil rights leader Martin Luther King Jr. used scriptural imagery and appealed to historic American ideals to overcome the legacy of slavery and racism. Furthermore, Hirsch contends, cultural literacy is not "the property of any group or class."

> To assume that this wider culture is static is an error; in fact it is not. It's not a WASP culture; it doesn't belong to any group. It is essentially and constantly changing, and it is open. What is needed is recognition that the accurate metaphor or model for this wider literacy is not domination, but dialectic; each group participates and contributes, transforms and is transformed, as much as any other group. . . . The English language no longer belongs to any single group or nation. The same goes for any other area of the wider culture.[46]

It may be illuminating to suggest that an emphasis on cultural literacy is another way of saying that the school's task is to prepare students for citizenship in a specific com-

munity, to mold character, and to encourage virtues consonant with the historic values of that community. The
assumption is twofold: that education is needed to overcome and restrain the natural human inclination toward
barbarism and that the values of our civilization are basically good. Teachers are thus the custodians of our civilization, and students are its heirs. The school is a specialized
community where the larger community, the nation, preserves and passes on its cultural memory. The importance
of its task is significantly increased when the broader society is highly volatile and rapidly changing. As Neil Postman puts it:

> Our own culture is overdosing on change. . . . The plain fact is
> that too much change, too fast, for too long has the effect of
> making social institutions useless and individuals perpetually
> unfit to live amid the conditions of their own culture. . . .
> Without at least a reminiscence of continuity and tradition,
> without a place to stand from which to observe change, with-
> out a counterargument to the overwhelming theories of
> change, we can easily be swept away—in fact are being swept
> away. . . . [I]n a culture of high volatility and casual regard for
> its past such responsibility becomes the school's most essen-
> tial service. *The school stands as the only mass medium capable of
> putting forward the case for what is not happening in the culture.*[47]

From even this brief overview, it is apparent that there is
a fundamental and perhaps irreconcilable conflict between
advocates of critical literacy and cultural literacy. In fact, it
is probably not too strong to say that North American society is currently involved in a significant cultural war, a
struggle over orthodoxy. The numerous and furious public
debates today—political correctness on university campuses
and in the news media; the content of the literary canon;
multiculturalism; claims by feminists, gay people, Native
peoples, and others that they are excluded from the domi-

nant culture—all signal that there is no longer a coherent, unified vision about American or Canadian society. There is lack of agreement about the past, the present, and the future. And if that is true, then a commitment to make public schools vehicles for inculcating community values inevitably leads to a cultural war between the two visions just considered. Here we come to what's really wrong with North American public education—it has lost its soul; there is no longer a coherent, consensual public philosophy available to guide it. As a consequence, education has become one of the most highly politicized institutions in North American life. In an increasingly politicized climate the prospects for improvement of education seem dim.

Culture Wars

The language of warfare may seem extreme to some readers. Yet that is precisely what University of Virginia sociology professor James Davison Hunter describes and documents in a brilliant analysis of American culture, entitled *Culture Wars: The Struggle to Define America*.[48] Hunter defines cultural conflict "very simply as political and social hostility rooted in different systems of moral understanding" (p. 42). It is "different moral visions" (p. 48) that are the source of conflict. "At stake is how we as Americans will order our lives together" (p. 34). The language of warfare, Hunter contends, is not too strong to describe what is happening. Even the protagonists in the conflict seem aware that it is indeed warfare:

> In all of this, the language of confrontation, battle, even war, then, is not merely a literary device but an apt tool to describe the way in which many issues contested in American public culture are being settled. It is no surprise that many of the contenders on all sides of the cultural divide use the very same language to understand their own involvement. The

National Organization for Women, for example, has a "War Room" in its national headquarters in Washington, D.C., a windowless room with charts, maps, a conference table, and a dozen or so telephones. Both sides of the new cultural divide could agree with the editor of *Publishers Weekly* who declared that the controversy over the arts and publishing was a "war"—"a war that must be won." So, too, activists on both sides of the cultural divide could agree with James Dobson of Focus on the Family, who announced, "We are in a civil war of values and the prize to the victor is the next generation—our children and grandchildren." Another activist observed that this "is a war of ideology, it's a war of ideas, it's a war about our way of life. And it has to be fought with the same intensity, I think, and dedication as you would fight a shooting war." (p. 64)

Who are the protagonists in this war? Hunter prefers to speak of conflicting tendencies or impulses rather than clearly articulated, coherent camps. "Though competing moral visions are at the heart of today's culture war, they do not always take form in coherent, clearly articulated, sharply differentiated world views. Rather, these moral visions take expression as *polarizing impulses* or *tendencies* in American culture" (p. 43). What are these two impulses? "To come right to the point, the cleavages at the heart of the contemporary culture war are created by what I would like to call the *impulse toward orthodoxy* and the *impulse toward progressivism*" (p. 43).

What Hunter has in mind here is not the specific doctrinal creeds of religious communities but what he calls *"formal properties* of a belief system or world view" (p. 44). "What is common to all three approaches to *orthodoxy* . . . is the *commitment on the part of adherents to an external, definable, and transcendent authority."* On the other hand, "within cultural progressivisms, by contrast, moral authority tends to be defined by the spirit of the modern age, a spirit of rationalism and subjectivism. Progressivist moral ideals tend, that is, to derive from and embody (though rarely exhaust) that spirit. From this standpoint, truth tends to be viewed as a process, as a reality that is ever unfolding. . . . In other words, what all *progressivist* worldviews share in common is *the tendency to resymbolize historic faiths according to the prevailing assumptions of contemporary life"* (pp. 44-45).

According to Hunter, these conflicting impulses affect the entire range of North American public life—family, education, law, the media, and of course politics. Hunter provides a fascinating sketch of specific conflicts in each area, but for our purposes we need only to note the battle in public education. The public schools play a significant role in the larger culture war. Persons on both sides of the cultural divide have placed the battle over public education at the center of the larger conflict. Hunter quotes an opponent of censorship, who says, "'This country is experiencing a religious crusade as fierce as any out of the Middle Ages. . . . Our children are being sacrificed because of the fanatical zeal of our fundamentalist brothers who claim to be hearing the voice of God. . . . In this religious war, spiced with overtones of race and class, the books are an accessible target'" (p. 201). From the opposite point of view, a spokesman for the National Association of Christian Educators claims that there is a great war waged in America—but not on the battlefield of conventional weapons. This battle is for the heart and mind and soul of every man, woman, and especially child in America. The combatants are secular humanism and Christianity.

I have called attention to this matter of cultural warfare for two reasons. On the one hand, similar impulses may be present in the communities that support Christian education. It is helpful to be aware of the cultural patterns and pressures that influence Christians in these areas. The Christian school movement, it seems to me, can ill afford its own version of cultural warfare. Equally important, however, is the need to be aware of the role that Christian schools play in the present culture war. If it is the case that education has become one of the most highly politicized institutions in North American life, the mere existence of alternative and distinctly Christian schools can affect the strategies of the combatants and can shape the outcome of the battle.

For many years the cultural legacy that fed the public school system included explicitly Christian themes. Thus a close correlation between the traditions and institutions of the U.S. and Canada and the Christian character of the two nations seemed obvious to many. The public schools were intended, albeit imperfectly in practice, to be functionally Christian—Protestant, specifically—in their value systems. Roman Catholics and Jews were encouraged to set up their own separate, parochial schools.[49] The legitimacy of a monopolistic, Protestant Christian public school system is questionable from a judicial point of view, and the orthodoxy of the Protestantism presented in the public schools was of a dubious quality.[50] But the situation has changed dramatically in recent years. Thanks to intensive lobbying by ardent civil libertarians advocating a radical church-state separation, the Christian religion is now the marginalized point of view in North American public education. The exclusion of devotional time, Scripture reading, and prayer is symptomatic, but more serious is the deliberate rewriting of textbooks to exclude traditional Christian values and even to eliminate direct references to the role of the Christian religion in public life.[51] Having carefully examined American social studies and literature texts, Paul Vitz notes how religion is ignored or trivialized:

In sum, then it seems that it is considered acceptable to mention America's less "typical" religions in textbooks, but mainstream Protestantism is for all practical purposes considered taboo. The effect of this is a denial of the fact that religion is really an important part of American life. Sometimes the censorship becomes especially offensive. One book, for example, devoted thirty pages to a discussion of the Pilgrims, noting that they celebrated thanksgiving because they "wanted to give thanks for all they had"—and yet it nowhere specifies that it was God that they were offering their thanks to. This sort of thing occurred again and again in the sample texts. It is permissible to refer to the Pueblo Indians praying to mother Earth, but Pilgrims can't be described as praying to God.[52]

Vitz concludes that the textbooks he sampled "clearly represented a systematic denial of the history, heritage, beliefs, and values of a very large segment of the American people."[53]

A clear, contemporary example of this can be seen in the "Hirsch project" to spell out the minimum shared knowledge that is needed to function in American society. After producing a large *Dictionary of Cultural Literacy*,[54] which included a significant section on Bible knowledge, E. D. Hirsch began a project that would attempt to set forth minimal cultural literacy for each elementary grade. What is striking about the first volume, *What Your 1st Grader Needs to Know,* is that it omits Bible stories. The teacher consultants of the Florida schools where the program was tested "deemed them unduly sectarian."[55]

The conflict between critical literacy and cultural literacy, as part of a larger cultural war, does not leave the arena of Christian education untouched. Leaders and influential people in Christian education may even find themselves sympathizing, to a greater or lesser degree, with one position or the other. There have been conflicts in some Christian school communities between teachers who are critical of American and Canadian institutions and parents who have confidence in those institutions. The Christian school also runs the risk of becoming politicized. We shall consider this, along with similar problems, in Chapter Three, "Christian Threats to Christian Education." The point in raising it here is simply to reinforce the fact that Christian education is not immune to the issues, debates, and conflicts in public education.

Conclusion

What implications can we draw for Christian school education? While the rest of this volume will explore many of these issues, for now, two specific matters come to mind. The first is that the concept of school choice must be broadened to include a pluralism of religious/philosophical viewpoints. School choice simply as a market mechanism, using consumer preferences to create more efficient education factories that produce skilled workers for our high-tech industrial machine, is an inadequate model. Creating a genuinely pluralistic system of public education, which is accessible to all and does not at the same time result in horrendous social fragmentation, will require much hard work and goodwill. Yet, unless this situation is faced head-on, the politicizing of the schools will increase along with their decline. Creative strategies for public education that foster basic cultural literacy—what it means to be an American or Canadian citizen—while also respecting the religious and philosophic individual differences of parents and communities must be developed if free and united national societies are to survive. Second, an observation and tentative conclusion: If the trend toward de-Christianizing the North American public square continues, if the secularizing drift continues to denude public conversation of a Christian presence and gives little or no room to sanctioned Christian values, then the role of Christian schools as custodians of the Christian heritage becomes even more significant. The mere existence of such schools is a necessary witness in an increasingly secular and pagan culture and society. What Christopher Dawson says about Christian higher education is also relevant to Christian elementary and high schools:

> So long as the Christian tradition of higher education still exists, the victory of secularism in a modern technological society is not complete. There is still a voice to bear witness to the existence of the forgotten world of spiritual reality in which man has his true being.[56]

Even beyond mere existence, it is also true that Christian schools, by preserving and transmitting the past wisdom of the Christian tradition, are performing an essential public task for our civilization. As long as Western civilization was living off the interest of its acquired Judeo-Christian moral capital, this preserving and transmitting function may have seemed less important than transforming the present culture. However, because the present culture is becoming increasingly anti-Christian, there is increasingly less to transform and the imperative to preserve the wisdom of the Christian past increases. Perhaps our situation today is more like that faced by medieval monks—in a darkening age, we and our schools must keep the lamp of Christian wisdom burning. To be sure that our Christian schools are doing what our Lord asks of us in our situation, we need to be aware of our context. Before we continue, therefore, we need to ask a penetrating question about our society and its culture. What kind of a world do we live in?

2

Critical Questions
About Our Culture

Introduction

In the previous chapter we concluded that the real problem of North American public education is that it has lost its soul. No consistent and coherent vision guides the enterprise as a whole. Instead, education has become one of the primary battlefields for cultural warfare as different groups seek to have their vision of the good life become the dominant one for education. In particular the battle is joined between advocates for critical literacy and cultural literacy, the former seeking radical transformation of North American institutions that are seen as oppressive, especially to the marginalized, the latter prizing what is considered to be the heritage of freedom and opportunity and desiring to incorporate all groups into the North American cultural and social mainstream. When one adds into this mix the concerns of business and industry for students learning marketable skills, the conflicting expectations for public education seem to create an unsolvable problem.

Our society lacks a coherent sense of purpose and task. The conflicts in educational philosophy are part of a broader cultural warfare and, as the Christian knows all too well, this conflict is serious because it is spiritual in nature. The struggle is really for the soul of North American civilization. Perhaps it is even true that Western civilization itself is losing its soul. But such grand thinking does not permit us to overlook what is at stake humanly: the souls of children and the souls of American and Canadian citizens. It is important, therefore, to examine North America's social and cultural situation more carefully. Exactly what kind of a world do we live in? What is the nature of the society and culture into which we send the graduates of our schools? For what and how are our schools preparing our children? And finally, if Christian schools are to be in some sense countercultural, what is the culture they must counter?

The task of analyzing and evaluating one's culture as a whole is a daunting task. We ourselves are so much a part of our own culture that developing a critical distance from it is very difficult. Missionary Lesslie Newbigin in reflecting on this problem cites a wonderful Chinese proverb: "If you want a definition of water, don't ask a fish."[1] In addition, an enormous range of learning across such fields as philosophy, history, sociology, politics, religion, literature, and art is required to be able to "read" a culture, to discern the spirit of the age. Personality factors, whether the critic is an optimist or pesimist, also play a significant role in reading the age. Apocalyptic visions of doom and decline compete with those of progress, growth, and future glory. Particularly since the publication, in 1918, of Oswald Spengler's extremely pessimistic *Decline of the West*, it has become fashionable in the twentieth century to engage in grand-scale, synoptic interpretations of what is wrong with Western civilization and where it is headed. Authors such as Alexander Solzhenitsyn have addressed significant warnings to the Western world[2] while others even speak of the suicide of the West.[3] Among perceptive observers there seems to be a growing consensus that Western civilization is dying. Symptoms of decay—religious, moral, legal, and artistic—are everywhere present. In fact, G. K. Chesterton suggests that the very language of decay is itself evidence of our problem: "Our fathers said that a nation had sinned and suffered, like a man; we say it has decayed, like a cheese."[4]

It is not my intention in this chapter to offer yet another independent global assessment. Rather, this chapter is more like a report that summarizes some key recent works that seem to shed light on our cultural situation. Leaning on the work of others, we shall examine some of the key characteristics of our contemporary world, including the following: modernism and postmodernism, individualism, relativism and pluralism, secularism, and paganism. In these seemingly diverse dimensions of our present cultural crisis there is an underlying common thread that anticipates the discussion in Chapter Five. I will argue in this chapter that loss of narrative unity—loss of a common story and a unified cultural memory—is the one consistent feature giving rise to individualism and secularism, while pluralism and paganism represent the rise of alternative narratives. Furthermore, this notion of common story is at the heart of recent criticism of modernism and the rise of postmodern thought.

Modernism and Postmodernism: From "No Story" to "All Stories"

The word *modern*, as in the expression "the modern age," is a loaded term. Popularly it has the positive emotional connotation of being up to date. Implicit is the conviction that the latest is the best, that chronological time represents progress. This popular usage is fully in harmony with a more philosophical use of the term also rooted in notions of progress. The modern era, in which science has been regarded as the way to all knowledge, has been judged to be superior to previous ages in which myth, superstition, and religion were the chief avenues to human understanding and guides to human conduct. The modern age is the age of human reason and human autonomy. Rational, autonomous humanity is the measure of all things.

It is helpful to consider briefly how this shift came about. During the Middle Ages, there was one Christian church, which taught the sinfulness of humanity and the need for revelation and divine grace. Human beings, it was believed, could not save themselves. They could not really know the truth about themselves and the meaning of the world apart from God's revealed word in Holy Scripture. Enlightenment came from the Holy Spirit; truth was to be found in God and in his Word. God was true; all men were liars. Furthermore, medieval thought was ultimately other-worldly. The remedy for the world's numerous ills, a dual destiny for the righteous and the unrighteous, was to be found in a world beyond the grave. In short, one could be certain about God, eternity, heaven, and hell; this world was the realm of uncertainty, change, and doubt.

This medieval viewpoint, which incidentally was fully shared by the Reformers, has been completely inverted in the modern era. God has become unknowable and thus the great question mark; autonomous, rational humanity is the locus of truth and certainty. This revolution in thought came about in part as a response to the seventeenth-century wars of religion. People asked if God's revelation in Scripture is the basis of human knowledge and certainty, why are Protestants and Catholics killing each other in the name of and for the sake of their version of the truth? Perhaps, it was suggested, the pretensions of religion are the problem. Is there not another way of getting knowledge and certainty that bypasses sectarian religious commitments? Is it not possible to find an order for life in community that transcends religious differences and that tolerates religious diversity? Can we not find a new foundation for certainty, for truth that is universal, that all human beings can accept, whatever their religion?

A solution to this quandary was suggested by the French mathematician-philosopher René Descartes (1596-1650), often considered the father of modern thought. Descartes sought mathematical-like certainty for thought itself and began by systematically doubting everything until he arrived at a foundational truth that could not be doubted. In his *Discourse on Method* he states his first rule:

> The first of these [rules] was to accept nothing as true which I did not clearly recognize to be so: that is to say, carefully to avoid precipitation and prejudice in judgments, and to accept in them nothing more than was presented to my mind so clearly and distinctly that I could have no occasion to doubt it.[5]

For Descartes then, certainty is to be found in the rational self. Systematic doubt finally removes everything except the one certain fact of Descartes' own personal existence. In his own words:

> I noticed that while I was trying to think everything false, it must needs be that I, who was thinking this, was something. And observing that this truth, *I am thinking, therefore I exist* [*Je pense, donc je suis*; Latin version; *cogito ergo sum*] was so solid and secure that the most extravagant suppositions of the skeptics could not overthrow it, I judged that I need not scruple to accept it as the first principle of [the] philosophy that I was seeking.[6]

Here is the truly Copernican revolution that begins typically modern thought. The human self is the starting point, the foundation for certainty, truth, and morality. Autonomous reason, not revelation, is the light upon modernity's path.

We need not explore all the interesting and important dimensions and consequences of this revolution, but for our interest in education we do need to briefly consider the political consequences. One of the fruits of the turn to the autonomous, rational self as the final judge of all truth was a new experiment in social, political life—liberal democracy. Prior to the modern era, rulers, governors, magistrates, and kings were considered in some sense servants of God, accountable to divine law. Their authority was religiously legitimated, and religious traditions were judged to be indispensable for maintaining public moral and social order. One feared God's servant, the king, because one ultimately feared God. Religious convictions were publicly expressed and deemed essential for public well-being. Liberal democracy, on the other hand, attempted to establish political order without religious sanction. The goal was to seek principles of justice and order on the basis of reason, universally available to all people, whatever their religious conviction.

The public square should therefore ideally be religiously naked or neutral. Religion was to be tolerated as a personal conviction, but in the public realm the language of conversation had to be restricted to universal, rational truth. Individuals have rights and consent to enter into a social contract with other individuals who also have rights, but no appeal may be made to moral order or truth that transcends the autonomous individual. Allan Bloom summarizes the liberal democratic experiment in this way:

> Human founders [of liberal democracy], looking only to universal principles of natural justice recognizable by all men through their unaided reason, established governments on

the basis of the consent of the governed without appeal to revelation and tradition.[7]

This separation of religion from reason can be restated in terms of the category of narrative. All human communities depend on shared stories if they are to function in an orderly way. The history of a people as told through key stories shapes a society's identity and character. Life together requires communication, and as E. D. Hirsh claims, "only by accumulating shared symbols, and the shared information that the symbols represent, can we learn to communicate effectively with one another in our national community."[8] But it is precisely this need for shared symbols and stories, for a common cultural memory, that liberalism rejects. Reason, which is universally the same, rather than particular stories and traditions (including, of course, religious stories and traditions), is the means by which communities are organized and run. Theologian Stanley Hauerwas sums this up nicely:

> Liberalism, in its many forms and versions, presupposes that society can be organized without any narrative that is commonly held to be true. As a result it tempts us to believe that freedom and rationality are independent of narrative—i.e. we are free to the extent that we have no story.[9]

Thus to the degree that our society and culture are modern, they are characterized by a deliberate effort to secularize, to remove the Christian story, tradition, and revealed moral order from public discourse. Religion has become something strictly private. This division, moreover, runs deeper than merely excluding the Christian religion as a legitimate conversation partner in public life. Our world in general creates a sharp division between our public and our private lives. Our public world is a universal one of facts, science, technology, bureaucracy, processes, and efficiency. Our private world is the particular world of values, opinions, beliefs, and religious convictions.

This split has had serious consequences for our society and culture. To begin with, as critics of technology such as French theologian Jacques Ellul and Canadian philosopher George Grant remind us, the world of facts, science, technique, and bureaucracy are hardly value-free and neutral. We are becoming increasingly aware of the tremendous impact on and threat that so-called neutral technology poses for our physical and social ecology. Technique, by its incredible depersonalizing power, has fundamentally altered our views of human nature. We even use the category of machine to understand our human functioning. Our notions of justice have also been profoundly changed by pragmatic notions such as "if it works, it is right." If we choose to be governed by pragmatic technocrats rather than divine-right kings, we are not repudiating a religious vision or ideology in favor of neutral, pragmatic processes. Rather, we are choosing an alternative religious vision.

We badly need more solid Christian reflection on this fact of our modern life. Those who are daily involved in the business of Christian education also need to reflect on the relationship between process and content. Is Christian education also being influenced by modernity's fascination with technique and process? Have Christians too accepted the split between public and private life and withdrawn their Christian faith to the inner, private chamber? Is the following observation by Lesslie Newbigin correct?

> Having lost the battle to control education, and having been badly battered in its encounter with modern science, Christianity in its modern form has largely accepted relegation to the private sector, where it can influence the choice of values by those who take this option. By doing so, it has secured for itself a continuing place, at the cost of surrendering the cru-

cial field. As an option for the private field, as the protagonist for certain values, Christianity can enjoy considerable success. Churches can grow. People can be encouraged, as the posters in General Eisenhower's day used to put it, "to join the church of your choice." All this can happen. And yet the claim, the awesome and winsome claim of Jesus Christ to be alone the Lord of all the world, the light that alone shows the whole of reality as it really is, the life that alone endures forever—this claim is effectively silenced. It remains, for our culture, just one of the varieties of religious experience.[10]

Any authentically Christian assessment of this modern development must therefore be mixed. On the one hand, it is undeniable that liberal democracy along with its economic partner, capitalism, has provided untold blessing for humanity. The democracies of the West provide unparalleled opportunity for many people. Religious freedom and the stability of political institutions are worth celebrating. Furthermore, these societies have been the engines of the most incredible wealth creation that the history of the world has ever known. Science and technology in politically stable, free-market economies have made twentieth-century human life for the vast majority of citizens light years better than in the entire past history of the human race. The benefits of liberal democracy are not to be sneezed at.

At the same time, many thoughtful people today are raising significant questions about the very heart of the modern project, particularly the attempt to establish and ground a moral order by reason alone apart from revelation or religious tradition. The project of modernity, which has been going on now for some two hundred years, survived as long as it was able to borrow freely from the leftover moral capital of the Judeo-Christian religious tradition. In other words, reason worked tolerably well in areas of science, philosophy, and law as long as its practitioners and the larger public were sustained in the moral convictions and practices that came from sources other than reason. As long as religion still taught men and women what it was to be truly human and truly good, an indirect influence on public life could still be observed. But when reason itself was relied upon to decide the ends as well as the means, the project of modernity began to come apart at the seams. The twentieth century, which was prophetically, and in hindsight ironically, named the "Christian century" by American social gospel theologians at the turn of the century, has turned out to be a time in which technologically brilliant but utterly immoral people have unleashed unspeakable horrors against their fellow human beings. Reason itself cannot provide a basis for being or doing good since reason on its own cannot determine the good. Ironically, as Bloom observes, "reason has discerned that all previous cultures were founded by and on gods or belief in gods. . . . There must be religion, and reason cannot found religions."[11]

Thus, there is a deep fissure, a fundamental contradiction, at the very heart of the modern project. This contradiction is not being noticed only by Christians or theists. Even non-theists are raising significant questions about modernity. The new watchword is *postmodernism*. This term is a catchall for many diverse intellectual and artistic expressions today, but at the very core of all postmodernism is a rejection of universal reason. One author summarizes it thus:

> For postmodernism has become a convenient rallying point around which Western intellectuals have gathered to debate the continuing worth or wholesale abandonment of the *universal propositions* that provide the ground for the enlightenment idea of politics and social transformation.[12]

Postmodern thought no longer holds that universal reason divorced from all religious, social, moral, political, or other commitments is possible. Prejudice and bias are unavoidable. All human thought is embedded in particular narrative traditions, and as Alan Ross states, "there is no point of view external to all traditions from which one can offer a universal judgment."[13] As a result one's personal experience or story is crucially determinative for how one thinks. Increasingly the argument is that the experience of blacks, other minorities, and women profoundly affects thought itself. Black, Asian, or feminist rationality is regarded as different from but just as valid as white, male, European rationality. The postmodern perspective fuels the debate about the literary canon as well as the push toward multiculturalism.

Postmodernism also significantly affects political life. As we have seen, modern liberalism sought to establish political society on the basis of a contract between autonomous, rational selves. This political project emphasizes the universal rights of man. Feminists have earnestly taken up the postmodern critique of this tenet. As feminist author Carole Pateman puts it:

> The idea of universal citizenship is specifically modern, and necessarily depends on the emergence of the view that all individuals are born free and equal or are naturally free and equal to each other. No individual is naturally subordinate to another, and all must thus have public standing as citizens, that upholds their self-governing status. Individual freedom and equality also entails that government can arise only through agreement and consent. We are all taught that the "individual" is a universal category that applies to anyone or everyone, but this is not the case. "The individual" is a man.[14]

Postmodernism rejects this universal abstraction. Since a society that acknowledges individuals still excludes certain sets of individuals, pluralism of groups or classes is the new point of orientation. Rights are viewed as belonging not to individuals but to diverse groups with their particular needs and interests. Pateman argues that

> The new rights that are being claimed today are the expression of differences whose importance is only now being asserted, and they are no longer rights that can be universalized. Radical democracy demands that we acknowledge difference—the particular, the multiple, the heterogeneous—in effect everything that had been excluded by the concept of Man in the abstract.[15]

What this means is that the language of rights must be specific rather than universal. Not the rights of the individual, but the rights of women, the rights of blacks, the rights of homosexuals, the rights of native people, and so on. The result is what may politely be called the politics of difference or the politics of interest-group formation. Less sanguinely it could be viewed as tribalism. Our culture seems to be moving beyond modern universal reason and denial of the importance of particular stories and traditions for public life to a viewpoint where the desire is to give all stories public space. However, it is still difficult to obtain public space for the Christian story. Even in an aggressively secular society there seems to be little recognition that Christians are a marginalized minority in the public arena. Clearly, genuine tolerance for all stories is lacking. Christianity—at least evangelical, conservative Christianity—is hardly politically correct.

What does this mean for Christianity in general and for Christian education in particular? In some ways the postmodern rejection of universal rationality in favor of prejudice and presupposition arising from particular stories may, initially at least, appear to be a welcome development. After all, Christian educators have been arguing for years against the notion that reason and thought are neutral or value-free. Public education, it has been said again and again, is not religiously neutral. Christian philosophers have insisted that all knowledge is influenced by religious commitments and specific narratives.[16] Some have also concluded that Christians should celebrate and promote pluralism as a way to greater social justice.[17] Others, however, worry that pluralism will only intensify the fragmentation of Canadian and American life,[18] sending Christians into ghettos and furthering the process of secularization in North America. As an alternative to pluralism, there are proposals to re-Christianize North America and reclaim its Christian heritage for the public arena.[19] Part of the problem with postmodern thought is that it denies the existence of any certain or universal truth. Everything is up for grabs. For Christians who believe that the gospel and God's moral law are universally true, this wholesale relativism presents a formidable challenge. Postmodernism, therefore, is not an unmixed blessing and Christians should not embrace it too enthusiastically.[20]

Modernization and Individualism: Habits of the Heart

Let us now move on to examine aspects of the conflict between modernism and postmodernism in greater detail by considering four important characteristics of contemporary North American society—individualism, pluralism/relativism, secularism, and paganism—and by concluding with some brief observations about the role of the media. These four important cultural and social patterns are somewhat at odds with one another. Individualism is the quintessential fruit of modernity while pluralism/relativism is the hallmark of postmodernism. Furthermore, although on the face of it the forces of strict secularism would seem to be dramatically at odds with a revived paganism, we shall see that they are really complementary phenomena. As the thrust toward secularization intensifies, it seems that paganism and pagan spiritualities again begin to flourish. The reason for this strange mixture and simultaneous existence of apparent opposites is to be found in the contradiction or dilemma that is at the heart of the modernization project itself.[21]

By "modernization" we mean the revolution in human thought and practice that deliberately applies reason to the transformation of economic, political, and social life. The truly modern society is what Jacques Ellul has called "the technological society,"[22] governed by the ideals of rational planning, efficiency, productivity, and utility.

Three characteristics distinguish a modern society from a traditional, or pre-modern, society. One is the removal of work from the home to the factory. Lesslie Newbigin says that "the home is no longer the place of work, and the family is no longer the working unit."[23] The personal and private world of home and family is thus split away from the public and anonymous world of commerce and industry. Another characteristic is the growth of cities: "Urbanization breaks up traditional family-based communities and introduces people into a world where there is a multiplicity of human networks, each controlled by different purposes. In traditional rural societies, each person is securely fixed in a single human milieu that embraces work, leisure, family relationships and religion. These all form part of a given world that is accepted as real and within which the individual person has a secure and well-defined identity. In a city the individual is in the presence of multiple possibilities."[24] A third feature is the growth of large bureaucracies, together with an increased role for powerful nation-states. In Newbigin's words: "Bureaucracy applies the principles of reason as understood at the Enlightenment to human life in the public sphere."[25]

This technological rationalism is seen by proponents of modernism as a liberator and the transformation of human life that it brings about as "the birth pangs of a better life for humanity."[26] And there is much to be said for such a view. Initially it seems so obviously true. The rise of modern, technological society has indeed improved the physical condition of a large majority of earth's population. It has vastly expanded the range of choices for people by liberating them from the ascriptivism of tradition, hierarchy, and class.

The availability of choice, in fact the necessity of choosing,[27] is precisely what makes life in the modern world so different from premodern, or traditional, societies. In premodern societies the ties of family, social class, and religion, not to mention region, bring clearly defined role expectations and social, political obligations. These give a person his or her identity. As Alasdair MacIntyre observes:

> In many pre-modern, traditional societies it is through his or her membership in a variety of social groups that the individual identifies himself or herself and is identified by others. I am brother, cousin and grandson, member of this household, that village, this tribe. These are not characteristics that belong to human beings accidentally, to be stripped away in order to discover 'the real me.' They are part of my substance, defining partially at least and sometimes wholly my obligations and my duties. Individuals inherit a particular space within an interlocking set of social relationships; lacking that space, they are nobody, or at best a stranger or an outcast. To know oneself as such a social person is however not to occupy a static and fixed position. It is to find oneself placed at a certain point on a journey with set goals; to move through life is to make progress—or to fail to make progress—toward a given end.[28]

This results in relatively stable communities with cohesive moral and social patterns. One need not or cannot choose to be something other than a participant in the community's story, to be true to its tradition, to be faithful to its expectations, and to be dutiful in carrying out communal obligations. Challenging the orthodoxy of the tradition is very difficult and makes one an outcast, a heretic. How different the modern person. No longer bound by physical or traditional fate and having incredible geographical and social mobility, the modern individual has become free to choose to be himself or herself, to become what he or she wants to be. Heresy is encouraged as a mark of authenticity. It is considered essential to find oneself.

This point about the necessity of choice, however, also underscores what is so problematic about modernity—the liberated individual self is also often a rootless, lonely self, a member of what David Riesman in his classic study called "the lonely crowd."[29] At the same time that our modern world maximizes rationality, choice, liberation, the future, and individual rights, this very range of options is seen to be dehumanizing and depersonalizing. In every dimension of modern life, the stable, personal, communal, traditional realities are set aside and are replaced by changeable, impersonal, anonymous, individual, immediate ones. The rational and anonymous efficiency of the shopping mall, the emergency room, and the state welfare office replaces the personal, ad hoc purchase from the local grocer, the housecall of the family physician, the visit to the widow or orphan by the deacons. The increased rationality and efficiency of modern urban life, in combination with the multiplicity of choices faced by the modern individual, results in a clear loss of identity. When identity is a matter of choice, it creates doubt and anxiety. As Newbigin has noted, "In the mulling crowds of the city, composed of individuals each pursuing goals of his or her own choice, the individual's sense of being in a world without landmarks is heightened—sometimes to the point of despair."[30] This is exactly the point made by Alasdair MacIntyre, who notes that modernity's accomplishments are often

> celebrated historically for the most part not as loss, but as self-congratulatory gain, as the emergence of the individual freed on the one hand from the social bonds of those constraining hierarchies which the modern word world rejected at its birth and on the other hand from what modernity has taken to be the superstitions of teleology. . . . [T]he peculiarly modern self . . . in acquiring sovereignty in its own realm lost its traditional boundaries provided by a social identity and a view of human life as ordered to a given end.[31]

It is for this reason that modernity has its critics as well as its celebrators. Countercultural critics have argued that the technological rationalism of modernity alienates and dehumanizes. Sociologists like Emile Durkheim speak of *anomie,* of the rootlessness and homelessness of the modern individual that arises from the high degree of specialization in the workplace and the separation of labor from the home and of productivity from communal meaning. Particularly when modern Western technological society comes face to face with "traditional" cultures in Africa, Asia, or the Middle East, serious conflict arises.

It is not surprising, therefore, that alternatives to modernity—especially to that quintessially modern system of liberal political-economy: democratic capitalism—are so attractive to many Western intellectuals. The dream of socialism, a political-economy that is ordered toward community and equality rather than contributing to the alienating individualism of liberal democratic capitalism, continues to have its appeal. However, supporters of socialism often forget that the total rationalization of economic life by centralized political managers—the socialist ideal—is in fact a modern phenomenon. Socialist bureaucracies are no more personal than capitalist ones, and there tend to be more of them. Many people, particularly during the sixties and seventies, rejected socialism, preferring to seek out alternative back-to-the-earth, communal lifestyles.[32]

For the Christian these challenges to modernity are provocative, even if their proposed solutions often seem unworkable and romantically naive nostalgia trips. If it is the case, as Christians confess, that human beings created in the divine image are communal, social beings who reflect the persons-in-relation of the Trinity, then Christians in particular need to ask this question as framed by Peter Berger: "Is the modern conception of the individual a great step forward in the story of human self-realization (as liberal thought since the Enlightenment has maintained), or is it, on the contrary, a dehumanizing aberration (as it would appear to be in the perspective of most non-Western traditional cultures)?"[33] The issue is whether the notion of the individual, predicated by the reality of choice, in fact enhances our humanity. As Berger notes, "Modernization entails a multiplication of options. One of the most seductive maxims of modernity is that *things could be other than what they have been.* This is the turbulent dynamism of modernity, its deeply rooted thrust for innovation and revolution. Tradition is no longer binding; the status quo can be changed; the future is an open horizon."[34] All this brings anxiety and uncertainty. In Berger's words, "There is an exhilarating quality to this liberation. There is also the terror of chaos."[35]

The chaos that Berger refers to is particularly noticeable in the realm of morality.[36] To be successful in the modern world requires a great deal of personal strength and disciplined habits, yet strengths and discipline are for the most part shaped by communities and social traditions. At the same time, the business corporation, the government bureaucracy, or the highly specialized academy tends to destroy the traditions that are essential to its own well-being. In other words, the individualism fostered by the modernizing process itself destroys the very base that makes free, liberal, democratic societies possible.

This inherent contradiction in modern societies has been described well by sociologist Robert Bellah and his associates in their widely read and much-discussed study *Habits of the Heart*.[37] The authors judge that "Individualism lies at the very core of American culture" and that some of our deepest problems both as individual and as a society are also closely linked to our individualism" (p. 142). They point to the irony of "the therapeutic quest for community," (p. 134) in which ideals of choice, self-realization, autonomy, and liberation are at odds with an emphasis on connectedness or belonging to a group. Many therapists, they suggest, "cry out for the very community that their moral logic undercuts" (p. 144). As the authors point out:

> The ambiguity and ambivalence of American individualism derive from both cultural and social contradictions. We insist, perhaps more than ever before, on finding our true selves independent of any cultural or social influence, being responsible to that self alone, and making its structures— multiversities, corporations, government agencies—manipulating and being manipulated by others. In describing this situation, Alasdair MacIntyre has spoken of "bureaucratic individualism," the form of life exemplified by the manager and the therapist. In bureaucratic individualism, the ambiguities and contradictions of individualism are frighteningly revealed, as freedom to make private decisions is bought at the cost of turning over most public decisions to bureaucratic managers and experts. A bureaucratic individualism in which the consent of the governed, the first demand of modern

enlightened individualism, has been abandoned in all but form, illustrates the tendency of individualism to destroy its own conditions.

But in our interviews, though we saw tendencies toward bureaucratic individualism, we cannot say that it has yet become dominant. Rather the inner tensions of American individualism add up to a classic case of ambivalence. We strongly assert the value of our self-reliance and autonomy. We deeply feel the emptiness of a life without sustaining social commitments. Yet we are hesitant to articulate our sense that we need one another as much as we need to stand alone, for fear that if we did we would lose our independence altogether. The tensions of our lives would be even greater if we did not, in fact, engage in practices that constantly limit the effects of an isolating individualism, even though we cannot articulate those practices nearly as well as we can the quest for autonomy. (pp. 150-51)

From a moral standpoint, the issue is clear. If the criteria for what is socially and culturally good are not established by community wisdom or tradition and for that reason affirmed and accepted, how can a society determine what is good? If it is all a matter of individual choice and preference, if it is simply my subjective value versus your subjective value, how can we decide on any communal good? This pattern of moral discourse is usually called emotivism, the conviction that our moral arguments are really statements of personal preference.[38] To say "this is good" is to say nothing more than "I approve of this." What happens when public moral discourse is reduced to this radical individualism? Not only does the conversation increase in shrillness as louder and louder voices compete for public attention, but moral decision-making becomes a matter of sheer arbitrary power. The strongest individual will prevails. Alasdair MacIntyre has observed that "emotivism entails the obliteration of any genuine distinction between manipulative and non-manipulative social relations."[39] Reasoned conversation about moral issues is impossible because no standard of right or wrong exists. There is nothing by which one can determine whether an act is just or unjust. In MacIntyre's apt phrase, moral conflicts become "the confrontation of one contingent arbitrariness by another."[40]

The political results of this are twofold. In the first place, the political process itself is reduced to nothing more than individual or interest-group confrontation. There is no public good—only competing preferences—and the strongest lobby group prevails. Second, society becomes increasingly legalistic and controlling; government becomes more intrusive. When the habits of virtue fostered by community tradition are lost, the only recourse for social order is an ever-increasing legal code. Alexander Solzhenitsyn accurately identifies this problem:

> Western society has chosen for itself the organization best suited to its purposes and one I might call legalistic. The limits of human rights and rightness are determined by a system of laws; such limits are very broad. People in the West have acquired considerable skill in using, interpreting, and manipulating law (though laws tend to be too complicated for an average person to understand without the help of an expert). Every conflict is solved according to the letter of the law and this is considered to be the ultimate solution. If one is right from a legal point of view, nothing more is required, nobody may mention that one could still not be entirely right, and urge self-restraint or a renunciation of these rights, call for sacrifice and selfless risk: this would simply sound absurd. Voluntary self-restraint is almost unheard of: everybody strives toward further expansion to the extreme limit of the legal frames. (An oil company is legally blameless when it buys up an invention of a new type of energy in order to prevent its use. A food product manufacturer is legally blameless when he poisons his produce to make it last longer: after all,

people are free not to purchase it.)

I have spent all my life under a Communist regime and I will tell you that a society without any objective legal scale is a terrible one indeed. But a society with no other scale but the legal one is also less than worthy of man. A society based on the letter of the law and never reaching any higher fails to take advantage of the full range of human possibilities. The letter of the law is too cold and formal to have a beneficial influence on society. Whenever the tissue of life is woven of legalistic relationships, this creates an atmosphere of spiritual mediocrity that paralyzes man's noblest impulses.

And it will be simply impossible to bear up to the trials of this threatening century with nothing but the supports of a legalistic structure.[41]

With all due respect to members of the legal profession, it may be the case that the level of a society's moral decline is directly proportional to the number of laws and lawyers. If so, America is in deep moral trouble.[42]

If modern individualism creates such profound moral problems for society, what is the antidote? While Bellah and his associates are unduly optimistic in their hope that a "republican and biblical" sense of community can be combined with the individualism of liberal democracy, they do introduce a category that is illuminating, especially for Christians. The category is "communities of memory." These communities provide an antidote to radical individualism and make it possible for individuals to find meaning and purpose in their lives.

Communities, in the sense in which we are using the term, have a history—in an important sense they are constituted by their past—and for this reason we can speak of a real community as a "community of memory," one that does not forget its past. In order not to forget that past, a community is involved in retelling its story, its constitutive narrative, and in so doing, it offers examples of the men and women who have embodied and exemplified the meaning of the community. These stories of collective history and exemplary individuals are an important part of the tradition that is so central to a community of memory.

The stories that make up a tradition contain conceptions of character, of what a good person is like, and of the virtues that define such character. But the stories are not all exemplary, not all about successes and achievements. A genuine community of memory will also tell painful stories of shared suffering that sometimes creates deeper identities than success. And if the community is completely honest, it will remember stories not only of suffering received but of suffering inflicted—dangerous memories, for they call the community to alter ancient evils. The communities of memory that tie us to the past also turn us toward the future as communities of hope. They carry a context of meaning that can allow us to connect our aspirations for ourselves and those closest to us with the aspirations of a larger whole and see our own efforts as being, in part, contributions to a common good.[43]

Christians will recognize this notion of communities of memory as a valid description of what the church in its preaching, teaching, and discipling tries to do. And, as I shall argue in Chapter Six, a community of memory is precisely what the Christian school is called to be.

Pluralism/Relativism: Mosaic Madness

Reginald Bibby defines relativism as "the inclination to see the merits of behavior and ideas not as universal or 'absolute' but as varying with individuals and their environments, and, in the end, as being equally valid because they are *chosen*."[44] Obviously relativism is the natural consequence of individualism. No objective standards of right and wrong can be used to judge individual acts. Each person has a right to his or her own lifestyle.

Yet our concern here takes us one step beyond moral relativism to cultural relativism, more positively called pluralism. Cultural relativism is more a group phenomenon than an individual one although it is also in many respects a natural extension of radical individualism. Here rights play a prominent role. Cultural pluralism acknowledges and even encourages the diversity and legitimacy of groups. Pluralism seeks to create a mosaic, a multicultural and multinational community of communities. Individualism is a typical characteristic of modern societies, and pluralism is more reflective of postmodern societies. And if, as Bellah and others have argued, the United States is the supremely individualistic culture and society, then its North American neighbor Canada, which prides itself on being a cultural and social mosaic rather than a melting pot, may be the premier example of deliberate and self-conscious cultural pluralism. That is the assessment of Reginald Bibby:

> Since the 1960s, one country has been leading the world in advocating freedom through pluralism and relativism. It has been carrying out something of a unique experiment in trying to be a multinational society, enshrining coexistence and tolerance. The preliminary results are beginning to appear. The news is not good.[45]

As Bibby sees it, this cultural and ethnic pluralism has run rampant in every aspect of Canadian life.

> Our mosaics have not stopped with the sphere of intergroup relations. Pluralism at the group and individual levels has become part of the Canadian psyche. Some time ago it left its cultural cradle. The pluralism infant has been growing up in the past three decades. It has been traveling across the country, visiting our moral, religious, family, educational, and political spheres. We now have not only a cultural mosaic but also a moral mosaic, a meaning system mosaic, a family structure mosaic, a sexual mosaic. And that's just the shortlist. Pluralism has come to pervade Canadian minds and Canadian institutions. (p. 9)

For many this pluralism is a wonderful prospect.[46] Bibby says, "At its best, Canada stands as a model to the world, a nation that can be a home to people of all nations and cultures, a microcosm of the harmony and peace that are possible when cultural diversity is tolerated and respected" (p. 10). Once again, at first glance there is much to be said for this. Majoritarian societies can be intolerant of all minorities, whether they be racial, ethnic, or religious minorities. Christians who are concerned about freedom thus understandably find pluralistic visions attractive.

In fact, however, the reality is often not as rosy as the ideal. Ideally, the deliberate encouragement of cultural and social (and moral as well as religious) diversity leads to tolerance and respect of other groups. Furthermore, the "expectation has been that fragments of the mosaic will somehow add up to a healthy and adhesive society" (p. 11). In fact, excessive cultivation of diversity, even when given a positive-sounding name such as multiculturalism seems to lead people to greater intolerance. "The evidence," according to McGill University sociologist Morton Weinfeld, "suggests a kind of ethnocentric effect, so that greater preoccupation with one's own group makes one more distant from and antipathetic to others."[47] Rather than easing racial tension, for example, such ethnic separatism only deepens racial divisions and sanctions racial tensions. The reason is that individual and group rights take a prominent front seat and the larger, public, well-being a distant back seat. Canadian columnist George Bain puts it this way: "Canadians have a lamentably limited capacity to see a national interest broader than the membership list of the occupational, economic, cultural, ethnic, gender, environmental, or other groups with which they identify in spirit if not formally" (p. 12). In fact, a preoccupation with group identity and group rights, when combined with a relativism that sees all group viewpoints as having equal validity, leads to a virtual impasse for any broader or national consensus. We are no longer able to generate a social responsibility to the well-being of the whole. This raises an important question. If the only thing we have in common is that we are diverse, is there anything really left in common? By making everything legitimate, does pluralism end in nothingness? To put it into narrative categories, does the validation of all stories result in the destruction of a national story?

Robert Bellah and company identify the threat of individualism to group life: "What has failed at every level—from the society of nations to the national society to the local community to the family—is integration. . . . we have put our own good, as individuals, as groups, and a nation, ahead of the common good."[48] Bibby observes that this critique may be more applicable to Canada than to the United States (p. 92). In Bibby's judgment, American individualism coexists with an intense commitment to group life. American national mythology unifies individual citizens while Canada lacks such mythology. "What has held our country together is not commitment to shared ideology but rather a tenuous willingness to coexist. While individualism in the United States is buffered by a group-endorsing ideology, in Canada there is no such ideological protection" (p. 95). The point is that with pluralism and relativism, the mere coexistence of diverse groups becomes an end in itself. It is this excessive pluralism, this focus on pluralism for pluralism's sake, that Bibby calls mosaic madness, an uninspiring visionless coexistence (p. 105).

Exploring Bibby's analysis of the Canadian mosaic is not intended as an in-depth exploration of cultural and social differences between the United States and Canada but rather as an illustration of cultural pluralism and relativism and its consequences as seen by one thoughtful observer in one country.[49] In fact, the cultural boundary lines between the two countries may not be as sharp as some suggest. Multiculturalism and the language of mosaic is making its presence felt in the United States, too.[50] In a recent work, one of America's foremost historians, Arthur Schlesinger Jr. raises serious questions about the "disuniting of America" that is the fruit of a growing insistence on multicultural-ism. Schlesinger is deeply concerned about the shift from an ideal of integration and assimilation to one of ethnic separatism:

> Instead of a transformative nation with an identity all its own, America increasingly sees itself as preservative of old identities. Instead of a nation composed of individuals mak-ing their own free choices, America increasingly sees itself as composed of groups more or less indelible in their ethnic character. The national ideal had once been *e pluribus unum.* Are we now to belittle *unum* and glorify *pluribus.* Will the center hold? Or will the melting pot yield to the Tower of Babel?[51]

Allan Bloom, in his bestseller *The Closing of the American Mind,* attacked the relativism of American higher education head-on. The opening line has been quoted often and is worth recalling: "There is one thing a professor can be absolutely certain of: almost every student entering the university believes, or says he believes, that truth is rela-tive."[52] And finally, it is clear that individualism and plural-ism/relativism, for all the nuanced differences between them, like modernism and postmodernism, are closely related and may be inseparable. Pluralism does not merely permit individual choices; instead, it encourages them and may even legislate them through state-sanctioned programs of multiculturalism. Individualism and pluralism can pro-vide freedom and opportunity, especially for marginalized groups, by checking the tyranny of majoritarian cultures. But when individualism and pluralism are carried to extremes, the end result is social anarchy, a collision of self-contained groups and stories, and no national vision or story. The Canadian experiment is instructive not only for the United States but also for Eastern Europe, the countries that made up the former Soviet Union, and even Africa. If a country such as Canada, with its peaceful history, prosperity, rich resources, and opportunity, cannot forge a national identity out of its diversity, is there hope for balkanized communities with long histories of warfare and ethnic conflict? Clearly relativism and pluralism, as ends in themselves, are not the solution to the group conflicts—ethnic, racial or religious—of the late twentieth century.

Education in North America must contend with a fragmented and relativistic culture, one in which a common narrative and a unified vision no longer exist. If education is the primary vehicle for civilization, for nurturing the character of a nation's citizens, and for shaping the public welfare, then the climate of individualism, pluralism, and relativism makes good education itself problematic, if not virtually impossible. And that, as we observed in the first chapter, is indeed the state of affairs today.

Secularism: The Naked Public Square

In all the commentary about contemporary society, there is probably no term that has been as frequently used as the word secular. Members of the so-called religious right, in particular, frequently use it in targeting their criticism of what they refer to as secular humanism. The term has also been used by devotees of modernity to celebrate life in "the secular city."[53] There seems to be agreement, by friends and foes of secularism alike, that our age is indeed a secular one. Precisely what does this mean?

Theologian Donald Bloesch, in a highly readable critical analysis of contemporary society and culture, argues that secularism is the distinctive characteristic of today's world:

> What makes contemporary culture qualitatively different from medieval culture is the phenomenon of secularism. There was unbelief, heresy, and apostasy in medieval times, but the distinguishing feature of the modern scene is that faith in God has been for the most part relegated to the private sphere of life. Christian values no longer permeate society but instead are generally regarded as archaic or even injurious to the social order.[54]

Similarly, Richard John Neuhaus, in a widely discussed volume, also points to the newness of secularism:

> What is relatively new is the naked public square. The naked public square is the result of political doctrine and practice that would exclude religion and religiously grounded values from the conduct of public business. The doctrine is that America is a secular society. It finds dogmatic expression in the ideology of secularism.[55]

In order for us properly to assess the rise of secularism, we need to understand it more precisely. How did this privatization of religion come about? What led to the removal of God from public civic, cultural and social life? What gave rise to the naked public square? Again, a contrast with pre-modern sacral societies is useful. In a sacral society the religious/cultic authority and power and the civil/political authority and power are virtually identical. The power of the priest and that of the ruler are practically indistinguishable. In the most extreme case, as with the pharaohs of ancient Egypt and the emperors of the Roman Empire, the political power was in essence the power of the deity itself. This is, of course, terribly convenient for the ruler. The ruler is god. At the same time, it is equally apparent that the divine legitimation of such consolidated power has the potential for horrid abuse.

In a real sense, it is one of the great political contributions of the Judeo-Christian tradition to separate the priestly and prophetic authority from the kingly. Beginning with the Hebrew prophets and continuing through the church-state conflicts of the Middle Ages and beyond, the Judeo-Christian tradition secularized the governing authority by clearly distinguishing and separating it from ecclesiastical authority. God, on whose behalf the prophets speak, is the ultimate authority. Both priest and king bow before him. Thus, in the spirit of the prophet Nathan, a fourth-century bishop, Ambrose, could discipline Emperor Theodosius, whose troops had massacred innocent civilians.

This kind of secularity, the separation of church and state, of civil and ecclesiastical authority—both under God—is undeniably a constructive and positive political development. In Christian terms, it is a blessing. It is also the case that the Christian church, from the time of the Emperor Constantine's conversion and the adoption of the Christian religion as the official religion of the Empire, has not always honored this separation in actual practice. All too often the power of the civil magistracy has been used for religious coercion. Enforced mass conversions and baptisms, the Crusades, the Inquisition, the religious wars of the seventeenth-century, and the rise of official state-churches in Protestantism are all examples of failures to be true to the separation vision. For, in principle, even a Christian theocratic ideal distinguishes between and separates royal and priestly authority.[56] In theory at least, the Christian tradition speaks of "two swords," not one.[57]

Actual practice, as we have noted, has fallen short of this ideal. It was the Anabaptists, having experienced persecution at the hands of other Christian magistrates, who insisted on "disestablishing" the church, on the church being a truly voluntary society.[58] Whereas Luther's Germany and Calvin's Geneva used the civil magistracy to effect reform in the church, the Anabaptist or Radical Reformation rejected civil authority itself as an appropriate vocation for Christians. For different reasons the philosophers of the Enlightenment, as they attempted to create a new foundation for political society on the basis of reason alone, also promoted disestablishment and voluntarism. The full realization of this vision politically and legally was not achieved until the framing of the U.S. Constitution with its non-establishment clause. American church life is strictly voluntarist; no church or religious body has preferred status or receives preferential treatment. Civic and ecclesiastical power are kept distinct. Once again, the religious liberty that such separation provides is undoubtedly a blessing. The American pattern has, by the end of the twentieth century, become the ideal to be emulated worldwide.

However, this basic principle of separation has become something quite different in recent years. The argument put forward by separationist secularists goes beyond the words of the U.S. Constitution: "Congress shall make no law respecting an establishment of religion, or prohibiting the free exercise thereof." Today many separationists wish to empty all public discussion of explicit religious content. Society must be totally secular, devoid of all display and all evidence of religious commitment and devotion. This is the reason for seeking to outlaw all public prayer; prohibiting religious symbolism such as creches, crosses, and menorahs in public places; and even removing references to religion from public school textbooks. The public square must be religiously naked. This aggressive secularism or secular humanism has provoked a great deal of public and legal controversy in recent years.

To the amazement of religious pessimists, the tide seems to be turning somewhat, albeit very slowly. Glenn Tinder's *The Political Meaning of Christianity* argues that the Christian religion is the basic source of the liberty enjoyed by citizens of the free world; an excerpt appeared in *The Atlantic Monthly*.[59] And even *Time* magazine had a cover story with the headline "One Nation, Under God: Has the Separation of Church and State Gone Too Far?" The article notes that for many Americans the answer is Yes.

> By isolating God from public life, they argue, the courts have replaced freedom of religion with freedom *from* religion. A nation's identity is informed by morality; and morality by faith. How can people freely debate issues like nuclear arms or the death penalty, how can children be educated without any reference to spiritual heritage?[60]

Thanks to a series of U.S. Supreme Court rulings, for the past forty years American society has been pushed in an increasing secularist direction. Odd results have been the consequence.

> In this nation of spiritual paradoxes, it is legal to hang a picture in a public exhibit of a crucifix submerged in urine, or to utter virtually any conceivable blasphemy in a public place; it is not legal, the federal courts have ruled, to mention God reverently in a classroom, on a football field or at a commencement ceremony as part of a public prayer.[61]

After a thoughtful discussion of the key issues in the debate between strict separationists and accommodationists, the *Time* writers come to a rather remarkable conclusion:

> For God to be kept out of the classroom or out of America's public debate by nervous school administrators or overcautious politicians serves no one's interests. That restriction prevents people from drawing on this country's rich and diverse religious heritage for guidance, and it degrades the nation's moral discourse by placing a whole realm of theological rea-

soning out of bounds. The price of that sort of quarantine, at a time of moral dislocation, is—and has been—far too high. The courts need to find a better balance between separation and accommodation—and Americans need to respect the new religious freedom they would gain as a result.[62]

It is remarkable for a magazine like *Time* to conclude that American society is becoming too secular. We may well ask, what is going on here? The answer is deceptively and profoundly simple: secularism simply doesn't work. In the first place, in spite of deliberate efforts to secularize, religion does not disappear.[63] It was the conviction and prediction of many philosophers that as science and technology prevailed in the modern world, religion would decline. That has simply not happened. Even in the Soviet Union, religion persisted through seventy years of aggressive official atheism. More important, it is becoming apparent, even to non-believers, that religion plays a crucial role in the order and well-being of any society.[64] The great Russian novelist Fyodor Dostoevsky was correct: "If God did not exist, everything would be permitted." Apparently, when people act as if God does not exist, the same is true. A remarkable volume in this vein was written by atheist-socialist Michael Harrington. In *The Politics at God's Funeral: The Spiritual Crisis of Western Civilization* Harrington sketches the consequences of the Judeo-Christian God's "dying"; the result has not been the final arrival of a new and better world but the rise of nihilism, hedonism, and moral anarchy.[65] When even atheists become worried about the acceptance of pervasive atheistic secularism, we need to sit up and take notice.

Secularism doesn't work. To put it differently, the naked public square is an impossibility. When one god is kicked out, another takes its place. In Richard Neuhaus's words:

The truly naked public square is at best a transitional phenomenon. It is a vacuum begging to be filled. When the democratically affirmed institutions that generate and transmit values are excluded, the vacuum will be filled by the agent left in control of the public square, the state. In this manner, a perverse notion of the disestablishment of religion leads to the establishment of the state as church. Not without reason, religion is viewed by some as a repressive imposition upon the public square. They would cast out the devil of particularist religion and thus put the public square in proper secular order. Having cast out the one devil, as noted earlier, they unavoidably invite the entrance of seven devils worse than the first.[66]

Aggressive secularism opens the door to fearful prospects, according to Neuhaus:

> More than that, the notion of the secular state can become the prelude to totalitarianism. That is, once religion is reduced to nothing more than privatized conscience, the public square has only two actors in it—the state and the individual. Religion as a mediating structure—a community that generates and transmits moral values—is no longer available as a countervailing force to the ambitions of the state. Whether in Hitler's Third Reich or in today's sundry states professing Marxist-Leninism, the chief attack is not upon individual religious belief. Individual religious belief can be dismissed scornfully as superstition, for it finally poses little threat to the power of the state. No, the chief attack is upon the *institutions* that bear and promulgate belief in a transcendent reality by which the state can be called to judgment. Such institutions threaten the totalitarian proposition that everything is to be within the state, nothing is to be outside the state.[67]

Let us consider the impact of all this on education, particularly public education. Once again the *Time* essay hits the nail on the head:

> The symbolic issues pale, however, compared with the heated debates about what can take place in the nation's

public schools. This has always been the central battleground for church-state conflict in America. On the one hand, children are viewed as more impressionable and vulnerable to peer pressure than adults and so should be protected from anything resembling religious indoctrination.

But on the other hand, many devout parents are eager to instill in their children the moral strength that they hope will deliver them from evil, whether it is sex, drugs or secular humanism. Such families also believe that faith is central to serious intellectual activity and should not be relegated to Sunday School. So the debate over what teachers can teach, what books may be used, what songs sung, even what clothes children may wear at school, strikes at the heart of many families' sense of spiritual freedom.[68]

And beyond the religious freedom of parents remains the issue of the public good. If a moral, disciplined citizenry is essential to the well-being of a society, and if religion is crucial to the formation of moral character, and if it is the school's task to prepare children to become productive, law-abiding citizens, then radically secular education is a recipe for social disaster. To many observers and commentators this is becoming increasingly clear. When we deliberately keep God out of the public square, we pay too high a price. It is much too soon to predict where this awareness will lead us, but clearly there is an opportunity now for Christians to enter the public square, as public Christians.

Paganism: Rebirth of the Gods in the New Dark Ages[69]

Richard Neuhaus contends that the naked public square cannot remain naked; in a secular society the state often becomes the new god. But it is not only a sacralized, deified state that replaces God in the public square. As Donald Bloesch points out, "When God is dead, the gods are reborn. New deities are beginning to fill the void created by soulless technology in the service of secular humanism and nihilism. . . . Dethroning the God of the heavens can only result in the emergence of a new divinity having its source in the depths of the earth."[70] Bloesch adds that the main challenge facing the church in contemporary society is "the rebirth of the gods of the earth, blood and soil, a return to the ancient gods of the pre-Christian barbarian tribes."[71] And further, "The Enlightenment desacralized the heavens; now society and nature are becoming the new domains of the sacred."[72] This rebirth of the ancient pagan gods is, according to Bloesch a direct consequence of secularism. "The gods of nation, race, class, military valor, nature, technique, sex—these and many others are competing to fill a void that has been spawned by an anti-religious secularism. Only Jesus Christ can fill the metaphysical vacuum in the human soul, but when Christ is absent, pseudo-deities or demons step forward to claim supremacy."[73]

There is ample evidence for Bloesch's contention. Some feminists are reintroducing pagan goddess worship,[74] some environmentalists are practicing Earth-Mother spirituality,[75] and New Age spiritualities as well as occult practices have become ubiquitous. Even the Christian church, at least its mainline ecumenical branch, is flirting with ancient spiritualities. At a World Council of Churches meeting during February 1991 under the theme "Come Holy Spirit, Renew the Whole Creation," Chung Kyung-Hyung gave a keynote address described as follows:

> Accompanied by a troupe of dancers with gongs, drums, and banners, and by Australian aborigines in paint and loincloths, she invoked ancestor spirits and indicated that the best "image of the Holy Spirit comes from the image of *Kwan In. . .* [who] is venerated as goddess of compassion and wisdom in East Asian women's popular religion."[76]

This rebirth of the gods is in many respects a fruit of secularism, pluralism, and relativism, but it takes us a step further. In Christian terms, paganism is idolatry, a deliberate substitution of false deities for the living God. Whereas a Christian can appreciate some features of secularity and pluralism (though not secularism and absolute moral relativism), there is nothing positive to say about idolatry.[77] All idolatry is a lie, destructive of all that is good in human life. It should be observed that the reason paganism is so destructive is that it removes all the restraints on the sinful impulses of human beings. At the core of neopagan critiques of Christianity is the charge that human freedom, human will, and desire are all curtailed. Christianity is seen as a repressive religion that does not permit natural impulses and instincts their free and spontaneous expression. Paganism destroys because idolatry is destructive. No one has explored this destructive character of modern idolatry with the thoroughness and clarity that Herbert Schlossberg has in his important work entitled *Idols for Destruction.*[78]

Schlossberg observes that critiques of culture in the modern era have predominantly tended to use spatial analogies—rise, decline, and fall—or organic ones in which "societies are thought of as being born, growing, decaying, dying" (p. 4). He then questions what analogy Christians ought to use and notes: "It is a curious fact that the Old Testament which describes the beginning, course, and end of a number of societies, never assesses them as being on the rise or decline, as progressing or regressing, as growing to maturity or falling to senescence" (p. 5). In fact, "Spatial and biological analogies are incompatible with biblical thinking because they are both quantitatively oriented and deterministic. . . . In place of these analogies the biblical explanation of the end of societies uses the concept of *judgment*. It depicts them as either having submitted themselves to God or else having rebelled against him" (p. 6). In sum, Schlossberg contends: "Idolatry in its larger meaning is properly understood as any substitution of what is created for the creator. People may worship nature, money, mankind, power, history or social and political systems instead of the God who created them all. . . . Our argument, then, is that idolatry and its associated concepts provide a better framework for us to understand our own society than do any of the alternatives" (pp. 6-7).

Idols destroy. The flirtation with paganism is not innocent. When sexuality, a good gift from the creator God, becomes an idol, it is a destroyer of sexuality itself and of human beings. When humanity is deified and becomes our ultimate criterion for right or wrong, we see horrors against actual human beings begin in earnest. Schlossberg's observations on this point are a direct commentary on contemporary news:

> It is no coincidence that humanitarian policy has reached the zenith of its influence at a time when death propaganda is so much in evidence. The arguments in favor of abortion, infanticide, and euthanasia reveal that the humanitarian ethic wishes to restrict the right to live and expand the right to die—and to kill. Humanism is a philosophy of death. It embraces death, wishes a good death, speaks of the horrible burdens of living for the baby who is less than perfect, for the sick person in pain. It is intolerable to live, cruel to be forced to live, but blessed to die. It is unfair to have to care for the helpless, and therefore merciful to kill. Those who wish to go on living, it seems, are guilty and ungrateful wretches dissipating the energies of the "loved ones" who have better uses for the estate than paying medical bills. (p. 52)

Scholossberg concludes,

> Humanitarianism is saviorhood, an ethic perfectly suited to the theology that divinizes man. But the theology that divinizes man, it turns out, only divinizes some men. The

objects of humanitarian concern become less than men, so that the humanitarian can exercise the prerogatives of a god. The god that failed is man. (p. 87)

Idolatry is thus not at all innocent. The divinization of man is really the "abolition of man."[79] The rise of paganism involves us in profound matters concerning the very future of Western civilization as it has been shaped (albeit imperfectly and incompletely) by the Christian gospel. To the degree that it is legitimate to speak of Western civilization as a Christian civilization, the rise of pagan deities suggests that the spiritual foundations of Western civilization are collapsing around us and that a new barbarism is taking its place. Charles Colson's comments on this are to the point:

> I believe that we do face a crisis in Western culture, and that it presents the greatest threat to civilization since the barbarians invaded Rome. I believe that today in the West, and particularly in America, the new barbarians are all around us. They are not hairy Goths and Vandals, swilling fermented brew and ravishing maidens; they are not Huns and Visigoths storming our borders or scaling our city walls. No, this time the invaders have come from within.
>
> We have bred them in our families and trained them in our classrooms. They inhabit our legislatures, our courts, our film studios, and our churches. Most of them are attractive and pleasant; their ideas are persuasive and subtle. Yet these men and women threaten our most cherished institutions and our very character as a people.[80]

Admittedly this language sounds somewhat gloomy, pessimistic, perhaps even apocalyptic. Yet here too, the truth sets us free. Can the truth of seeing our age as one of growing barbarism be doubted? Is Peter Kreeft's observation that "a modernist is someone who is more concerned about air pollution than soul pollution. . . . who wants clean air so he can breathe dirty words"[81] not an accurate and telling judgment about our values? And here is the important point: Categories such as idolatry and judgment are more hopeful than those of decay and decline. It is possible to repent of idolatry. Conversion and renewal, of individuals and society, have taken place and can again. A sense of opportunity and challenge should be the church's response.[82]

Media Messages

After all this sober and even somber cultural analysis, I was tempted to give this section the heading "How *Sesame Street* Has Made Elementary School Teaching Impossible" or, for high school and college students, "How MTV Makes Teaching Impossible." It is undoubtedly true that at the practical level of classroom teaching television and the other electronic media have had a profound and direct impact on education. The random, unconnected television images of *Sesame Street* present an enormous challenge to conventional classroom teaching, in terms of both content and process.

To begin with, television pushes and pulls teaching to become another branch of entertainment. As educator and media critic Neil Postman notes, when schools and teachers follow the lead of television, the result is that "drawing an audience—rather than teaching—becomes the focus of education." Postman asserts that "School is the one institution in the culture that should present a different way of knowing, of evaluating, of assessing." His worry "is that if school becomes so overwhelmed by entertainment metaphors and metaphysics, then it becomes not content-centered but attention-centered, like television, chasing 'ratings' or class attendance." This would have disastrous consequences. "If school becomes that way, then the game may be lost, because school is using the same approach, epistemologically, as television. Instead of being something different from television, it is reduced to being just another *kind* of television."[83] In other words, the argument of some educators that *Sesame Street* is "an imaginative aid in solving the growing problem of teaching Americans to read, while, at the same time, encouraging children to love school" really boils down to this: "*Sesame Street* encourages children to love school *only* if school is like *Sesame Street*."[84]

We must consider the distinction between word and image, but first we need to reflect on some broader cultural aspects of the media's role in our lives. To begin with, the media of mass communication, of which television may the most pervasive, unavoidably shape and define the way we experience the reality of the world around us. By selecting what images or stories make the news and what dramas fill our primetime, as well as by selecting the content or substance of such images, stories, and dramas, television serves as a filter through which we see the world and by which we order our experience.[85] As Carol Tavris, a social psychologist and columnist, observes:

> People are affected not only by what they see but also by what they don't see. They don't see counterbalancing stories of what used to be called character. They don't see problems solved other than by violence. They rarely see stories of real people—the kind who know each other longer than two minutes before they jump into bed or commit murder with chainsaws.[86]

It is precisely here that one encounters massive complaints by those on the orthodox or conservative side of the contemporary cultural divide. Conservatives deliver jeremiads "that the media and arts establishment is unfairly prejudiced against the values they hold dear."[87] On such issues as abortion, homosexuality, and pornography, the "liberal" media, it is felt by many, is simply out of touch with the mainstream of North American values. The following statement about the film industry is typical of this attitude: "The people in Hollywood are so far removed from the people of middle America. They have a hostility toward people who believe anything at all. They live in a hedonistic, materialistic little world."[88] James Davison Hunter notes that these comments may be exaggerated, "but the general perceptions are not totally born out of illusion." In fact, he insists, there is solid empirical evidence that such accusations are based on fact and that the media playing field is not at all even. "Studies of the attitude of media and entertainment elites, as well as of television news programming and newspaper coverage of various social issues and political events, have shown a fairly strong and consistent bias toward a liberal and progressivist point of view."[89]

The first point that must be made about the media, therefore, is that they are hardly value neutral and that there is overwhelming evidence that the content of much that is now shown on television and in contemporary films is hostile to the Christian faith and to Christian moral sensitivities. This clearly suggests, according to communications professor Quentin Schultze, "that Christian viewers must become far more discerning about how stories influence their lives and shape their faith. Too many Christians wrongly believe that the tube is merely entertainment for mindless diversion. Every story is not just a diversion from the world, but also a door to another world. Stories are part of the language of the culture, and the tube is a popular voice."[90]

Recognizing that television is more than an entertaining diversion, that its images and narratives instruct as well as amuse, leads us to acknowledge with Schultze that "Television is one of the major educators of modern society. . . . Television is not usually a formal educator, such as with telecourses offered by colleges, but an informal, implicit, often unconscious educator. . . . Viewers learn from the tube, even if they aren't interested in education. Televised stories teach many things."[91] Neil Postman, a critic of the phenomenon, similarly contends: "One is entirely justified in saying that the major educational enterprise now being undertaken in the United States is not happening in its classrooms but in the home, in front of the television set, and under the jurisdiction not of school administrators and teachers but of network executives and entertainers."[92] Postman believes that it is not inaccurate to speak of television as a "curriculum," a curriculum that in fact nearly "obliterates" the school curriculum.[93]

Some critics of television go beyond an examination of the content of television stories to a critique of the very medium itself. While it may be true that, to a large extent, "TV shapes culture by telling stories,"[94] it is also true that much of television, by the very nature of the medium, is hostile to the narrative mode. The popularity of MTV, for example, can be attributed, at least in part, to its deliberate use of a non-narrative presentation. MTV's inventor Robert Pittman "describes how he had to explain the concept of MTV to executives who wanted a beginning, a middle and an end to their television." Pittman's response: "I said, 'There is no beginning, middle, and end. It's all ebb and flow,'" adding that the executives failed to realize that "this is a non-narrative generation."[95]

The result is television that "does away with narrative and replaces it with what filmmakers call montage: a rapid sequence of loosely connected images. This is the perfect fit of medium to music because rock is about the flow of experience, not about making sense out of experience."[96] Similar criticism has often been made of television newscasts depending on sound bites and images and lacking the time or the will for more in-depth, narrative-like exposition. What this suggests is that the medium itself imposes certain limits on television's use of stories to shape culture. Even many television stories, it could be argued, do not contribute to a larger narrative framework of meaning but only provide very small slices of self-contained narratives, a succession of images. Television is more an image medium than a story medium.

This has led some to draw a sharp distinction between image and word[97] and to reach the conclusion that while word is the appropriate vehicle for communicating truth, image is by its very nature illusory and deceitful. In the words of perhaps the most famous exponent of this view, the British Christian journalist Malcolm Muggeridge, the camera "always lies."[98] Muggeridge, in fact, contends: "The media have, indeed, provided the Devil with perhaps the greatest opportunity accorded him since Adam and Eve were turned out of the Garden of Eden."[99] When it was pointed out to him that this well-articulated critical perspective on the media was inconsistent with his own rather active, even very successful involvement in it, his reply was vintage Muggeridge: "[A]s a television performer, I see myself as a man playing a piano in a brothel, who includes 'Abide With Me' in his repertoire in the hope of thereby edifying both clients and inmates."[100]

What is at issue in this debate about word and image? A brief glance at a fascinating recorded dinner conversation between Neil Postman and Camille Paglia is illuminating.[101] Postman's argument is "that reading is an ordered process requiring us to sit at a table, consume ideas from left to right, and make judgments of truth and falsehood. By its nature, reading teaches us to reason. Television with its random, unconnected images, works against this linear tradition and breaks the habit of logic and thinking" (p. 44). Paglia does not disagree with Postman's analysis but insists that human life is far too rich to be reduced to the Apollonian and Protestant categories of word and reason. The Dionysian, pagan, and, in her judgment, Roman Catholic attention to image and icon is necessary to express the dynamic and even chaotic dimensions of human experience such as sex and violence.

Paglia's comments on the biblical prohibitions against images and the bias toward word is also interesting. The Postman-Paglia dinner began, we are told, "with a blessing in the form of two readings from the Bible: Exodus 20:4—'Thou shalt not make unto thee any graven image.'—and John 1:1—'In the beginning was the Word, and the Word was with God, and the Word was God.'" In Paglia's judgment, this priority of word and the prohibition of image, with its accompanying repression of pagan ritualism and eroticism, was an overreaction, if not an error. In fact, the word is not first. Paglia says,

> "In the beginning was nature." That's the first sentence of *my* book. Nature—violent, chaotic, unpredictable, uncontrollable—predates and stands in opposition to the ordered, structured world created by the word, by the law, by the book-centered culture of Judeo-Christianity. The image—which is pagan and expressive of nature's sex and violence—was outlawed by Moses in favor of the word. That's where our troubles began. (p. 45)

Postman and Paglia, thus, are in agreement about the correct description and analysis of contemporary culture. Where they differ is in their evaluation of it. Paglia sees popular culture and its return to images as "an eruption of paganism," a return to "the age of polytheism," "a rebirth of the pagan gods." She celebrates it as a liberating development.[102] Postman, on the other hand, while agreeing with the analysis, sees the development of an image-oriented popular culture not as liberating but as an ominous "triumph of idolatry" (pp. 47, 54). What is remarkable is that both insist that television must be controlled and that schools should not become like TV but should remain counter-culturally logocentric. Postman insists that schools "should supply what the rest of the culture is not supplying. In this case, I think the only defense against the seductions of imagery is a literate education. If children are educated in the traditions of the word, then perhaps they will be able to make discriminating choices in the chaotic realm of the image" (p. 54). Paglia agrees: "To me the ideal education should be rigorous and word-based—logocentric. The student must learn the logical, hierarchical system. Then TV culture allows the other part of the mind to move freely around the outside of that system. . . . Education is, by definition, repressive" (p. 54). In conclusion, Paglia notes: "Our dialogue has reached one major point of agreement. I want schools to stress the highest intellectual values and ideals of the Greco-Roman and Judeo-Christian traditions. . . . [W]e agree on this: We need to reinforce the logocentric and Apollonian side of our culture in the schools. It is time for enlightened repression of the children" (p. 55).

This snapshot of an important debate about word and image requires a much larger framework than we are able to provide here. Educators in particular must reflect further on the issues that have been sketched in the preceding passage. Any discussion about the context within which Christian education takes place today simply cannot avoid carefully examining the mass media. It is also apparent that discussions about the media cannot be separated from the larger cultural questions that we have considered in this chapter. Television, it seems, is the perfect vehicle for expressing and disseminating the values of postmodernism and even, perhaps, a revived paganism.

Conclusion

We have undertaken a fairly extensive survey of some recent literature that attempts to analyze and assess the key ideals, themes, and issues of our contemporary world. What does all this mean for Christians in general and for Christian education in particular? We are now better equipped to address the issues raised somewhat tentatively at the end of our opening chapter and to come to more definitive conclusions. To begin with, Christians today must recognize that the Christian religion is no longer the privileged faith of the West but a public minority religion. We do not thereby forfeit our right to make policy claims in the public arena, but we are forced to do so by competing with other vocal religions in the public marketplace. Our situation is indeed increasingly more like that of the early church—a minority religion. Whether this has really sunk into the consciousness of most Christians in North America remains to be seen. At any rate the implications are significant for Christian education.

In the first place it means that Christian schools as an alternative to public education are more important today than ever before. The very existence of such schools is a terribly important witness. Once again, Christopher Dawson's words about Christian higher education are also relevant to the Christian elementary and high school:

> So long as the Christian tradition of higher education still exists, the victory of secularism in a modern, technological society is not complete. There is still a voice to bear witness to the existence of the forgotten world of spiritual reality in which man has his true being.[103]

Second, Christians do not give up on public schools—just as we do not give up on our culture and society—but we recognize that we cannot be satisfied with the education they offer our children.

Finally, conserving the wisdom of the Christian tradition becomes an increasingly significant public function of the Christian school. It is now doubly clear that our situation is increasingly like that of the medieval monks. In a darkening age, Christian schools are called to keep the lamp of Christian civilization burning. Alasdair MacIntyre describes the hope that we may be able somehow to preserve the virtues of our civilization from the encroaching dark ages: "[I]f the tradition of the virtues was able to survive the horrors of the last dark ages, we are not entirely without grounds for hope. This time however the barbarians are not waiting beyond the frontiers; they have already been governing us for quite some time. . . . We are waiting not for a Godot, but for another—doubtless very different—St. Benedict."[104] Another educator also appeals to the example of St. Benedict, founder of Western monasticism. Noting that in the classical tradition the only education worthy of the name was an education in virtue, Jeffrey Holland, President of Brigham Young University, claims,

> Even during the very darkest moments in our history that philosophy endures. St. Benedict, living at a time when Rome was threatened and finally overrun by vandals, simply retreated behind the stone walls of Monte Cassino, taking with him the spirit and valued traditions of Christianity. "While the barbarian invaders ran wild," notes Calvin Woodard, "pillaging and destroying everything in sight, St. Benedict and his monks gently nourished the flickering flame of civilization."
>
> St. Benedict's example reminds us that one of the purposes of education is not only to resist the wicked, the tawdry and the profane, but to stand unalterably for the higher values of

civilization—Plato's truths, if you will—and, when the turbulent world will not accept them, to preserve and keep them alive for the future—when and after the vandals have exhausted themselves.[105]

We shall explore this theme more thoroughly in Chapter Six, "The Christian Story and the Christian School."

3

"Christian" Threats to Christian Education

Introduction

The title of this chapter requires some explanation. In the previous two chapters we considered the condition of and external threats to North American education in general. We examined the cultural context and the various competing forces, including spiritual ones, that have turned education into a battleground. Since Christian education is an enterprise of faith, it is vulnerable to the external spiritual threats faced by all ventures of faith in contemporary society. The pressures of modernity, the fragmentation of postmodernity, the process of secularization, and the hostility of a secular culture to Christian civilizational claims are threats to the Christian school as well as to the church. Furthermore, the relativization of public moral values is not only a threat to the Christian family. An increasingly pagan civilization profoundly influences the cultural sensitivities and appetites of all members of our Christian school communities.

In addition, the Christian school faces some distinct threats of its own. Externally, the rising cost of Christian school education threatens its universality; a Christian education that is available only people who are well-to-do is not deserving of its name. And if financial assistance from the government were forthcoming in the United States—as is the case in all Canadian provinces except Ontario—the involvement of government in matters of accreditation and curriculum supervision potentially threatens the independence and integrity of Christian education. Internally, as Christian schools have improved in quality and become an accepted part of the North American educational landscape, the danger is that there will be a loss of commitment to the basic vision that gave birth to the Christian school movement. Spiritual and educational complacency may set in. This problem of a loss of vision is exacerbated because Christian schools are not isolated from the debates, fads, and reform movements of the education industry in North America. Christian school teachers and Christian professors of education must come to terms with and critically evaluate the latest in contemporary educational philosophy, psychology, or pedagogy. And parents are not immune to the vocational pressures that come from business and industry to place marketable skills at the head of a list of educational objectives for the Christian school. In sum, Christian education exists in the world of the North American educational enterprise and must face the threats posed by contemporary culture.

Our concern in this chapter, however, is with a different set of threats to the Christian schools, ones we have labeled "Christian" threats. These are tendencies that on the surface reflect deeply held and appropriate Christian convictions yet, through distortion or isolation from other beliefs and practices, unwittingly undermine either the Christian or the education component of Christian education. For example, devotional exercises—Scripture reading, meditation, and prayer—are important aspects of the Christian life of discipleship and valid also within the school setting. Yet, as former Calvin College English professor Henry Zylstra pointed out more than forty years ago, devotions are not what make the school distinctively a *Christian school*. Although devotions are important, Zylstra argues that "they do not constitute the school a school: for this precious devotional element is just as proper to the home, to Christian industry, Christian recreation, places of Christian mercy, and the like." While the teacher who interrupts a geography lesson to remind her class of the gospel has her priorities in the right order, Zylstra continues: "But we ought not to go on to infer from this that a Christian school is a Christian school because it offers such wonderful opportunities for church or mission work. It is a precious by-product. Our schools must be schools."[1] A valid Christian practice can become a threat to the Christian school as school when it is mistakenly seen as the *raison d'être* of the school or as the hallmark of distinctively Christian education. Similarly, the Christian character of the school is threatened when through overemphasis or distortion a valid belief or practice is no longer recognizably or distinctively Christian. Although seeing the school as a place for indoctrination, evangelism, or prophetic social critique undermines the school as school, indoctrination and a disproportionate emphasis on excellence also threaten the Christian character of the school.

Before we examine each of these points in greater detail, we need to make an additional observation of a more general nature. Parents who sacrifice for Christian education are concerned that it be distinctively Christian, but this ideal is notoriously elusive. One of the major obstacles to distinctively Christian education is the phenomenon of identification and accommodation—the tendency to identify a specific educational philosophy, curriculum, or pedagogy as the Christian approach to education. Thus one encounters, for example, the contradictory claims that phonics or whole language is the Christian approach to teaching reading at the primary school level. Some have put forth arguments that the classical medieval model is the way to structure a Christ-centered curriculum.[2] Similar claims have been made for open education and cooperative, or first-step, learning.[3] Also, to repeat an observation from our first chapter, it is possible to find supporters of cultural or critical literacy as the Christian approach to school. Our response to this phenomenon of identification and accommodation is not to argue that choices should be avoided in matters of educational philosophy, psychology, or pedagogy, nor that such choices should not be warranted by Christian beliefs and commitments. On the contrary! Rather, we must take great care that we do not too quickly identify specific philosophies or pedagogies as the Christian approach and thereby close down needed conversation. Excessive claims and positions usually need to be modified or even abandoned. When this is repeated too often, as has happened in the cycle of reforms in public education during this century, the stability and health of Christian education as a whole is threatened.

Threat Number One: Indoctrination

We now move on to examine four different but related sets of threats to Christian education. The first one is the threat of indoctrination.

The charge of indoctrination is the favorite of secular critics of Christian education.[4] The ideals of human autonomy and free, open inquiry seem to many people to be diametrically at odds with the deliberate, self-conscious attempt to nurture children in a specific religious tradition. An obvious rejoinder to this is that the ideals of human autonomy and free, open inquiry are as much a dogma as the doctrine of original sin and human need for salvation by grace in Jesus Christ. The Christian simply judges one to be true and the other false. Furthermore, it seems incomprehensible that parents would desire an education for their children that deliberately avoided all standards, rules, values, and commitments. Christian parents who desire that their children acquire a Christian worldview may have different goals from those of secularly oriented humanistic parents, but then the debate is about which doctrine, not doctrine versus no doctrine at all.

Yet, there are two levels at which the charge of indoctrination must be taken seriously as a threat. Indoctrination, in its positive sense as teaching the specific confessions of the Christian church, is the task of the institutional church, not the school. On this score the Reformed tradition's approach to Christian education[5] differs from that of Roman Catholic, Lutheran, and parochial schools, those that are operated by a church for the purpose of raising children in the tenets of that church's specific faith.[6] Although teaching Bible and Christian theology is appropriate and necessary in every Christian school curriculum, it is not the primary task of the school as school to catechize.

There is, however, a second and perhaps more troubling level at which the issue of indoctrination must be faced. The ultimate goal of Christian parents is that their children willingly and joyfully embrace the Christian faith. Passing on the Christian faith from generation to generation, however, is a complex process and fraught with potential pitfalls as well as pain, especially for parents of children who repudiate the faith. The tradition can be passed on and appropriated in a thoughtless and wooden fashion. Then tradition stops being the living faith of the dead and becomes traditionalism—the dead faith of the living.[7] In evangelical communities, where personal commitment to the Christian faith is considered a matter of one's eternal salvation, children may feel intimidated by fear of judgment or even simple peer pressure to conform to the religious expectations of parents, other Christian adults, or the community as a whole. As Christian psychologist Donald Sloat has observed, since "Christian values cannot be easily or automatically transferred from one generation to the next. . . . parents (and the church as well) may instill so much fear and guilt along with values that youngsters are afraid to sort out their beliefs in order to stand on their own."[8] The practice of encouraging testimonies in evangelistic meetings, school assemblies, and youth retreats, often pressures young people to conform to expectations of the community. Furthermore, faith produced under such pressure is often fragile because the individuals have not seriously wrestled with difficult questions and personal doubts. Sloat asserts that "A . . . problem exists when youngsters accept what their parents have taught them without questioning or evaluating it. They are then simply following hollow beliefs that can crumble easily under pressure. This is especially true when Christian parents either do not teach children to think for themselves or do not even allow them to do so. It is easy for succeeding generations to go along with their parents' teachings, and as a result they live out traditions that have little or no personal meaning."[9] Such indoctrination fails to meet the test of proper Christian education—namely, that the truth of the Christian faith must become meaningful and experientially real for each generation anew. The only way to avoid indoctrination in this negative sense is to give children the space to test their own faith in the crucible of human experience. Parents, therefore, need to allow their children "to have experiences from which they can learn, not overly sheltering them. . . . [E]ach of us is different and has to come to grips with his own faith and make it real through personal experience. . . . Personalizing our faith and value system is necessary for us as Christians to be strong, positive, fruitful people."[10]

Sloat points out that good intentions on the part of parents and church leaders are not enough to provide an environment in which healthy spiritual growth and maturation take place. Some of his comments about churches and families are also applicable to the Christian school, where there is a self-conscious effort to pass on a religious tradition and inculcate in children a specific worldview rooted in that tradition. Christian education does run the risk of becoming mere indoctrination, a mindless repetition of stale and dead doctrines for their own sake, without any genuine, living, experiential relation to those doctrines.

Some critics of Christian education believe that all committed education is indoctrination. In the words of one such critic, "No school governed by ideology—any ideology whatsoever—can afford to educate its students; it can only indoctrinate and train them."[11] Education, in this understanding, must be utterly free and open inquiry. This common assumption and accusation against Christian education is one that must be answered. Two points need to be made. In the first place, as Douglas Wilson notes, "[T]eaching students to think in terms of a fixed reference point is not the same thing as indoctrination. It is more than devout propaganda. . . . A fixed reference point does not blind Christians to the existence of objections; it enables Christians to answer them. . . . It is not propagandizing when teachers give their students a place to stand. Relativism has only the appearance of openness; in the end, it always frustrates the one who wants to acquire knowledge."[12] In a secular world, a Christian worldview opens up new vistas for students by providing a coherent framework in which the reality of the world can be examined and understood. Good Christian education is not only a matter of standing in the truth, it must also be a matter of seeking out and testing the truth. This is what Christian discernment is all about. A recent manifesto on Christian education affirms the following: "Trusting the Holy Spirit's guidance in the students' lives, the Christian school community offers opportunities and fosters responsibilities to exercise discernment—the making of informed Christian choices based on God's Word."[13]

It must be frankly acknowledged that not all Christian education meets these criteria. Douglas Wilson puts it forthrightly: "Now it is true that some who claim to hold to Christian truth are unreasoning ideologues."[14] Wilson also devotes an entire chapter of his book on Christian education to "the problem of 'pious' ignorance," a euphemism for "the strong anti-intellectual sentiment that exists among some conservative Christians."[15] His conclusion is clear. He disparages the loss of what Harry Blamires has called "the Christian mind," the loss of Christian thinking by reducing it to "spiritual things" and the Sunday School curriculum:

> Wisdom is not confined or imprisoned. Although many conservative Christians have withdrawn into an evangelical ghetto, the wisdom of God has not gone with them. Rather, wisdom stands at the gates of the city and cries out to the sons of men (Proverbs 8). What she offers is more than spiritual insight about spiritual things; it is spiritual insight about *all* things. She speaks about political science (v. 15) and economics (vv. 18, 20-21). She knows all about the origin of the universe because she was there (vv. 22-31). All who hate her love death (v. 36). Those who build any school without her build on a poor foundation.[16]

In *The Closing of the American Heart: What's Really Wrong with America's Schools* Ronald Nash makes a similar observation about the anti-intellectualism pervasive in many Christian school communities, particularly in the fundamentalist and charismatic subcultures of North American evangelical Christianity.

> If there is one major weakness in some elements of the Christian school movement, it is related to the seemingly unlimited evangelical propensity for superspirituality and anti-intellectualism. There is absolutely nothing wrong with a proper emphasis on spirituality. But what must be abandoned is a thoughtless, mindless type of otherworldliness that denigrates the importance of truth.
>
> Too many Christian schools still offer a curriculum that stresses simple memorization of information presented in less than adequate teaching material. The Christian church needs young people who have been exposed to the best of Western culture and who are able to interact thoughtfully and reflectively with the literature, history, philosophy, and science of that culture. In short, we need Christians who have broad minds that have been sharpened to the point of usefulness.[17]

One of the ways in which this matter of anti-intellectualist indoctrination comes to expression is in the use of standardized curricula, such as those offered by the Accelerated Christian Education (A.C.E.) program. Susan Rose, in her critical assessment of one of these schools, concludes:

> The education offered at the Baptist Academy appears to anticipate the future of efficient, corporate-oriented instruction. The emphasis on orderliness and discipline at the "office" learning station realistically mirrors the working stations of many present and future jobs. The increasingly automated and computerized clerical or office job requires someone who is willing and able to sit at a word processor or computer terminal for an entire day with little or no interaction with fellow workers. Progress in the factory means more automated or robotized machinery operated or watched by soli-

tary people who are attentive to sporadic requests from the control board.

The A.C.E. program stresses the extreme self-discipline and isolation required of each student at his or her "work-station." The pre-packaged learning program of A.C.E. creates a monologue of instructions rather than a dialogue; no longer is the teacher needed to communicate knowledge to or engage in joint activities with students. Thus, A.C.E. is keeping up with the times. It uses a system of transmitting information through manuals under the direction of adults who are more like supervisors than teachers, who are not as well educated or well paid as public-school teachers. This correlates nicely with the standardization of production and procedures now practiced by many large corporations in the service, manufacturing, insurance, and banking fields.[18]

The results, according to Rose, are graduates who will compliantly fit into the automated, routinized world of corporate America.

If we consider the Baptist school as a corporate franchise, the minister is the educational entrepreneur in the modern corporate sense; he brings A.C.E. to his community the way someone else brings a McDonald's or Wendy's fast food franchise. The minister may get some financial rewards for his efforts, but his major gain is his increased control over the spiritual and educational lives of his congregation. The owner of a McDonald's can feel like an independent businessman at the same time he is purveying the same low quality food that thousands of others are feeding to millions of Americans on behalf the same corporation. So too, the independent Christian school can feel as if it is breaking free from the "secular humanist" stranglehold on education—only to buy a repetitive, programmed meal of knowledge which fits the needs of corporate society (or the military-industrial complex) much more efficiently than do the public schools.[19]

According to Ronald Nash, "while the parents may think the schools are helping to keep their children out of the hands of 'Satan' (the godless humanism that presumably controls public education), the children are really being delivered into the hands of another 'Satan,' which for Rose is the materialistic god of corporate America and the military-industrial complex."[20]

The anti-business ideology and rhetorical flourishes aside, it must be granted that what Rose describes is the sort of indoctrination that could happen in certain kinds of educational settings.[21] It is also clear that what she describes is not what Reformed Christian educators want. Rose describes a charismatic Christian school ("Covenant") in terms that Reformed Christians would be much happier with:

> In contrast, the middle-class charismatic parents and educators challenge their students to think more critically. Like all parents, they want to instill their values and beliefs but the process of instruction is more important than the specific content. Group work, discussions that examine a spectrum of values and beliefs, and various strategies for formulating and resolving problems characterize school life. Challenge and interpretation rather than conformity and security are stressed.
>
> Covenant people are communicating their view of the world as a place in which individuals are actors who, in cooperation with one another, can transform the world. In contrast to the Baptist emphasis on individual discipline, the middle-class charismatics stress self-directed and cooperative work in their children's education. The charismatics anticipate their children entering roles that will enable them to act on the world.[22]

By now our point should be clear. Passing on the Christian faith, tradition, ethos, and worldview from one generation to the next should never degenerate to mere indoctrination. Unthinking, unexamined, and uncritical traditionalism is always a danger in religiously committed and intentional education, but it is most decidedly not the goal of a good Christian education. There must be room in

Christian education for thoughtful examination of the Christian tradition, an examination that must take seriously the objections raised against the Christian faith and worldview as well as alternatives to it. However, some critics claim that Christian education shelters children from the real world. Are Christian schools greenhouses that protect and isolate children from broader society and culture? Susan Rose quotes a Baptist mother:

> "Some people say we are protecting them from the world, sheltering them. Well, that's right. I don't want them in the world. I want them to go into Christian service. It's like tomatoes in a greenhouse; you have to protect them and nourish them until they grow strong before you put them in the garden."[23]

This parent has a valid point. Taking the developmental levels of children seriously does mean that Christian parents want to shelter young children from the moral decadence and sinful, secularist, or pagan values of our cultures. What is the real world? In the judgment of Christians, the world of violence, sexual immorality, and general hedonism is an unreal world, and it is the desire of Christian parents that children learn to live in the real world of peace, justice, monogamy, and loving service as they grow into their involvement with the so-called real world. Christians acknowledge, however, that sheltering is both a strategic move and a temporary one. Permanent sheltering or withdrawal from the world is impossible, primarily because we all carry the world in our hearts. No wall is high enough to keep the world completely outside.

In another sense, too, sheltering is an ill-advised strategy. We live in God's world; this is his creation. Good Christian education explores the entire range of human experience in order to equip children to a life of full, trinitarian discipleship. This exploration of all dimensions of creation also means exploring the cultural products of those who are not Christians and those whose culture differs significantly from white, North American culture. To ignore this wider range of human experience is to miss opportunities to acknowledge and praise the Spirit of the Creator God in his lavish giving of gifts to humanity. As John Calvin says,

> Meanwhile, we ought not to forget those most excellent benefits of the divine Spirit, which he distributes to whomever he wills, for the common good of mankind.
>
> If we regard the Spirit of God as the sole fountain of truth, we shall neither reject the truth itself, nor despise it wherever it shall appear, unless we wish to dishonor the Spirit of God. For by holding the gifts of the Spirit in slight esteem, we condemn and reproach the Spirit himself. . . . Those men whom Scripture [1 Cor. 2:14] calls "natural men" were, indeed, sharp and penetrating in their investigation of inferior things. Let us, accordingly, learn by their example how many gifts the Lord left to human nature even after it was despoiled of its true good.[24]

A Christian school in the Reformed tradition does not shelter students from the full range of human experience or from the cultural products of non-Christians. The desire is to have students critically interact with the best of Western and other civilizations. Nor should the Reformed Christian school shelter students from the challenges to the Christian faith presented by such issues as evolution and atheism and such thinkers as Marx, Darwin, and Freud. The goal is not indoctrination but an examined, thoughtful, mature Christian faith and worldview.

Threat Number Two: Evangelism

From the outset I wish to reiterate a point I have made elsewhere, namely that the Christian school has an evangelical role to play in the life of the Christian community as a whole. It is true that Christian education "is designed to promote Christian *cultural* or *creational obedience*" and "is not in the first place designed to evangelize students or to prepare them for evangelism and missionary service."[25] However, to overlook the concern of the home and church that students become full-orbed living disciples of our Lord Jesus Christ would be a failure to live up to the name Christian. Since, as Henry Zylstra states, "Christian education must be both education and Christian if it is to justify itself and successfully meet the secular challenge,"[26] a school cannot ignore the missionary command of our Lord and still be considered Christian. In a nutshell,

> Christian day school education also takes place in the New Testament age which is dominated by the missionary mandate. For this reason it should not be considered a violation of the school's proper sphere or jurisdiction of Christian day school teachers also press the *missionary* claim of the gospel. In Christian day schools, too, students must be confronted with the call to Christian discipleship and need to have the urgency of world evangelism placed before them. Failure to do either or both will have (or already may have had) an adverse effect on Reformed Christian day school education in North America. Reformed Christian day schools do not exist exclusively or even chiefly for purposes of evangelism and mission, but they ignore their evangelistic role at the peril of being less than truly Christian schools.[27]

And again:

> The school cannot leave the mission mandate to the church alone. Not in *our* day. Not only do teachers when teaching subjects such as geography and history have an obligation to point out the importance of Christian missionary activity, but the schools must themselves serve in a mission capacity. Students who pass through Christian schools ought to be confronted with the call to Christian commitment.[28]

This, it should be noted, is also the conclusion of Professor

Henry Zylstra:

> I think that devotional exercises, Bible reading, prayer, medi-
> tation, the service of song, and Biblical study seriously pur-
> sued, pursued also with evanglical emphases, and not merely
> as so much scientific data—I think that these are very pre-
> cious. Without them a school could hardly be designated
> Christian.[29]

Taking an evangelical role seriously means that a vibrant
and open Christian testimony is one of the most important
requisites for a teacher in the Christian school. Modeling
evangelical enthusiasm is perhaps even more important
than explicitly including an evangelical objective in a geography lesson plan. It is also worth considering at this point
whether the Christian school should permit the enrollment
of a restricted number of children from non-Christian
homes as an evangelistic strategy. This opens up a host of
questions, not to mention difficulties, but if schools in mission situations on foreign soils can be used in such a way,
there should be no principled reason why North American
schools, now also increasingly in a "mission situation,"
could not do the same. Safeguards must be adopted, of
course, that will ensure the integrity of the school as a
Christian school. Non-Christian parents would have to
indicate a willingness and desire to have their children
instructed within a Christian worldview.[30]

Having emphasized one part of the equation (Christian
schools that want to be Christian do have an evangelical
role), we must now stress the other side. When evangelism
is the primary reason for the Christian school, it becomes a
threat to the school as school. In addition to the fact that
indoctrination, understood as explicitly teaching the confessions or doctrines of a particular church, is not the task
of the school, three other observations must be made here.

In the first place, evangelism as the rationale for Christian education runs contrary to a Reformed understanding of children as members of the covenant community. Reformed people do not regard their children as lost pagans, outside the family of God. On the contrary—they believe that their children, "though sinful by nature, are received by God in Christ as members of his covenant."[31] This covenantal presumption has often been misunderstood by Reformed and non-Reformed Christians alike. It does not mean that baptism regenerates or that covenant membership makes calls to committed Christian discipleship irrelevant and unnecessary. It does mean that our children are considered in Christ as members of God's family, that their spirituality is taken seriously, and that the integrity of their faith is treated with respect. Not only does this free the school to be fully a school, but it also frees the Christian community at large from the guilt manipulations and pressure tactics often used in evangelistic settings. Treating our children out of a presumption that they are lost and spiritually crippled does them a disservice and disregards God's covenantal promises to his people.

Secondly, life is more than evangelism. Being saved is not all that there is to Christian discipleship. Here a trinitarian vision or perspective is helpful and needed. God is our Redeemer in Jesus Christ. Yet redemption is in some sense the means to a greater end. Salvation is the restoration of humanity and creation to the ordered purpose intended by the Creator God. For Reformed people in particular, the most important question in life is not What must I do to be saved? but How can I glorify God? As the Westminster Catechism so beautifully puts it: "the chief end of man is to glorify God and enjoy Him forever." To be sure, fallen, sinful human beings need to be saved from their lostness before they can truly glorify God and enjoy him forever. Yet salvation in this sense is a means not the end. Abraham Kuyper, in his *Lectures on Calvinism,* put it this way: the dominating principle of Calvinism "was not, soteriologically, justification by faith, but in the widest sense cosmologically, *the sovereignty of the triune God over the whole cosmos,* in all its spheres and kingdoms, visible and invisible."[32]

This distinction is crucially important for the Christian school. It is this trinitarian, catholic vision that is the heart of the rationale for Reformed Christian education. It is the conviction that our world belongs to God, that Christians are called to vocations in God's world where they are to be humanly and culturally active as saved disciples of Jesus Christ. And it is the specific task of the school to make that connection between vocation and discipleship a real and living one. Schools prepare students for citizenship in the kingdom of our Lord Jesus Christ, a kingdom that is more than the church. To be saved is to be called to serve in God's world. When schools thus take evangelism in the narrow sense as the reason for their existence, they endanger their own identity and calling as schools. Once again, Henry Zylstra makes the point eloquently:

> I repeat: the schools must be schools. It is the very strength of the Reformed profession of Christianity not solely in the isolatedly religious but in the religious commanding the naturally and culturally human. It is as human beings that we are Christians, in our human nature expressing itself in a natural environment, expressing itself also in cultural activity of all kinds, and, further, in a particular historical situation here on earth. Our being called to be saints does not exempt us from being human, nor exempt us from cultural activity, nor exempt us from social and political obligation, nor render reason superfluous, nor permit an indifference to art and literature, nor lift us out of history. On the contrary, it is in and through these things that our moral and religious choice for the spiritual kingdom of Christ becomes concrete, real, and

meaningful. And that is why our schools must be schools, our education education.[33]

Finally, it is necessary to reflect on the consequences of the school taking on roles and tasks traditionally served by other social institutions such as the family or church. If evangelism is indeed the real task of the church, what happens, when the school simply becomes an arm of the church? We have already noted that when this happens, the school tends to lose its distinct identity as school. But the reverse process also may take place. When the school increasingly takes on the tasks of the church, it may also undermine the integrity of the church's distinct mission. This is perhaps the key thesis of Neal Postman's book *Teaching As a Conserving Activity*. Postman contends that "schools should not, except under the most extreme provocation, try to accomplish goals which other social institutions traditionally serve." Postman points to the limited competence and resources of teachers. They cannot do the work of priest, psychologist, therapist, political reformer, social worker, sex advisor, and parent. He also notes the institutional consequence: "The more one social institution encroaches upon the functions of another, the more it weakens it. This idea . . . comes from the field of ecology, where it is understood that as one system begins to preempt the purposes of another, the functional capacity of both is undermined." Postman concludes: "[A]s the school blurs the lines of authority between itself and other institutions, it tends to weaken not only its own capability but the capabilities of other institutions as well."[34]

While the sensitive Christian teacher cannot overlook an evangelical dimension to all teaching, he or she must be foremost a teacher and not an evangelist. While the school should be open to evangelical opportunities, it must be a school and not a church.

How the Christian school can play a legitimate evangelical role as school will become more apparent when we consider a narrative approach to Christian education in Chapter Six.

Threat Number Three: Prophecy

I have labeled the third threat to Christian education prophecy. The word *prophetic* has in recent years been used especially for vocal criticism of alleged sinful deformations in North American social, economic, and political life. To be prophetic is to be critical of capitalism, militarism, racism, and sexism. Hence, *prophetic* is simply another term for what I referred to as critical literacy in the first chapter. I prefer *prophetic* in this context because we are considering Christian threats to Christian education, and it is especially in religious or ecclesiastical circles that such social and cultural criticism is referred to as prophecy.

We begin by noting that prophecy, even when understood narrowly as social and cultural critique, is a valued activity and a necessary dimension of Christian discipleship in the world. Christians are indeed called to an antithetical relationship to what the New Testament calls the world. They are called to be countercultural agents of God's kingdom. This seems even more urgent today in light of our cultural analysis in the previous chapter. As our society and culture become increasingly hostile to the Christian religion and its truth claims, Christians will increasingly be regarded as "resident aliens,"[35] and the prophetic countercultural attitude will seem increasingly to be an imperative.

To put it into more biblical categories, true prophecy exposes and challenges idolatry. As we noted in Chapter Two, idolatry and judgment are essential categories for interpreting the crisis of our society and culture. We noted the contention of Herbert Schlossberg that "idolatry and its associated concepts provide a better framework for us to understand our own society than do any of the alternatives."[36] Schlossberg identifies idolatry as "any substitution of what is created for the creator. People may worship nature, money, mankind, power, history or social and political systems instead of the God who created them all."[37] Prophecy is thus clearly an essential ingredient of Christian discipleship, and the Old Testament prophets have much to teach us in our idolatrous and destructive age.

But what about prophecy in the school? One author who pleads for "Christian schooling as prophetic witness" also takes note of the threat involved.

> Righteousness can be advanced in society through schooling only as we both recognise and respect the distinctive educational structure of the school. Its use, for example, as a political instrument or as an ecclesiastical instrument is an abuse of the structural identity of the school. The inevitable result is a blunting of the school's educational effectiveness. Pursued consistently it will destroy the school, transforming it into a political or ecclesiastical agency.
>
> Again it is to be stressed that it is proper, indeed essential, that the school address political and ecclesiastical questions. In doing so it will have political and ecclesiastical input. However, the faithful practice of Christian schooling will be careful to ensure that this is done in a way that respects the distinctive educational identity of the school.[38]

We need, therefore, to ask some tough questions at this point. Should the school curriculum be shaped by prophetic categories? Should the school itself be an instrument of social change? Should Christian teachers think of themselves as prophets who consider social-cultural criticism to be their chief task? Has the Christian school failed in its task if its students don't picket nuclear power plants, attend anti-abortion rallies, protest against war, write letters for Amnesty International, and join marches on Earth Day? The authors of a famous 1960s tract asked if teaching should be a subversive activity. Their answer was clear and unequivocal: "We believe that the schools must serve as the principal medium for developing in youth the attitudes and skills of social, political, and cultural criticism."[39] Should Christian schools join in here? Is this the necessary next stage in the evolution of Christian education in North America?

One Christian educator who has eloquently pleaded for greater prophetic activity is Nicholas Wolterstorff. In an address to the Ontario Christian School Teachers Convention in the fall of 1984, Wolterstorff insisted that Reformed Christian education must go beyond traditional and classic neo-Calvinist models of developing a Christian mind to a more holistic goal of equipping the student for active discipleship in Christ's kingdom, for discipleship that goes beyond the cultural mandate to include a concern for justice.[40] Society as well as culture must be taken seriously. Wolterstorff asks whether classic neo-Calvinism in its concern to legitimate vocations in culture and society has in fact been indifferent to the concerns of the suffering and oppressed because it has been an ideology of the powerful and comfortable or "perhaps because the neo-Calvinist has given insufficient recognition to the *fallenness* of our world." Whatever the reasons, Wolterstorff is convinced "that the life for which we educate must be a life seeking justice and showing mercy as well as a life of wresting culture from nature." Acknowledging his own change of heart, Wolterstorff states his case eloquently:

> Once I did not know, but now I do know, that a program of Christian education which grounds itself only on the command to have dominion and not also on the command to

free the people cannot be an acceptable program of Christian education. Once I did not know, but now I do know, that a program of Christian learning which seeks only to develop abstract science in Christian perspective and not also to develop praxis-oriented science of service to Christian social action can be of only limited use in Christian education.

According to Wolterstorff, the neo-Calvinist vision must be expanded to a view that includes the struggle against sin and oppression as well as "celebrative delight in all that is good." All of this, he judges, can be brought together in the biblical notion of shalom:

> I have come to think that the most promising concept for capturing God's and our mission in the world is the biblical concept of shalom. Shalom is the content of that Kingdom which Jesus said was breaking in and whose ultimate presence his death and resurrection have secured. We now are to delight in the shalom we experience and to share in God's cause of advancing its presence. There is no shalom without justice. But beyond that, shalom is delight in all one's relationships: with God, neighbor, nature, and self. Shalom unites the fulfillment of culture with the liberation of justice. Life in the City of God is a life committed to struggling for shalom and to appreciating the flickers of shalom that already brighten our existence. Christian education is education for shalom.

How does one teach for shalom? How does one shape the actions of students into prophetic directions? Beyond awareness raising and thinking, Wolterstorff suggests discipline that will increase the tendency of a person to act in appropriate ways by reward and punishment, modeling and giving reasons.[41]

On the face of it, it is hard to quarrel against shalom. What Christian wants to be on record as being for militarism, racism, and sexism, and against peace, justice, equality, and earthkeeping. Refusing to join the prophetic chorus seems an act of bad faith, if not bad taste. Yet Wolterstorff's vision does arouse opposition. To begin with, there is the objection that reforming society is an improper goal for Christian education because society is irreformable. David Engelsma puts it this way: "The Christian school does not evangelize—only the church does. Christian schools do not exist to reform society, because, as is the A, B, C, of the Reformed religion, society is irreformably depraved, reserved for fiery destruction."[42] Actually, in fairness to Wolterstorff, he is more concerned with obedience and alleviation of pain and misery than he is optimistic or triumphalistic about reforming society.[43] Nonetheless, other questions also surface.

Part of the difficulty with Wolterstorff's plea is that it is not always concrete and specific, especially with respect to the Christian elementary or high school. Indeed most of his suggestions—internationalization of the curriculum and programs in peace and war, nationalism, poverty, urban ugliness, ecology, crime and punishment—appear more suited to curricular discussions at the university or college level than to the elementary school or even the high school.[44] A second general difficulty arises from the present preoccupation with political correctness in North American education, as well as in the churches. Although shalom is a wonderful Old Testament concept, the peace and justice agenda of some mainline churches has been so captured by leftist political ideas that the currency is thoroughly debased. Much of it is shallow, one-sided, anti-business, anti-Western ideology that reduces very complex issues to slogans and simplistic categories: us/them, peacemakers/ militarists, those for the poor/those who oppress the poor, earth keepers/despoilers, equalitarians/racists. Consequently, when this ideology is pushed into education, the school is politicized. True education ought to prepare a student for

serious, engaged reflection on these complex issues. A highly politicized school merely indoctrinates.

While this is problematic at all levels of education and in
all schools, the problem is even more acute in Christian
elementary and high schools, particularly since younger
children are highly vulnerable to political manipulation.
Not only does the politicizing of the school threaten the
school as school (where students should be taught good
socio-political analytic skills and not merely acquire political habits by indoctrination), but the Christian dimension
of the school is also threatened. What passes as prophetic
in Christian social justice circles often turns out to be little
more than proof-text frosting on secular humanitarian-
ism.[45] The social teaching of most mainline liberal churches in North America today usually differs little from the
policy of the left-wing in the Democratic party in the United States or the socialist New Democratic Party in Canada.
Resentment and altruism are confused with Christian justice and love. What claims to be radically Christian is often
trendy, simple accommodation to conventional, secular
socio-political criticism. What is called prophecy, therefore,
often not only impedes good education; it is not always
even all that distinctively Christian.

To the degree that such prophecy is utopian or apocalyptic in its tone it presents additional problems. Utopian
thinking is opposed by Christian orthodoxy because it is
presumptuous of God's timetable and counterproductive to
the social good. Utopianism is the conviction that the final
shalom of God's kingdom is achievable today. All that
stands in its way is ignorance and bad faith. Thus utopians
are perpetually in the position of complaining about the
status quo, whatever it happens to be.[46] Utopians are all-or-
nothing thinkers. They consider penultimate judgments
and affirmations to be a capitulation, a moral lapse. Either

North America is the kingdom of God or it is Babylon. Clearly it is short of the new heaven, so it must be Babylon. No careful discrimination between ultimate good and a relatively good society is possible. Since good Christian education should teach the skill of discriminating between what is relatively good and what is relatively evil in a given culture or society, what is improvable and what may be the best we can do short of the kingdom of God, utopian-prophetic thinking stands in the way of good education. More than that, however, it also stands in the way of a good society. By failing to acknowledge that there is much that is good in Western civilization and in North American society, utopian thinking undermines the good that is there. Traditions of freedom, political stability, equality before the law, opportunity to profit from one's labors and be a responsible, productive participant in society—all these and more are, we now know with stark certainty, fragile and not to be taken for granted. Unless prophecy is accompanied by affirmation and conservation of that which is good, much of what we take for granted can and will be lost in revolutionary change. Socially and politically, the perfect is in fact the enemy of the good.

When prophecy becomes apocalyptic in its tone, it creates a climate that is educationally *and* socio-politically counterproductive. Herbert London, in an analysis of social studies textbooks published in recent years, has documented this one-sided apocalyptic tendency.[47] When children and adolescents are bombarded with this apocalyptic material, what happens to their worldview? Is it any wonder that suicide rate among teenagers is as high as it is? Is it any wonder that many have little or no hope about the future? The opposite all-is-wonderful mentality is not suitable, either. Real problems should not be ignored. However, an overemphasis upon the apocalyptic-prophetic often ignores the developmental levels and capacities of children to absorb crisis thinking. Frightened children neither learn nor develop a framework that encourages them to gain skills which could help ameliorate the very real ills of our world.

The use of prophecy to politicize the school also betrays a fundamental lack of trust in adult institutions to reform society. It also runs the danger of exploiting children by enlisting them in adult crusades. This is to turn a Reformed covenantal emphasis on the proper responsibility of young persons on its head. The school should not intrude upon the social function of the family, the church, the medical profession, and community and political organizations. In the Christian community, politicizing the school intrudes particularly upon the responsibility and sensitivities of parents. Those who favor politicizing the school do so only when their political views are promoted.

Finally, when education becomes prophetic in its actual practice, the distinctive calling of a student is lost. Education is not life; it is preparation for life. Education allows for a certain detachment from life, a time for reflective and analytic distance. When education itself becomes immersed in socio-political activism or when education is solely seen as developing marketable job skills, then the comprehensive education that opens up many different dimensions of experience for the whole person is lost. The calling of a student is to be a student, not an evangelist or social activist.

Raising these objections to prophecy is a somewhat uncomfortable responsibility. Themes such as justice, peace, and earthkeeping are biblically appropriate and even necessary in Christian education. Their debasement in our day does not invalidate their true importance. Nicholas Wolterstorff is quite correct when he observes that "the Christian college cannot neglect the suffering of humanity. . . . It cannot burrow into culture while neglecting society."[48] What is true for the Christian college is no less true for the Christian elementary and high school.

Threat Number Four: Excellence

Perhaps it seems odd to consider excellence a threat to Christian education at a time when the universal complaint about education is that standards are declining and quality is eroding. Recently *The Atlantic Monthly* published an article on "the other crisis in American education," the failure to educate the gifted among us, which the author contends is as serious a challenge to education as is the poor quality of education received by those who are disadvantaged.[49] If excellence is a problem in public education, how can it be a threat to Christian education?

In part, the question itself hints at the answer. In a large measure, Christian schools have not suffered the same kind of erosion of quality that some public schools have because they do not live with the same social trauma and disadvantage. Most children attending Christian schools come from relatively stable, middle-class family settings in which disciplined habits of study and reading are encouraged and even modeled. There are exceptions, of course, and even children who do come from such homes are still subject to social and cultural pressures that discourage excellence. Nonetheless, home and community involvement in and support for the work of the school and its teachers are significantly higher in Christian education than in public education as a whole. Consequently, Christian schools often develop a reputation for excellence. I would judge that the quality of Christian schools affiliated with Christian Schools International (CSI) matches or surpasses that of most public schools. Professional qualifications and development of teachers in these schools at all levels is at a high level. These are good schools, even excellent schools.

Here is precisely the problem. At face value, excellence in learning is a good thing; it is even a Christian value. Various slogans reflect this thought: "God deserves our best;" "Christ is Lord, also of education;" "As image bearers of God himself we glorify him by using our talents fully." Even excessive athletic competition is often connected to such biblical notions as "Our bodies are temples of the Holy Spirit." It should be said from the outset that merit and competition are not intrinsically evil. Yet, the danger is real that Christian schools begin to define their *raison d'être* in terms of quality, excellence, and the general success of their graduates. When excellence and success are defined in worldly rather than truly Christian terms, the foundational vision of the Christian school is threatened. For Christians, excellence is pursued because God's work is underway,[50] success is measured in terms of the good done in and for Christ's kingdom. Applying these standards, Mother Teresa is a success; Donald Trump is not. It ought to be a matter of concern to practitioners and supporters of Christian education that this is not always clear in Christian school communities.

In short, excellence is a threat to the Christian character of the school when it is defined in worldly terms of achievement rather than in terms of discipleship to Jesus Christ. Clearly, achievement and discipleship must not be seen as mutually exclusive. The Reformed doctrine of vocation, a sense of calling from God and a desire to glorify him in whatever he calls us to do, makes that abundantly clear. The Christian lawyer or investment banker, no less than the Christian missionary, is called to discipleship. Yet there is something wrong with a Christian education that produces many successful lawyers, engineers, doctors, and businessmen but relatively few missionaries, inner-city pastors, or long-term service volunteers. We must always be on the alert that we define excellence in a Christian way, in terms of valuable service to Christ's kingdom. Otherwise, excellence is a threat to the integrity of Christian education.

An emphasis on excellence or competence can also become a form of unchristian elitism. Excellence, when defined in terms of intellectual dexterity, can result in the marginalizing of slower learners. Excellence must not neglect the joy of the cross. It must be nurtured in a climate of care and compassion for the suffering world, a care that is directed toward the world beyond our affluent North American society but also to the suffering that takes place within the school itself. Christian schools need not apologize for striving for academic excellence, provided they also show care and compassion for those who find learning more difficult. If Christian schools only salute the academic and athletic achievements of the highly accomplished and are unable to rejoice with the accomplishments of the less talented or differently gifted, then excellence has become an idol and Christian education has lost its soul. For this reason competition in Christian schools should be focused less on external competition between students and more on the internal competition that the student experiences with his or her own personal mastery of a subject or activity.[51]

Conclusion

In the first half of this volume we have looked at the problems facing Christian education, problems arising out of our social and cultural context as well as those more endemic to the Christian school itself. We are now in a position to consider an answer to the question, Why should we have Christian schools, and what should they be like?

4

The Christian Mind: Necessary But Not Sufficient

Introduction: Why Christian Education?

Why should there be Christian schools, and what is their task? Why do parents, in many instances with considerable financial sacrifice, send their children to such schools? Various answers have been given to these and similar questions. Parents and communities that establish Christian schools do so for different, and sometimes even contradictory, reasons. For some, Christian education is primarily a protest against and shelter from the secular humanism alleged to be predominant in public schools. For others, a parochial model, where children are trained in the basic doctrines, beliefs, and practices of a particular church tradition, is the basic reason for a Christian school. For still others, concerns about quality and parental control of education weigh more significantly than fears about secular humanism or denominational loyalty. Christian schools have excellent academic standards and are more directly accountable to parents.

The question of motivation for Christian education is complicated by the fact that the real reasons for sending one's children to Christian schools may differ from stated ones. Critics of private Christian schools often include such changes as racism, ethnocentrism, and classism in their arsenal of attacks. Perhaps, in some cases, there is truth to such charges.[1] Perhaps there are Christian parents whose primary reason for supporting Christian schools is that they serve "our kind." The human heart is complex and its deepest motives inscrutable. It is not always possible to explore the regions beneath the layers of self-deception and to sort out reasons that are appropriate from those that are not. Yet it is important to be aware of the real possibility of impure motives and to explore good, positive, and appropriate reasons for Christian education.

Some patterns of stated reasons can be discerned in Christian school communities. It is also possible to discern shifts in emphasis. Reasons given for Reformed Christian education today are not the same as those given prior to World War II or even World War I. Let me illustrate this with an extended and personal metaphor.[2]

I grew up in Ladner, British Columbia, then a small quiet town, now a bustling bedroom suburb of Vancouver. Tourists who travel from Vancouver to Victoria by way of the Tsawwassen-Schwartz Bay ferry will pass through it. My grandparents had a dairy farm near what is now the causeway and Tsawwassen terminal of the ferry. On summer Sunday afternoons, when visiting my grandparents' farm, we would often walk along the dike that ran around Tsawwassen Bay and Robert's Bank. On the dike was a small fortresslike, two-story tower that obviously had been used for some military purpose. As children we loved to climb to the second floor, which provided a magnificent view of the entire Georgia Strait. I realize now, better than I did then, the significance of that tower. It was built during World War II, undoubtedly shortly and hurriedly after Pearl Harbor, as a watchtower to provide warning against Japanese warships if they were to sail through the Strait of Georgia

on their way to invading Vancouver. Of course, the warships never came.

There is a delightfully ironic outcome to this chapter of
paranoia and subsequent shameful treatment of Japanese-
Canadian citizens. Today the watchtower is gone, and in its
place stands one of the world's largest coal superports—the
Robert's Bank terminal. And what nation sends its enormous ships up and down the Strait of Georgia? None other
than Japan, the former enemy, now a friendly and very
welcome trading partner in one generation!

What happened on Robert's Bank is a useful, albeit over-
simplified, metaphor for understanding what has happened
to North American Reformed Christian education in this
century. Reformed Christian education in North America,
primarily the United States, was in its origins, I believe,
dominated by a watchtower mentality. Undoubtedly, the
Dutch ethnic identity as aliens in North American culture
played an important role. Intertwined with such social factors, however, was an important theological principle—that
of a spiritual antithesis. Christians were called to be separate from the world and its culture. Sometimes antithesis
and ethnicity were joined in what seems to us today to be a
rather quaint argument, namely, that the very principles of
Reformed Christianity or Calvinism could be articulated
only in the Dutch language. The Anglo-American tempera-
ment and culture, reflected in its language, so it was
argued, was too preoccupied with the practical, the busy.
The Anglo-American mind was superficial, and Methodist,
or Arminian. Church historian, Henry Zwaanstra in his dissertation *Reformed Thought and Experience in a New World*,
discusses the raging debate about the use of the English
language in Christian Reformed worship earlier this century:

. . . [According to one thinker] The whole future of Calvinism
in the Christian Reformed Church depended on the way the
problem was solved. A quick change to English would
amount to losing the best, most valuable and highest thing
the church possessed—the Calvinistic view of life and the
world. Behind the language there was a spiritual world, a
world of ideas. Before the language could safely be changed, a
spiritual soil consisting of the old, well-proven and recently
reborn Calvinism had to be prepared. Into this soil coming
generations could be planted and confidently expected to
thrive. The Christian Reformed Church, he observed, was different from the other churches in America, because it had
remained outside the stream of American life and the good it
still possessed was in no small measure the result of its retain-
ing the Holland language. Those families in which Holland
Reformed literature was read were the most distinctively
Reformed and Calvinistic families in the church while those
that were completely Americanized were superficial in matters of principle and lacked sympathy for doctrinal truth. The
English-speaking congregations in the church were very weak
in their attachment to Calvinism.[3]

This argument about language, incidentally, is not so
outdated as it initially appears. In fact, it has a contemporary ring to it. Although originally public education had
"de-ethnicizing" high on its list of priorities, multicultural
education today has as its goal the cultivation of ethnic
identity and pride. Real separatists, such as the Amish or
Old Order Mennonites as well as ethnic groups such as the
French-Canadian Quebecois, insist that retention of language is essential to the preservation of their religion or
culture.

The separatist mentality has not died in the Reformed
community and may even be on the upswing today as
increasing numbers of Christians wake up to the perceived
threat of secular humanism. Furthermore, some CSI
schools, especially in Canada, are still considered Dutch

schools by the general public. However, the watchtower metaphor no longer accurately describes what takes place in most CSI schools. Today they are much more like superports through which the latest and best educational activities and cultural products flow freely, accompanied by varying degrees of critical commentary. Christian schools, too, have moved from a posture of hostility toward the surrounding culture to one of being a relatively friendly trading partner. A shift has taken place.

It is possible to see this shift quite easily when one compares what critics and defenders of Christian education said about it seventy-five years ago with what they say today. Some years ago *Christian Educators Journal* reprinted a 1919 article entitled "The Christian School and American Society." The author was responding to concerted attacks, including even persecution of private and parochial Christian schools by civil authorities. He summarizes this opposition as follows:

> It cannot be gainsaid that most of the opposition against the private school in general and against the Christian school in particular roots in the assumption that these schools are not in harmony with the spirit of America and with American ideas, that, instead of tending to unify the American people, they embody a tendency toward clannishness, toward the formation of groups or clans living side by side with other citizens but having no sympathy for them and not entering into their spirit. It is evident that in a country such as ours an institution that would exert an influence toward such isolation would tend to disrupt society and would therefore be harmful. Since, according to the assumption, such is the effect of the private or parochial school, the sooner the doors of such schools are closed the better.[4]

The Christian school, its detractors were arguing, did effectively what contemporary proponents of multicultural education say should be done—cultivating ethnic identity

and pride. The author's response to this opposition is interesting. "Our schools," he notes, "are no Dutch schools;
they are American schools, and at least so far as their language is concerned they satisfy the demands of the state
and are adapted to American society." In terms of what is
taught he notes, "The American Christian school is not
inferior to any other school, and is therefore adapted to
American life and society as well as any other." Furthermore, the Christian school can teach the virtues of patrio-
tism and good citizenship "even more efficiently than can
any other school, because we have the opportunity of bas-
ing our teaching not only on the grounds at the disposal of
the public school, but also on the higher and truer and
firmer ground, the Word of God." A good Christian, thus,
"cannot be other than a good citizen, a true American."
The school, therefore, which has as its aim to give its pupils
a Christian education, to fit them for Christian life, will, in
the same measure as it succeeds in this aim, train them to
be good citizens. The Americanism in the child is not weak-
ened by the elements of Christianity in the school but is
strengthened thereby.[5]

While the author grants that Christian schools are
indeed separate schools, he dismisses the argument that
they are socially divisive:

> It would seem, therefore, that the Christian school, with
> respect to its language, with respect to the instruction therein
> given, with respect to the inculcation of good citizenship, is
> as thoroughly adapted to American society as are the public
> schools of the state, and can therefore in no way be harmful
> to American society. And since, in the inculcation of Christ-
> ian morality, they can appeal to higher motives than can the
> non-Christian schools, it even appears that they can be an
> influence for good in our country. So long as they keep in the
> foreground their distinctively Christian character, and so
> long as they continue to adapt themselves to American soci-

ety, will they be ever more able to produce generations of good Christian citizens of America, men and women who are loyal to the principles of Christianity and who are lovers of American institutions and of American ideals.[6]

The objection to Christian education here is that it is too different, too distinctive, too hostile to American culture, and the reply seeks to downplay the distinctiveness and affirm what the two have in common. This objection has not gone away.[7] But the major question addressed to Christian schools today is, What's so distinctive about them?

Those of us who want to defend Christian education constantly face the question Why should I pay all that tuition when I see no perceptible difference in the teaching techniques, classroom activity, student behavior, and vocational goals? When a study appears suggesting that the values of Christian school graduates differ very little from those of Christians who have graduated from public schools, Christian school supporters get very nervous.[8] We buttress our rationale for Christian education by trying to articulate how our teaching in every subject is distinctive and informed by a Christian perspective. It is precisely the features used to defend the enterprise of Christian education in 1919 that trouble many Christian educators today. Many of today's critics denounce the lack of distinctiveness in Christian education and its failure to produce radical Christian disciples. In the words of one such critic,

> The further development of an integrated Christian curriculum around a truly biblical vision of life, the restoration of the child to the office of learner, education for radical discipleship: these are the educational challenges faced by a Christian community in a disintegrating secular society. Return to the basics, indeed! Our temptation is to join hands with a reactionary conservatism, prodded by religious anxiety about the future. Our challenge is to build a faithful, courageous, and prophetic Christian community which supports an alter-

native way of schooling, so that we and others may find healing and know the reality of God's salvation while it is still the
day of grace.[9]

What this suggests is a shift from a concern to be like public education to a concern to be distinctively Christian.
Christian schools have shifted, some believe, from being
watchtowers to superports.

Steven Vryhof confirms this analysis by suggesting that
in the history of Reformed Christian education in North
America it is possible to observe three distinct impulses—
isolation, imitation, and transformation.

> Historically, Reformed Christian schools have tended to
> isolate and protect. To maintain doctrinal and ethnic purity,
> they segregated Dutch-immigrant children from the rest of
> society. . . . This desire to isolate and protect [from the secular
> culture of a new land] was the first impulse of the Christian
> Reformed schools, and it remains strong today.
>
> World War I brought a new impulse—a rush to American-
> ize. The Christian Reformed community dropped the Dutch
> language, accommodated various dimensions of American
> values and lifestyles, and worked to increase the quality of
> the "Dutch Schools.". . . This desire to accommodate and imi-
> tate the surrounding culture was the second impulse charac-
> teristic of Christian schools; it too, remains today.
>
> After World War II, under the influence of a new wave of
> immigrants from the Netherlands, Christian school educators
> proposed a "transformational" agenda for Christian schools.
> To teach transformationally was to teach "from a Christian
> perspective."
>
> These three impulses—isolation, imitation, and transfor-
> mation—remain in tension in the Christian school commu-
> nity. We continue to pursue all three, though at different
> times and in different areas.[10]

My analysis earlier in this chapter is in basic agreement
with this. My only minor quarrel concerns the third
"impulse." I would argue that transformation and Christian

perspective, while closely related, do need to be distinguished. Or perhaps better, a distinction needs to be made between a Christian social-cultural perspective, which I would term transformational, and what could be called a Christian worldview, or a "Christian mind."

The Christian Mind: Thinking Christianly

An obvious answer to the question, Why Christian schools? would seem to be to develop Christian minds. After all, the primary task of a school, it could be said, is teaching students how to think, and thus a Christian school should teach students to think Christianly. Thinking Christianly is often expressed in such visual imagery as a Christian perspective or a Christian worldview.[11] The Christian mind is one that sees the world as Christ sees it. Thus, a Christian perspective on the environment sees the world as God's creation to be taken care of by human beings, rather than as raw material to be exploited greedily for personal consumption and comfort. A Christian perspective on human sexuality proceeds from the dignity of people as responsible image bearers of God, rather than as centers of animal instincts and drives, and speaks of sexual intercourse between husbands and wives, not just partners. A Christian view of wealth and riches neither curses nor blesses material prosperity but seeks to understand them within the larger picture of God's providence and the coming of his kingdom, a kingdom in which stewardship, justice, righteousness, and charity are the norm. Examples of such Christian thinking could be multiplied. The goal to inculcate Christian thinking is laudable, particularly in an increasingly secular and pagan world, which shuts out the Christian perspective on reality.

The issues raised here could be stated differently in terms

of truth. One classic definition of education states that its goal is to discover truth. A utilitarian appeal concerning the benefits of education is sometimes made, even by non-Christians, to a passage in the gospel of John: "The truth shall set you free." This text is mistakenly said to mean that education is a liberating process, setting us free from the chains of ignorance, superstition, poverty and so forth.[12] The Christian indeed believes, with Wheaton philosophy professor Arthur Holmes, that ultimately because God is the creator and sustainer of the world and its order, all truth is God's truth. In Holmes' words,

> The early church claimed that all truth is God's truth wherever it be found. The *focus* here is on truth. But the ultimate *locus* of truth is God. If he is the eternal and all-wise creator of all things, as Christians affirm, then his creative wisdom is the source and norm of all truth about everything. And if God and his wisdom are unchangingly the same, then truth is likewise unchanging, and thus *universal.* If all truth is his, and he understands fully its interrelatedness, then truth is *unified* in his perfect understanding. . . . The truth about every area [of life] is interrelated as coherent whole in God's wisdom, so that for man, "the fear of the Lord is the beginning of wisdom." That is to say, the believer has a starting point which gives perspective on life both in its parts and as a whole.[13]

It is the Christian conviction about God's revelation that makes specifically Christian thinking a possibility. God's Word in the Bible is "a lamp to our feet and a light for our path" (Psalm 119:105). Life in all its fullness, as created by God, is discovered and enjoyed in the light of God's revelation. "For with you is the fountain of life, in your light we see light" (Psalm 36:9). Christian education is scripturally directed education, learning that is rooted in revelation. Because God has spoken and to the extent he has, we are able to see things from his point of view.

This goal of Christian education—to teach students to see things from God's perspective—has become familiar to the point of being a slogan in Reformed Christian education circles and even beyond. Particularly at the Christian college level, discussions about Christian worldview and the integration of faith and learning have become ubiquitous.14 From this it would seem that laments about a dearth of Christian thinking are no longer entirely valid. Some thirty years ago, a British writer and student of C. S. Lewis published an essay entitled *The Christian Mind*. He begins with the following now oft-quoted lament:

> There is no longer a Christian mind. It is a commonplace that the mind of modern man has been secularized. . . . Tragic as this fact is, it would not be so desperately tragic had the Christian mind held out against the secular drift. But unfortunately the Christian mind has succumbed to the secular drift with a degree of weakness and nervelessness unmatched in Christian history. . . . [A]s a *thinking* being, the modern Christian has succumbed to secularization. . . . Except over a very narrow field of thinking, chiefly touching questions of personal conduct, we Christians in the modern world accept, for the purpose of mental activity, a frame of reference constituted by the secular mind and a set of criteria reflecting secular evaluations. . . . [T]here is no public pool of discourse fed by Christianly committed thought on the world we live in. . . . The mental secularization of Christian means that nowadays we meet only as worshipping beings and as moral beings, not as thinking beings.15

How valid are Blamires' observations? Does the growing list of books about Christian worldview along with those that seek to understand biology, sociology, business, literature, and psychology through the eyes of faith not suggest that the Christian mind is a healthier reality today, at least among Christian academics in North America? Perhaps. However, Blamires' contention that "there is no *public* pool of discourse fed by Christianly committed thought on the world we live in" continues to be a valid concern for two reasons. In the first place, the Christian mind is divided along lines that parallel those in secular society. Politically, for example, Christians line up on the right and on the left. Similar alignments can be found in Christian academia. To mention just one example, it is possible to find Christian economic theorists on both sides of the question about the welfare state. For some, Christian compassion makes some form of the welfare state imperative, for others a Christian concern for freedom makes it undesirable.[16] Similar divisions can be observed about such contentious matters as science and faith, the role of women in church and society, and the kind of literature that is suitable in Christian schools.[17]

The division, even fragmentation, of the evangelical Christian community does make it difficult to speak of the Christian mind. Futhermore, as we noted earlier in Chapter Three, what passes for a Christian perspective is sometimes difficult to distinguish from similar non-Christian positions. Christian defenses of capitalism or socialism, for example, are barely distinguishable from their non-Christian counterparts. The only difference is often the scriptural proofs accompanying them.

There is, however, another and perhaps even more formidable obstacle to the development of a disciplined Christian mind. The modern Western world was built on the assumption that reasonable and autonomous individuals would be able to put their religious beliefs on a private backburner and construct a society and culture based on public, universal reason and contract. Religious convictions would remain personal and private; the public square would ideally be naked of religious claims. In the words of Allan Bloom:

> Human founders [of modern, liberal, democratic societies],
> looking only to universal principles of natural justice recog-
> nizable by all men through their unaided reason, established
> governments on the basis of the consent of the governed
> without appeal to revelation or reason.[18]

In this context a Christian mind that serves as a public pool of discourse and insists on public recognition is thus a challenge directed at the very heart of our modern, secular world.

From this it is clear that developing Christian minds is difficult not only because of divisions and fragmentation within the Christian community but because of overwhelming opposition from the modern secular world. The difficulty is exacerbated by the fact that the very notion of seeking truth is in trouble. The thesis of Allan Bloom's *The Closing of the American Mind* is that American education today fails to produce any kind of mind, or minds, let alone a Christian one.[19] All points of view are tolerated; all are considered equally valid. Instead of opening minds, this loss of any shared vision, this denial of any possibility of knowing the truth, of distinguishing good and evil, produces empty, undiscriminating, closed minds. Schools today, Bloom argues, are "technical smorgasbords," utterly incapable of distinguishing "between important and unimportant in any other way than by the demands of the market."[20]

The real crisis in education today is the denial of truth, a denial of universal truths about nature, about human nature, about moral law, about society. The crisis is in the contention that there are only relative values, values created by the autonomous will rather than encountered and discovered by reason and experience. Bloom is not alone in this diagnosis. Roman Catholic historian Christopher Dawson complained in 1961 about a loss of vision that reduced education to "a disintegrated mass of specialisms and vocational courses." According to Dawson, our "modern Western society does not possess a civilization, but only a technological order resting on a moral vacuum."[21] Similarly, Arthur Holmes attributes the loss of a unified Judaeo-Christian worldview to the fact that "men and women no longer believe in truth. It is not simply that they no longer believe Christianity to be true—that is obvious—but rather that one adequate conception of truth itself is largely lost."[22] Holmes lists three dimensions of this loss of truth: a loss of focus on truth (people really are not as concerned about truth as they are about pleasure or success), a loss of the universality of truth (acceptance of the utter relativism of viewpoints), and a loss of the unity of truth (fragmentation and incoherence that arises from a loss of awareness that the universe is God's creation and that reality is interrelated and coherent).[23] For Holmes the only antidote to this fragmentation is a theistic worldview in which "the truth about every area is interrelated as a coherent whole in God's wisdom, so that for man 'the fear of the Lord is the beginning of wisdom.' That is to say, the believer has a starting point which gives perspective on life both in its parts and as a whole."[24]

If the diagnosis of Blamires, Bloom, Dawson, and Holmes is correct, then the task of Christian education—teaching students to think in accord with a coherent, scripturally based, comprehensive worldview—is a daunting one. We live in a world that is hostile to the Christian faith, and—if Blamires is correct—in which Christians have lost their nerve. It should be observed at this point that Christian educators should not be sanguine about the inroads of cultural relativism into their own communities. In a review of Allan Bloom's book, Calvin College English professor Edward E. Ericson observes that in our Christian educational institutions, too, "even as we are genuinely committed to trying to bring a Christian perspective to bear on our disciplines, our minds have been saturated at deep levels by the kind of modern academic mindset which Bloom delineates. . . . Thus, despite our best intentions, what we serve up in the name of bringing Christian perspective to bear upon our teaching and writing turns out in practice to be merely laying a thin veneer over a rotten surface."[25] Blamires puts it similarly when he notes that much of our so-called Christian thinking is basically "secular thinking turned with pious platitudes."[26]

Supporters and practitioners of Christian education need to be aware of these real difficulties. Furthermore, questions need to be asked about our commitment to developing a disciplined Christian mind. Is there as much concern among Christian educators about Christian thinking as about students' performance in the Iowa or Canadian Basic Skills Test? Are parents who support Christian education as excited about Christian worldview questions as they are about their school's performance in athletic contests?

The Christian Mind in Action: The Two Kingdoms

It is important to underscore that this concern for the development of a Christian mind is not merely to satisfy the needs of the intellectually curious or gifted. The Christian worldview shapes the way Christian people live, helping them make decisions and choose vocations. In short, the Christian mind shapes concrete Christian discipleship. The basic conviction here is that "ideas have consequences," that civilizations are shaped by their fundamentally religious convictions, choices, and visions.[27] The difference between a Christian education and a non-Christian

education is that they are rooted in fundamentally different religious visions of life. No education is religiously neutral. In the words of former Calvin College philosophy professor William Harry Jellema,

> All formal education, then, even such as profess to be neutral,
> reflects some *civitas*. That it cannot escape doing so is but a
> phase of the fact that man cannot escape answering the ques-
> tion who God is, and articulating the answer in life; that is to
> say, cannot escape religious decision and allegiance to some
> kingdom. . . . The difference between Christian and non-
> Christian education is, therefore, not that religious faith is
> present in the one and not in the other; the difference is
> between the Christian definition of God and a non-Christian
> definition; and is thus a difference and opposition between
> kingdoms.[28]

This notion that all education is for a kingdom or *civitas*
and reflects the fundamental religious conflict between
kingdoms is, of course, rooted in St. Augustine's famous
distinction between the *civitas Dei* (the city of God) and the
civitas mundi (the city of this world or of man). This
antithesis between two cities or kingdoms was also a
favorite theme of the Dutch neo-Calvinism of Abraham
Kuyper, profoundly influencing North American Reformed
Christian education at all levels. According to Kuyper, the
Christian mind or "life-system" was opposed by the mind
of modernity, and the stakes in this conflict were ultimate.

> There is no doubt then that Christianity is imperilled by
> great and serious dangers. Two life-systems are wrestling with
> one another, in mortal combat. Modernism is bound to build
> a world of its own from the data of the natural man, and to
> construct man himself from the data of nature; while, on the
> other hand, all those who reverently bend the knee to Christ
> and worship Him as the Son of the living God, and God him-
> self, are bent upon saving the "Christian Heritage." This is
> the struggle in Europe, this is the struggle in America, and
> this also, is the struggle for principles in which my own

country is engaged, and in which I myself have been spending all my energy for nearly forty years.

From the first, therefore, I have always said to myself,—"If the battle is to be fought with honor and with a hope of victory, then principle must be arrayed against principle; then it must be felt that in Modernism the vast energy of an all-embracing life-system assails us, then also it must be understood that we have to take our stand in a life-system of equally comprehensive and far-reaching power. And this powerful life-system is not to be invented or formulated by ourselves, but is to be taken and applied as it presents itself in history. When thus taken, I found and confessed and I still hold, that this manifestation of the Christian principle is given us in Calvinism. In Calvinism my heart has found rest. From Calvinism have I drawn the inspiration firmly and resolutely to take my stand in the thick of this great conflict of principles.[29]

In sum then, all education reflects and lives out of a specific mind and seeks to educate for citizenship in that kingdom. Christian education is determined by the Christian mind and is for discipleship in the kingdom of God. Nicholas Wolterstorff has summarized this view well:

The goal of Christian education is not just the formation of a way of thinking. Nor is it that plus the development of moral character. Nor is that plus the cultivation of a mode of piety. Nor is that plus the transmission of one and another part of humanity's knowledge. Education is for the totality of life in a kingdom.[30]

In order to accent this emphasis upon a totality vision of Christian discipleship, some have preferred to use the biblical category of wisdom in place of a potentially misleading cognitivist or intellectualist emphasis on mind. An excellent summary of this can be found in John Van Dyk's booklet *The Beginning of Wisdom: The Nature and Task of the Christian School:*

What is wisdom? According to the Bible, a wise person both *understands* and *does* the will of God (Eph. 5:15-17). In other words, wisdom is not merely collecting and amassing theoretical or factual knowledge; nor is it simply gaining technical skills. Wisdom is knowledge and understanding deepened into spiritual insight and expressed in loving service (James 3:13). Wisdom originates in the fear of the Lord and is enhanced by faith, hope, love, knowledge, spiritual insight, and active discipleship. "The fear of the Lord," the Bible teaches, "is the beginning of wisdom; all who follow His precepts have good understanding" (Ps. 111:10).

Thus a Christian school is a place where Christian educators refuse to be satisfied with providing only factual knowledge and marketable skills. Rather, teachers in a Christian school seek to transform all activities and studies into an expression of biblical wisdom, training the students to walk as disciples of Jesus Christ.[31]

The Christian Mind: Basic Contours

A Christian worldview is an attempt to understand and explain the world from the vantage point of God's revelation in the Bible. Part of the problem that Christian educators face is that there are significant differences among Christians in terms of their understanding of Scripture and thus their worldviews. A famous typology by American theologian H. Richard Niebuhr lists five basic types, or perennial answers, to these differences in terms of the Christ and culture question.[32] Similarities and patterns notwithstanding, it is true that worldviews are to some degree as original and different as individual faith. For our purposes we do not need to consider all the varieties and dimensions of the worldview discussion. For maximum benefit to Christian educators and supporters of Christian education, it might be helpful to set forth one example of a statement of faith, namely the one recently published by Christian Schools

International. The statement consists of two parts: a basic statement of belief and specific implications for Christian schools and Christian education.[33]

A Statement of Belief for Christian Schools International and Its Schools

Every school is based upon a specific system of belief, whether it is governed and guided by the government, a private board or society, or a church or denomination. CSI schools are no exception. They are based upon the following understanding of God and his world, which in turn gives shape to the purpose of the school.

On the foundation of God's infallible Word, the Scriptures of the Old and New Testament, as explicated in the ecumenical creeds and the confessions of the Reformed tradition, we declare the following summary of the Christian faith.

God. There is one infinite, holy, loving, personal God who speaks to us in Scripture and reveals himself to us in his acts of creation, salvation, and renewal, as Father, Son, and Holy Spirit. As finite human beings created in God's image, we declare that it is our purpose and privilege to worship, honor, serve, and obey him.

Creation. The world belongs to God, who created it and faithfully sustains it by his providence. Creation is the theater of God's glory, displaying his power and majesty. God calls us to discover creation's resources, to receive these gifts with thanksgiving and delight, and to use them wisely as stewards and caretakers who are responsible to God and to our neighbor.

Sin. Our ability to carry out our human calling to honor God, serve our neighbor, and care for the creation is marred by the corrosive effects of sin, which touch every part of life. When our first parents listened to Satan's lie, questioned God's Word, and rebelled against him, they brought his judgment upon themselves, their posterity, and the creation. Brokenness, disease, hate, arrogance, alienation, abuse of creation, and ultimately death are the inevitable fruits of sin in our world.

Covenant. However, God has not rejected or abandoned

his world but has turned to it in love. He gave the rainbow sign to Noah as a pledge of his promise to care for all creatures. He made a covenant with Abraham, promising to be a faithful God to him and his children, and through them to bless all nations. Through his servant Moses, God disclosed his law for the human community, promising rich blessing as the fruit of obedience. God always keeps his promises. We acknowledge with gratitude and joy that he is our God and the God of our children, that we are his people, and that this is his world.

Redemption. As he promised, God in love sent Jesus Christ into the world to save it from sin and its consequences. The atoning death of the Son of God is the only payment for the debt of human sin, and Christ's resurrection is the only liberation from the powers of evil and death. The victorious Lord sends the Holy Spirit to create faith, cleanse and renew hearts, and build a community of love and holiness. It is this community's mission to proclaim and live this good news and to make disciples of the nations.

Kingdom of God. Jesus Christ is King of Kings and Lord of Lords. His kingdom is an everlasting kingdom, and he reigns over all things for our good. To be a citizen of this kingdom is a privilege, a joy, and a responsibility. Led by his Spirit, we place our every thought, word, and deed in the service of Christ's present and coming reign, and we live daily in the confident hope of his triumphant return.

A Statement of Purpose for Christian Schools

On the foundation of God's infallible Word, the Scriptures of the Old and New Testament, as explicated in the ecumenical creeds and the confessions of the Reformed tradition, we affirm the following summary of the mission of the Christian school.

Community. The Christian school, as an enterprise of the entire community, enables and equips all its children to serve the Lord, to love their fellow human beings, and to care for God's creation. The school community provides an environment of love and care within which students are nurtured. As an indispensable partner with the home and the church, the

Christian school leads children to live according to biblical wisdom.

Staff. Staff members of the Christian school, living in joyful fellowship with God, model the love of Christ to children. Empowered by the Holy Spirit and dedicated to the highest standards of excellence and professionalism, Christian teachers view their work as a vocation. The calling of a Christian school teacher is to pass on the wisdom of the Christian tradition to students and to help them understand and apply the transforming power of the gospel to contemporary society and culture.

Students. Children are God's image bearers, entrusted to parents and the Christian community as his gifts. The Christian school encourages students to develop their gifts in response to God and in loving service to fellow human beings. Students are led to to know God and to respond to him in every dimension of the creation and in every aspect of their lives.

Curriculum. The Christian school curriculum is developed and organized so that children may come to know God more deeply and richly and live for him more faithfully. Since human experience in all its rich variety is a good gift from the Creator, who remains involved in his world, the Christian school curriculum explores all dimensions of creation. God's design for the creation and his will for human society and culture must be understood and obeyed. This is the way of godly wisdom. Students are taught to recognize the brokenness that sin brings to God's carefully designed world and are challenged to bring the healing power of Jesus Christ to a fallen world.

The Christian Mind: Some Reconsiderations

It seems incontrovertible that one of the particular tasks, perhaps even the chief one, of the Christian school is the cultivation of distinctively Christian ways of thinking. After all, teaching the basic skills for thinking is what schools are supposed to do. Yet putting it this baldly may point to the inadequacy of this formulation. Characteristic is Nicholas Wolterstorff's objection:

> It used to be said, particularly in the Calvinist tradition, that the goal of Christian education is to impart to the student the Christian "world and life view." The intent behind putting it this way was to affirm that the gospel pertains to all of life and not just to some "religious" part. But this formulation is inadequate, for it puts too much emphasis on a "view," that is, on what we have called cognition. To be identified with the people of God and to share in its work does indeed require that one have a system of belief—call it "the Christian world and life view." But it requires more than that. It requires the Christian *way of life*. Christian education is education aimed at training for the Christian way of life, not just education aimed at inculcating the Christian world and life view.[34]

We have already noted that this goal—a Christian way of life in and for the kingdom of God—is what we mean by the Christian mind. What Wolterstorff challenges is the assumption that Christian thinking will lead rather directly to Christian acting. Wolterstorff doubts that "the Christian way of *thinking about* the world will just naturally express itself in the Christian way of *being* in the world."[35]

The question raised here is not a new one. It is an issue that religious people who attempt to pass on their faith must face. The practice of catechetical instruction—having students learn the rudiments of the faith by memorizing its doctrines, often in a question and answer format—is a valuable strategy for passing on knowledge about the faith, but it does not guarantee an active faith. Knowing doctrine is not, it is worth trumpeting today, inimical to a living faith; it just must not be identified with it. Similarly, knowing the rudiments of a Christian worldview is a crucial part of Christian education, but if preparation for a Christian way of life is the real goal, it clearly is not sufficient. More is necessary. The question that must be faced is whether this "more" is the task of the school or whether the school's task is limited to the cognitive dimension.

Wolterstorff has been one of the more eloquent spokespersons for the "more" argument, pleading for Christian schools to include a social justice dimension to preparation for kingdom service. In Wolterstorff's words, "a program of Christian learning which seeks only to develop abstract science in Christian perspective and not to develop praxis-oriented science of service to Christian social action can be of only limited use in Christian education."[36] Hence, it is useful to distinguish a Christian perspective from transforming practice. Not only has Wolterstorff pleaded passionately for Christian schools to teach for justice; he has also provided a rather substantive strategy for what he calls tendency learning, learning that shapes action as well as thought. In Wolterstorff's words, "To cultivate action one must cultivate the tendency or disposition or inclination—call it what you will—on the part of the person to act in the manner deserved in the relevant circumstance."[37] He suggests three processes for the formation of action: discipline, modeling, and giving reasons. In sum,

> The main point to notice here is that just initiating students into the Christian mind . . . is not likely to have much effect on their actions unless it actually incorporates reasons for acting on certain quite specific ways, and unless it makes appropriate use of discipline and modeling. If the schooling of our children focuses just on mind-formation, then we must expect that when they emerge from school and take up their adult lives, they will *talk* the Christian mind and *live* the mind of the world.[38]

It is clear that action cannot proceed purposefully apart from knowledge. He continues, "If we do genuinely wish a person to act in a certain way, customarily we will regard some knowledge as relevant; and if the person does not already have that knowledge we will do what we can to insure that he or she acquires it."[39] In other words, the Christian mind is necessary, but it is not sufficient.

Wolterstorff raises yet another objection to the exclusive focus on the Christian mind as the goal of Christian education. In his judgment, "what gets lost in this way of looking at things is delight and gratitude and worship: delight in God's creation, delight in humanity's works of art, grateful worship of God."[40]

Nicholas Wolterstorff is not the only philosopher who has raised objections to the notion of worldview or Christian mind as the focal point and goal of Christian education. Redeemer College philosopher Theodore Plantinga also has reservations.[41] To begin with, Plantinga judges that language of worldview and perspective do not adequately describe what takes place in Christian schools, particularly, we could note, at the elementary school level. Preschool and kindergarten teachers who guide young children into the world of numbers and language by teaching them to count, recognize letters and sounds, and even put words together do not ordinarily have a highly articulated philosophy of mathematics or advanced knowledge in linguistic theory. To speak of a Christian perspective on these matters is to raise the discussion to a level of abstraction more appropriate for a Christian graduate school than for an elementary classroom. Plantinga judges that it is our discourse about Christian education that is more in need of correction than the practice, for, he says, "I regard our practice as healthier than our theory" (p. 2).

Plantinga's objection goes further than this, however. It is his contention that the notion of "Christian perspective" is a legacy of the modern ideal of universal knowledge, knowledge that overlooks the particular. The assumption of those who seek universal knowledge is that it is possible for human beings through their reason to acquire an absolute viewpoint. Plantinga in turn argues that limited local knowledge is all that is available to us. This suggests, according to Plantinga, that teachers are dependent on others for their material: "they do not have time to examine everything for themselves; they have to rely on the work of others" (p. 24). It is here that he sees a conflict with the worldview approach to Christian schooling:

> But this account of teaching as bound up with the notion of local knowledge does not fit in well with the idea often voiced that the Christian teacher builds a—or perhaps *the*— Christian point of view into every lesson. The point-of-view emphasis is a hangover from the science ideal and Greek visualism. The thinking behind it—never expressed in quite the words I will use here—is this. Secular thought is a complete body of knowledge whose internal structure is determined by a point of view, or perspective, or philosophy, or perhaps worldview. Christian thought is an alternative body of knowledge (also complete—in principle, at least) which derives its structure from the "Christian perspective" (or point of view, or worldview). Thus when the Christian teacher tells his class about Burma (where he himself has never set foot), he is really expounding one small segment of the universal body of Christian thought. (p. 24)

Plantinga raises three objections to this account of things. First, it assumes an absolute point of view "of a universal body of Christian thought unified and structured by a single perspective" (p. 24). Such an absolute point of view is not available to the teacher. Second, it makes it impossible for students to enter imaginatively into other cultural worlds in order to view them from within. The Christian perspective tends to distance concrete reality by forcing it through a predetermined philosophic grid. Third, it makes teaching of non-Christian literature difficult in Christian schools. Often the focus turns away from the text to the author's worldview, and the study of literature becomes a journey into intellectual history (p. 25).

Plantinga's thesis is that selection of subject matter is the primary distinguishing feature of a truly Christian school.

> My suggestion is that we should give up the illusion that we are imposing a Christian perspective on every bit of subject matter we take up in our schools. Instead we should understand the uniqueness of the Christian teacher and school primarily in terms of the selection of subject matter. Given that there are more books than we can ever read, more organisms that we can ever study, more historical eras than we can ever investigate, which ones do we focus on as significant for Christian awareness?
>
> Christian schools have won a measure of acceptance in our society by claiming to teach the same material as secular public schools—but from a different point of view. In effect they claim that they are just the same—only different. What I am suggesting is first that the difference between the two types of schools lies more in subject matter than in point of view, and secondly that Christian schools should seek more independence from the prevailing secular curriculum than they already possess. (p. 25)

Plantinga is convinced that "teaching is telling." Note the shift here from a visual to an oral metaphor. This notion underscores the authoritative and fiduciary character of the task. The teacher does not merely pass on information. He or she has been entrusted with shaping the lives of the community's children. The teacher's credibility and moral character are thus crucial qualifications for the task of telling (pp. 41-48).

Conclusion

These reconsiderations of Christian perspective at the very least caution us against excessive claims about them.

Christian educators need to be sensitive to the dangers of cognitivist assumptions—that simply knowing what is right will lead to doing what is right, that a Christian worldview will lead to Christian obedience. They need to be cautioned about grandiose and global claims concerning Christian perspective and relieved of the unnecessary guilt that accompanies inevitable failures to provide a distinctive Christian perspective on everything from spelling to multiplication tables. Alternative educational strategies such as modeling and selection enrich our understanding of what is possible and useful in Christian education.

At the same time, a word of caution is in order about the critiques of the worldview approach. It is not constructive to disparage the development of a Christian way of viewing the world.[42] The resources available to Christian teachers in a host of disciplines should not be ignored or dismissed. There is already far too much anti-intellectualism in evangelical and Reformed Christian communities. Learning to think Christianly is also a form of Christian discipleship. It is, to be sure, not the whole of it, but it is a part—and an important part.[43] Forming Christian minds is one thing that the Christian school can do well, and the Christian school is the most obvious, if not the only, place where learning the skill of thinking Christianly can be nurtured. It takes hard work, but it is also a rewarding calling. In short, while acknowledging some of the qualifications spelled out in the previous section of this chapter, I would still argue that the formation of a Christian mind remains an essential task of the Christian school. It is a necessary but not entirely sufficient goal. The goals of, as well as the qualifications and concerns raised about, the formation of a Christian mind can be addressed by reformulating the task of the school in terms of narrative categories. It is to this subject that we now turn.

The Rediscovery of Narrative

Introduction: Story Problems

In this and the following chapter we will be considering the idea of "story," or "narrative," as an avenue for exploring the reason for and the content of Christian education. In several places earlier in this volume we have contended that the idea of narrative provides a solution to many of the problems and dilemmas facing education in general and Christian education in particular. Before we set forth the solution, it is helpful to provide a brief summary.

In Chapter One we examined the critical questions facing public schooling and concluded that the root problem is an unresolved debate about North American culture itself. Cultural warfare between progressives and traditionalists and between advocates of critical literacy and cultural literacy is really a conflict about story. Traditionalists for the most part affirm the North American story, insisting that it is large enough to include even groups that consider themselves marginalized. The school is then seen as a community of cultural memory, as a vehicle for inculcating the community's basic values. An educated person is one who is literate in the language and symbols of the mainstream culture. Good education produces citizens who know and live the mainstream story.

On the other hand, advocates of critical literacy repudiate the mainstream story and, usually in the name of multiculturalism, seek to tell alternate stories, in particular the stories of those said to have been marginalized and oppressed by mainstream culture. The result of this plurality and polarity of visions has resulted in a culture war in North America. The crucial question for education is, thus, who tells the story and how it is to be told. Consequently, education has become one of the primary battlefields for the very soul of North American culture. A clear and consistent vision, a coherent story, is not present. We seem to be, to paraphrase Matthew Arnold, living on a "darkling plain" where stories clash by night and day.

In Chapter Two we reported in some detail on the general state of our culture and society. The underlying theme of modernity, we argued, was a loss of narrative unity, of a common story, and of a unified cultural memory. This common feature helps explain the individualism and secularism so characteristic of the modern age. As theologian Stanley Hauerwas has observed, the dominant love of universal rationality in liberal political thought tends to obliterate particular stories and traditions. Communities are to be organized by universal reason rather than the accumulated wisdom represented by community traditions and symbols:

> Liberalism, in its many forms and versions, presupposes that society can be organized without any narrative that is commonly held to be true. As a result it tempts us to believe that freedom and rationality are independent of narrative—i.e. we are free to the extent that we have no story.[1]

This universalizing goal of reason is particularly hard on narrative-based faiths such as Christianity. Modernity deliberately secularizes by removing the Christian story, tradition, and revealed moral order from public discourse. Religion becomes a strictly private affair; the public square remains religiously naked.

The postmodern movement, which seems to be moving beyond universal reason to a reaffirmation of particular stories, still makes little public room for the Christian stories. The Christian story, at least in its evangelical, conservative form, is not yet politically correct. It is not included among the options in the clamor for multiculturalism. While there appears to be growing tolerance for many more stories, including pagan stories, not all stories have equal access to the public square.

What is at stake in all this is the reality of community. In an anarchic society, characterized by individualism, relativism, and alienating fragmentation, can any sense of community or any guiding moral vision remain? A statement of Robert Bellah and his associates is worth recalling at this point:

> Communities, in the sense in which we are using the term, have a history—in an important sense they are constituted by their past—and for this reason we can speak of a real community as a "community of memory," one that does not forget its past. In order not to forget that past, a community is involved in retelling its story, its constitutive narrative, and in so doing, it offers examples of the men and women who have embodied and exemplified the meaning of the community. These stories of collective history and exemplary individuals are an important part of the tradition that is so central to a community of memory.[2]

The problem, of course, is that differing "communities of memory" are warring with each other. And when it comes to the core story that has shaped Western civilization, we may be suffering from what columnist George F. Will has called "cultural amnesia."

Today there is a potentially fatal idea in circulation: that there should not be in this pluralistic society any core culture passed on from generation to generation. To those who say we are threatened by a suffocating "hegemony" of Western civilization's classic works, I say the real danger is cultural amnesia. It is withdrawal from the challenge of finding common ground on which Americans can stand together—not the little patches of fenced-off turf for irritable groups, but the common ground of citizenship in the nation.[3]

Finally, we suggested in Chapters Three and Four that a concept of narrative could help resolve some of the problems involved with maintaining distinctively Christian education. Now let us examine more closely the notion of story itself, beginning with the contemporary rediscovery of stories and their importance.

The Rediscovery of Stories

Human beings throughout all ages and in all cultures are storytellers. We tell stories to entertain, to stave off boredom, to escape. We tell other stories, such as Aesop's fables, to teach moral lessons to our children as well as to amuse. We tell our own personal stories in psychotherapy in order to heal our emotional wounds. We read stories for all these reasons and for guidance in our lives.[4]

Stories, it has been suggested, are an essential part of our very humanity. Elie Wiesel put it this way: "God made man because he loves stories."[5] The ambiguity of the pronoun *he* in this oft-quoted line is explored nicely by John Shea:

If God made man because he loves stories, creation is a success. For humankind is addicted to stories. No matter our mood, in reverie or expectation, panic or peace, we can be found stringing together incidents, and unfolding episodes. We turn our pain into narrative so we can bear it; we turn our ecstasy into narrative so we can prolong it. We all seem to be under the sentence of Scheherazade. We tell our stories to live.

But there is a deeper suggestion in Wiesel's phrase. God not only loves to hear our stories, he loves to tell his own. And quite simply, we are the story God tells.

We are born into a community of stories and storytellers. In interpreting our traditional stories of God we find out who we are and what we must do. In telling the stories of God we ourselves are told.[6]

Shea's observations about the key role of story in religious experience alert us to the remarkable resurgence of interest in narrative today.

I do not suggest that storytelling ceased for a time and now has resumed. Rather, I have in mind a remarkable current scholarly interest in the notion of narrative, an interest that spans many fields, from biblical studies to theology to developmental psychology to moral philosophy. Narrative is now a popular topic in many disciplines and fields, particularly as these relate to education in general and and even more specifically to moral education or character formation. In the words of William Kilpatrick, a vigorous advocate for character education, "In the past ten years a number of exciting new developments in theory and research have done much to substantiate the case for character education. Philosophers, psychologists, and educators, working separately and pursuing different lines of inquiry, have been arriving at similar conclusions about the need for stories and models in moral formation."[7]

What accounts for this renewed interest in narrative? William G. Doty suggests an answer:

Stories have to be told, to be expressed, for they are the part of the narrative quality of existence that can be shared and that therefore compensate for all that cannot be shared. No matter how jaded we are, we have our own stories to live out, and other people's stories to hear. In our stories we extend ourselves toward becoming other than we are, we learn to experiment with possible futures as well as to gain perspective on where we have been. As the rational rules us more and more—the cloture of science, the emptiness of mass-speak—we need story to guide our emotions and capabilities and morals.[8]

Here we have at least a beginning of an explanation that makes a great deal of sense. Since so much of human life today is dominated by rationality and much of that rationality is unsatisfactory when it comes to our religious, emotional, and moral life, we are recovering the importance of story. The motto of modernists was Descartes' motto "I think, therefore I am." Postmodern men and women know that we do not live by reason alone—we need stories.

Theologian Michael Novak takes us a step further by insisting that ordinary cognitive methods are not able to provide full accounts of the human experience of change or conversion. "Story," he argues, "articulates a change in experience. It is a particularly apt method for expressing the sort of experience that alters one's fundamental 'standpoint' or 'horizon.'" In sum, "Story then is a method. It is an ancient and altogether human method. The human being alone among the creatures on the earth is a story-telling animal: sees the present rising out of a past, heading into a future; perceives reality in narrative form."[9]

Novak also judges that story is in some ways at odds with rationalism. Its resurgence is in some sense a reaction against rationalistic expression and interpretations of experience.

> During every high tide of rationalism—a phenomenon as recurrent in its way as the rising of the oceans—story is not a highly valued method. In rationalistic periods, the human subject is self-effacing. What counts is not the experience which occasioned insight, nor the moment (if one has occurred) of conversion, nor the altogether individual, unique, and contingent details of autobiographical narrative; no, what counts, in the rationalist self-image, is that the mind be conformed (1) to *universal* principles (2) to *general*

rules of evidence, and (3) to *clear* and *distinct* concepts accessible to any inquiring and adequately disciplined mind. As a
method, story runs against the grain of these criteria. Elements of the universal, the general, and even of the clear and
the distinct idea figure in almost all stories. But whereas in a
story these elements are recessive and implicit, in a more
rationalist method they are salient, explicit, ruthlessly dominant. Elements of story are an embarrassment to a fully rationalistic period; rationalism attempts to "demythologize."
When encountered in undigested form, not fully imagined,
not utterly concrete, not thoroughly experiential, elements of
the universal, the general, and the conceptual are an embarrassment to a good story.[10]

The Quarrel between Philosophy and Poetry

The suggestion that stories are an alternative to reason
seems plausible when we realize that the tension between
stories and philosophy is an ancient one. Not only is excessive conceptuality an embarrassment to a good story; the
reverse is also true. Philosophers tend to be suspicious of
storytellers because stories are seen to be less truthful than
the fruits of philosophical or rational inquiry and discourse. To see why this is so and how it affects education, it
is instructive to consider the first significant writing that
could be called a philosophy of education, namely Plato's
Republic.[11]

Plato observes that storytelling is a significant part of the
education of the young because children readily identify
with and imitate the heroes of stories. Because children are
so easily influenced by stories, it is important to censor stories that deceive or encourage immorality. The critical discussion on this point between Socrates and Adeimantus
proceeds as follows:

"Then shall we so easily let the children hear just any tales fashioned by just anyone and take into their souls opinions for the most part opposite to those we'll suppose they must have when they are grown up?"

"In no event will we permit it."

"First, as it seems, we must supervise the makers of tales; and if they make a fine tale, it must be approved, but if it's not, it must be rejected. We'll persuade nurses and mothers to tell the approved tales to their children and to shape their souls with tales more than their bodies with hands. Many of those they now tell must be thrown out." (377B)

Among the tales not to be told are those that depict the gods as deceitful, vengeful, warlike, or weak. Only stories that edify and ennoble are to be told. Because the young are so impressionable, "we must do everything to insure that what they hear first, with respect to virtue, be the finest told tales for them to hear" (378D).

Plato assumed that stories have a powerful impact on the young; thus, people who are concerned about the well-being of the city will carefully superintend the stories told to children. Yet at the end of the *Republic,* Plato goes a step further. He not only desires to censor the poets, he wishes to expel them from the city. To understand this final repudiation of poets and storytellers, it is necessary to be aware of Plato's own version of what he calls "an old quarrel between philosophy and poetry" (607B). According to Plato, truth and knowledge do not come from perception alone or even from particular examples, but by philosophical reasoning and abstraction. True knowledge, which is the ultimate goal of all education, requires an idea (the form) of the good, the just, the beautiful. True knowledge is conceptual and thus universal in nature, not narrative and particular. According to Robin Barrow, Plato claims "that real understanding of such things as courage, religion and morality in general requires *philosophical* enquiry."[12] Barrow summarizes Plato's viewpoint:

His fundamental objection to artists is that they pose as, and are taken to be, what they are not. It is the fact that they are revered as sages which troubles him. The poet writes about things about which he does not know and is taken to be an authority on matters about which he is basically ignorant. True knowledge can only be acquired through study of the forms. Only the forms are real. The everyday world of sense-experience is one removed from reality. But the artist, dealing as he does in representations of the sensible world, which are themselves merely representations of the ideal forms, is two removes from reality. He is trafficking in imitations of imitations.[13]

Plato's attack on stories is thus twofold. First, he wishes to censor the stories told to the young so that only stories contributing to appropriate virtues will be told. Second, he raises a philosophic objection to the use of story itself. The very medium of narrative stands in the way of true—that is, conceptual—knowledge. In Plato's judgment, the storyteller knows how to tell a tale well but does not really know the truth "about the gods, about warfare, about human relationships, human conduct and other such intricate and momentous questions."[14]

How does one acquire such knowledge? Again Barrow's summary is instructive:

According to the theory of forms, as I have interpreted it, to make informed comment on such matters it is necessary to have considerable ability in abstract thought and conceptual analysis. To know about warfare requires, besides practical experience of, and accurate information about war, reflection on it and above all consideration of such key concepts as courage, cowardice and war itself. Similarly to talk with understanding about the gods, the plausibility of claiming they exist, and so on. Above all there is the ethical content, which can never be hidden for long, which, if it is to derive from knowledge rather than the mere opinion of the author, presupposes contemplation of the form of the Good, or more prosaically, the study of moral philosophy.[15]

Poets or storytellers, by the very nature of their medium, are several steps removed from the reality, knowledge, and truth that is the stock in trade of the thinker or philosopher. This quarrel between the poet and the philosopher has been repeated in the history of Western thought. In Christian theology the quarrel has focused on the relationship between doctrine and story. Is doctrine—intellectual abstraction stated in propositional form—more true, more precise, more real, than the narrative itself? Protests against the intellectualizing of the Christian faith have often come from artists and storytellers. Some regard stories and even visual art forms as better vehicles for communicating the gospel than the allegedly barren and cold propositions of Christian theology.

Yet is there not an obvious resolution to the quarrel, a resolution suggested by Plato's own desire to censor the poets? What if the poet is also a philosopher? What if the poet has, through philosophic inquiry, acquired adequate knowledge and then seeks to communicate this knowledge in narrative form? Barrow summarizes Plato's likely response:

> Of course Homer, or any other author, may as a matter of fact be more than merely an artist. If this is the case, if he happens also to be a philosopher and to have thought in the right way about such issues, then these strictures would not apply to him. But even here Plato would oppose the notion of the artist's work being an entirely desirable medium for revealing his own knowledge to others. For the manner of his presentation is not conducive to enhancing the understanding of the reader, since it does not involve straightforward rational argument or discussion.[16]

The implication of Plato's intellectualism for education is obvious:

> Here there is a serious challenge to the view that literature (or

the fine arts in general) are a potent medium of teaching. They may have their place as influences for the good, if they enshrine right opinion. But they do not represent a path to true knowledge. For the path to knowledge is paved by the mastery of concepts and rational argument, not by the seductive form of art.[17]

Let us now consider a relevant contemporary application of this quarrel between philosophy and poetry in the area of moral education.

Application: Moral Reasoning Versus Moral Imagination[18]

Thanks in large measure to the work of Swiss psychologist Jean Piaget and Harvard social psychologist Lawrence Kohlberg, there is growing interest in the study of personal moral development—how a person develops moral judgment as well as the capacity to act in moral situations. The claim is made that all persons move through several stages of moral reasoning and that they do so in a patterned way. As Nicholas Wolterstorff points out,

> Human beings, so it is claimed, confront life and reality not with random thoughts but rather with integrated *patterns* of reasoning—about causality, about morality, and the like. These patterns are the common property of humanity. Nobody reasons in private, idiosyncratic patterns. However, people do proceed from one such integrated pattern of reasoning to another. They go through stages. They develop. Two persons may in fact be reasoning about morality with two quite different patterns. But that is not because they have their own private patterns. It is because they are in different stages.[19]

Apart from the reference to development and stages,[20] the operative word here is *reasoning*. Wolterstorff notes that "Kohlberg's concern is exclusively with the form of a person's moral reasoning, not the *content*."[21] Craig Dykstra refers to this approach to moral life as "juridical ethics." In juridical ethics, the focus is on making judgments about the rightness or wrongness of particular acts as a judge in a lawcourt might do. According to Dykstra, for Kohlberg "the moral life is primarily the life of making choices about how to act in situations where people's claims about rights and duties conflict. Moral development is the development of the ability to provide increasingly more principled reasons and justifications for the choices one makes in such situations."[22]

This approach to the moral life is sometimes referred to as quandary ethics. "The moral landscape," notes Dykstra, "is seen to consist largely of problematic circumstances. Morality becomes the enterprise of social problem solving, and ethics becomes the discipline of finding the most adequate ways to solve those problems." The moral agent is "a problem-solving agent."[23] This approach is thus highly rationalistic. The virtuous person is the one who has the capacity for clear moral reasoning. "Virtue is knowledge, the psychological structure of morality is cognitive, and the testing technique involves eliciting and analyzing people's cognitive judgments and patterns of reasoning."[24]

The highly rationalistic structure of the Piaget/Kohlberg approach to moral development becomes even more apparent when we take note of that which allegedly triggers the move from one stage to another; namely, the desire to eliminate "cognitive dissonance." Wolterstorff provides a good summary:

> Why do people move from one stage to another? Piaget and Kohlberg repudiate some of the explanations for this which others might suspect. People do not move from one stage to another because of some innate programming which works itself out if they simply live long enough. Nor do they

move because they have been taught the concepts belonging
to a later stage. Nor do they move because they are subtly
conditioned to do so or because they observe models in their
environment operating at a higher stage. According to this
theory, people move from one stage to the next because of a
certain sort of interaction between their environment and
the particular pattern of reasoning in which they find themselves. Development is the result of interaction between pattern and environment.

Specifically, Kohlberg and Piaget claim, everyone wants to
eliminate "cognitive dissonance" to attain "cognitive equilibrium". This, they say, is what underlies stage advancement.
Each successive stage in a particular hierarchy is "more highly
differentiated" and "more thoroughly integrated" than its
predecessors, and is thus better able to cope with experience.
Experience confronts the later stage with less dissonance.
Accordingly, when the dissonance between one's environment and stage of reasoning becomes sufficiently severe, one
moves on to a higher stage in order to attain equilibrium.
There the person rests, until that stage, too, yields an intoler-
able amount of dissonance in interaction with that part of
the environment to which the concepts of that hierarchy
apply.[25]

In other words, moral growth occurs when our reasoning
comes to a dead end, when it no longer seems adequate to
the new set of moral dilemmas with which we are faced.
The highest stage of moral growth is achieved when a person is able to reason morally in terms of universal, comprehensive, and consistent principles of justice and right.[26]

Critiques of the Piaget/Kohlberg approach, Dykstra
explains, focus on the rationalistic presuppositions concerning human nature and morality and the implication
that one needs to "be a moral philosopher in order to be a
moral person."[27] To begin with, this does not take the reality of sin and the bondage of the human will seriously. "It
pictures moral difficulties to be difficulties of thinking

rationally, and suggests that moral progress is attainable by a combination of increased reasoning power plus sincerity or strength of will."[28] As important, reduction of the moral life to rational problem solving involves a very truncated view of the moral life itself. Stanley Hauerwas notes,

> But moral behavior involves more than simply the decisions and choices men make about specific problems; it also includes the kind of men they are (their character and virtues), the kind of beliefs they hold, and the way that they integrate and organize their resources and energies to form a coherent life plan. The moral life is not simply a matter of decision governed by publicly defensible principles and rules; we can only act in the world we see, a seeing partially determined by the kind of beings we have become through the stories we have learned and embodied in our life plan.[29]

Craig Dykstra contrasts this more holistic approach to the moral agent, focusing on character and vision, with the Kohlberg approach: "For visional ethics, [moral] action follows vision, and vision depends on character—a person thinking, reasoning, believing, feeling, willing, and acting as a whole."[30] Here the key to moral growth is not the capacity for moral reasoning at high levels of abstraction and universality, "but the capacity for imaginal thought. . . . Our moral judgments are the way we look at things. They have less to do with particular cases, decisions, and logical reasons than they do with our general moral vision and quality of perception."[31] Instead of using the language of moral reasoning, Dykstra prefers to speak of imagination, revelation, and conversion. The key to moral growth for Christians, then, is the capacity for our imaginations to be transformed by the image of Christ, by the metaphors, stories, and images of the Christian faith. This involves a different kind of rationality. Dykstra notes:

> But the rationality of the imagination is not always the logic

of deduction. Because revelation illumines selves and history, its rationality will be of a kind appropriate to selves and history; a dramatic or narrative rationality. Revelation will help us to see connections between persons, events, evaluations, and descriptions that we had not been able to see before, because our evil imaginations . . . hid them from us.[32]

The contrast is thus drawn sharply between an approach to moral development that emphasizes reasoning (and considers the highest stage of moral growth to be the autonomous, rational person capable of universalizing thought), and one that emphasizes story, character, and virtue. In Craig Dykstra's "visional ethics" moral reasoning has its place. "But it is neither a necessary nor a sufficient condition for moral virtue. It can be a very considerable asset in helping us to think through moral perplexities."[33] But reasoning is not enough. The content of our moral life, the vision that governs it, and the character of the moral agent are also significant.[34]

An exclusive emphasis on moral reasoning ignores the unity of the person, the orientation, attitude, and particularly the character of the moral agent, a character that is not shaped by moral reasoning and is certainly not reducible to it. Hauerwas points out,

> But our moral lives are not simply made up of the addition of our separate responses to particular situations. Rather we exhibit an orientation that gives our life a theme through which the variety of what we do and do not do can be scored. To be agents at all requires a directionality that involves the development of character and virtue. Our character is the result of our sustained attention to the world that gives a coherence to our intentionality. Such attention is formed and given content by the stories through which we have learned to form the story of our lives. To be moral persons is to allow stories to be told through us so that our manifold activities gain a coherence that allows us to claim them

for our own. The significance of stories is the significance of character for the moral life as our experience itself, if it is to be coherent, is but an incipient story.

Our character is constituted by the rules, metaphors, and stories that are combined to give a design or unity to the variety of things we must and must not do in our lives. If our lives are to be reflective and coherent our vision must be ordered around dominant metaphors or stories.[35]

The shift, therefore, from character education to moral reasoning or values clarification has, according to Boston College professor of education William Kilpatrick, had a disastrous effect on education. Although values clarification began with good intentions—to help students think independently and critically about values and lead them to a commitment to self-discovered values—the actual consequence has been to "create an educational system with a de facto policy of withholding from children the greatest incentive to moral behavior—namely, the conviction that life makes sense—a policy of doing everything possible to prevent them from learning the larger purpose or stories that give meaning to existence." Kilpatrick concludes: "In failing to impart these stories, schools have deprived children of both moral content and moral energy."[36]

A wonderful example of how stories can transform the moral imagination is provided by Harvard psychiatrist Robert Coles in *The Call of Stories: Teaching and the Moral Imagination*.[37] Coles recounts his parents reading "to each other from novels by George Eliot and Dickens and Hardy and Tolstoy during my elementary years" and growing to share their literary enthusiasm (xi). His own interest in medicine was inspired by the poetry and prose as well as personal acquaintance with William Carlos Williams. Along with practicing psychiatry, Coles has also been teaching literature "in hopes of doing moral and social inquiry" (xvi).

In particular, he has "taught Harvard medical students in a seminar called 'Literature and Medicine,' where we read [Flannery] O'Connor, [Walker] Percy, and the 'doctor stories' in which William Carlos Williams gave an account of his experience as a physician working among the poor in northern New Jersey." Furthermore, Coles adds, "We have also called upon Anton Chekhov, another writing physician, and Leo Tolstoy" (xvii).

Coles's conclusion from this teaching is in line with observations from Dykstra and Hauerwas:

> As I have continued to do psychiatric work with children, I have gradually realized that my teaching has helped that work along—by reminding me how complex, ironic, ambiguous, and fateful this life can be, and that the conceptual categories I learned in psychiatry, in psychoanalysis, in social science seminars, are not the only means by which one ought view the world. (xvii)

Not only did stories enhance his ability to understand and relate to his patients, Coles recounts that "I gradually found myself more interested in the concrete details of a given person's narrative than in aggressively formulating her or his 'problems'" (14). One of Coles' teachers helped him think of his patients as storytellers: "The people who come to see us bring us their stories. They hope they tell them well enough so that we understand the truth of their lives. They hope we know how to interpret their stories correctly. We have to remember that what we hear is *their story*" (7). He adds, "Their story, yours, mine—it's what we all carry with us on this trip we take, and we owe it to each other to respect our stories and learn from them"(30).

Much of Coles' *The Call of Stories* is itself a narrative of discovery as he takes us through many of his favorite writers and writings and recalls numerous conversations with students about the impact of literature on their own life journey. Particularly gripping is Coles' account of the humanizing effect that prose and poetry had on the medical students he was teaching:

> Meanwhile, too, my medical students try to make sense of their stage of that journey, make sense of the long struggle they will soon have with death. Already, in school, they know the burdens and obstacles: so many facts to master; so various the professional possibilities to consider; so many diseases yet to be understood. Time was already their adversary in the premedical years and will never let go of their lives, given all the things to know and do, the tests that follow tests, and even in middle age, when every possible certificate covers every available office wall, the test that any disease can offer the person who takes it on seriously. Time is a prize fought for on the medical battlefield, the doctor trying to obtain it for someone, and death anxious to take it away, the sooner the better. With such a combative future for these apprentices, no wonder a poem can have such a powerful meaning. . . .
>
> Medical students keep learning to concentrate, to get to the very heart of this or that matter. They keep struggling to tame life itself, in its excesses, its madness. And they keep being stopped in their tracks by moments of tragedy or great bad luck. No wonder, as some of them tell me, their minds ache to give sharp, pointed expression to what they have seen and heard and felt. Poets try to sharpen the sight, to nurture language carefully in the hope of calling upon it for an understanding of what is happening. Poets give us images and metaphors and offer the epiphanies doctors and patients alike crave, even if it is in the silent form of a slant of late afternoon light. (98-101)

Coles has a special place in his heart for the writings of William Carlos Williams:

> I heard him many times confronting his flaws, and I read his efforts to render that aspect of his life insofar as it informed his medical practice, in a series of stories, first published in 1937 as Life along the Passaic River. When I began teaching

college students and medical students, I found those stories powerful in their impact upon those young men and women who, like Williams, struggled with ambitious intelligence as a force that can demolish the "heart's reasons"—namely, a warm empathy, a considerateness toward others, a willingness, even, to let them become one's teachers, however humble or troubled their lives. (p. 107)

At one point Coles recalls a conversation with Williams about medical ethics. Competence and knowledge were not enough, and even courses on medical ethics would not do the trick. "Again he posed the matter of 'conduct' (as opposed to 'ideas'), repeating, as he had in his writing, that the ultimate test of a person's worth as a doctor or teacher or lawyer has to do not only with what he or she knows, but with how he or she behaves with another person, the patient or student or client" (119). However, the awareness that ideas are not enough, Coles insists, does not mean that ideas are somehow to be disparaged. He recalls a seminar discussion on this matter:

We pointed out to one another that a story is not an idea, though there most certainly are ideas in stories; that reading a story is not like memorizing facts. We talked of the mind's capacity to analyze. This capacity—to abstract, to absorb elements of knowledge, and to relinquish them in statements, verbal or written—is an important part of what we are: creatures of language, of symbols galore. But we need not use ourselves, so to speak in only that way. We have memories; we have feelings. We reach out to others. We have the responsiveness that one sees in preliterate infants who cry when others cry, smile when others smile, frown when others frown; or the responsiveness of youngsters, even preschool ones, who sing in response to the sound of others singing, who get choked up when shown a sad picture or told about a sad event. That side of ourselves is not set apart from our intellect. In order to respond, one remembers, one notices, then one makes connections—engaging the thinking mind as well as what is called one's emotional side.

How to encompass in our minds the complexity of some lived moments in a life? How to embody in language the mix of heightened awareness and felt experience which reading a story can end up offering to the reader? Not that a novel cannot, also, be an occasion for abstraction, for polemical argument. But it can, as well, insinuate itself into a remembering, daydreaming, wondering life; can prompt laughter or tears; can inspire moments of amused reflection with respect to one's nature, accomplishments, flaws. (127-28)

Coles gives a particularly poignant example of the capacity of stories to transform. He tells of reading Tolstoy with a difficult patient and notes, "The more I become immersed yet again in Tolstoy's stories, in Tolstoy's own story, the less unyielding I become to my patient, still on the ward, whom I began to approach with a friendly, even searching smile, and maybe a bit of shame" (171-72). In a nutshell, "a compelling narrative, offering a storyteller's moral imagination vigorously at work, can enable any of us to learn by example, to take to heart what is, really, a gift of grace" (191). Moral character and conduct is to a large extent therefore shaped by stories, "a person's moral conduct responding to the moral imagination of writers and the moral imperative of fellow human beings in need" (205).

Narrative Knowing and Human Experience

What we have been pursuing in this chapter, more or less anecdotally, is a consideration of story as an alternative way of human knowing. Stories take us beyond reason and discursive thinking to new levels of awareness about human experience. We will now move on to some more theoretical observations about narrative knowing. What exactly is it? What is its appeal and exactly how does narrative work?

A perceptive reader cannot help but be aware of a certain

irony here, an irony not absent from the extensive literature about narrative.[38] If story is a superior form of knowing, how is it necessary or even possible to gain greater clarity on the nature of narrative itself by means of analysis? A
full answer to these legitimate questions will have to be
given by the analysis itself. For now, suffice it to say that
narrative should not be seen as an alternative to discursive
thought in the sense of eliminating it, but rather as complementary in some way.

Let us begin with some attempts at defining narrative
and noting its characteristics and component parts. Theologian Gabriel Fackre describes it as follows:

> Narrative, in its encompassing sense, is an account of events
> and participants moving over time and space, a recital with
> beginning and ending patterned by the narrator's principle of
> selection . . . an account of characters and events in a plot
> moving over time and space through conflict toward resolu-
> tion.[39]

Narrative is thus a conceptual tool for understanding
human activity, particularly activity that is intentional and
purposive. It is a way of providing an intelligible pattern or
organization to human activity. As psychologist Donald
Polkinghorne, whose own interest in narrative arose from a
concern to bridge the gap between academic psychology
and clinical practice, has observed,

> The narrative organizational scheme is of particular impor-
> tance for understanding human activity. It is the scheme that
> displays purpose and direction in human affairs and makes
> individual human lives comprehensible as wholes. We con-
> ceive our own and others' behavior within the narrative
> framework, and through it recognize the effects our planned
> actions can have on desired goals. . . .
>
>   In summary, narrative is a meaning structure that orga-
> nizes events and human actions into a whole, thereby
> attributing significance to individual actions and events

according to their effect on the whole. Thus, narratives are to be differentiated from chronicles, which simply list events according to their place on a time line. Narrative provides a symbolized account of actions that includes a temporal dimension.[40]

What is striking about this last citation is that it points to narrative as a form of "cognitive functioning."[41] It is itself a scheme, a pattern of organization, sometimes even referred to by psychologists in narrative terms as a "life-script."[42] Polkinghorne formulates the thesis of his book as follows:

> The core of the argument I make in this book is that narrative is a scheme by means of which human beings give meaning to their experience of temporality and personal actions. Narrative meaning functions to give form to the understanding of a purpose to life and to join everyday actions and events into episodic units. It provides a framework for understanding the past events of one's life and for planning future actions. It is the primary scheme by means of which human existence is rendered meaningful. Thus, the study of human beings by the human sciences needs to focus on the realm of meaning in general, and on narrative meaning in particular.[43]

To see one's life in narrative terms, then, is to acknowledge that there is an observable coherence or meaning to one's activity—in narrative terms, a plot or script. But narrative also underscores a certain open-endedness or indeterminacy to our human activity. At crucial junctions in our life story, we make choices that affect and change our futures. To some degree we choose or alter our story and its script. Furthermore, there are dimensions to our life story that defy neat, precise analysis. There is always an element of mystery. The story can be told, but it cannot always be fully explained. That is why the story must be told as a story. In sum,

A story, thus, is a narrative account that binds events and agents together in an intelligible pattern. We do not tell stories simply because they provide us a more colorful way to say what can be said in a different way, but because there is no other way we can articulate the richness of intentional activity—that is, behavior that is purposeful but not necessary. For as any good novelist knows there is always more involved in any human action than can be said. To tell a story often involves our attempt to make intelligible the muddle of things we have done in order to have a self.[44]

Stories give us an identity, a selfhood. We are our stories. Or perhaps it is better to say that "We live in our stories," as John Hoffman puts it:

We understand ourselves though complex narratives composed of actual or imagined memories from our personal past or from the history of our community. We relate to myths, legends, and ordinary fictions, setting forth our heroes and our dreams. Through story we keep telling ourselves who we are, and what we must do, what we may hope for, where we are going. Such messages do more than set expectations and direct voluntary conduct. They significantly determine the future. They are self-fulfilling prophecies even when we are not fully conscious of them.[45]

In other words, we are characters in a plot, acting according to a life script that is rooted in the past—memory—and oriented to the future—vision.

Our very experience as human beings is thus narrative-like.[46] Says John Hoffman, "We understand ourselves and our world largely in terms of a collection of tales and significant events, perhaps collapsed into symbols, drawn from our personal history and cultural traditions. These tales and events become welded into a personal story within which we live."[47] If this is true, and the point seems obvious, then it is easy to understand the appeal and attraction that stories seem to have for all people in all places. It also underscores the pilgrim or journey character of Christian experience. Theologian Sallie TeSelle puts it well:

> Why does everyone love a good story, and how is story related to theological reflection? The answers to these two questions are, I believe, related. We all love a good story because of the basic narrative quality of human experience; in a sense, any story is about ourselves, and a *good* story is good precisely because somehow it rings true to human life. Human life is not marked by instantaneous rapture and easy solutions. Life is tough. That is hardly a novel thought, but it is nonetheless the backbone in a literal sense—the 'structure'—of a good story. We recognize our own pilgrimages from here to there in a good story; we feel its movement in our bones and know it is 'right.' . . . We love stories, then, because our lives are stories and we recognize in the attempts of others to move, temporally and painfully, our own story. . . . For the Christian, the story of Jesus is *the* story par excellence. . . . That God should be with us in the story of a human life could be seen as a happy accident, but it makes more sense to see it as God's way of always being with human beings *as they are*, as the concrete, temporal beings who have a beginning and an end—who are, in other words, stories themselves.[48]

If it is thus true that stories define us as selves, as intentional, purposive creatures, if we all live in a story, then the variety of stories that confront us as human beings are in effect invitations to participate in different worlds. John Hoffman suggests that

> language—and especially, the hearing of stories—inevitably offers the listener a world in which to live. It is an invitation to experience reality from a particular perspective, to worship a certain God, to follow one way, to adopt heroes, to celebrate hope or sink in despair.[49]

Good narratives engage us because they are true to the tensions, complexity, ambiguity, and even indeterminacy of life itself. Narratives take seriously not just who we are now, but seek to place our "now" in the larger framework of our past and future. Narrative underscores the pilgrim character of our experience. We are on a journey, which has to some degree been scripted by our past and yet remains somewhat open to future possibilities. It is thus no accident that lack of awareness or loss of memory can result in psychopathologies. Healthy selfhood requires a narrative awareness involving both memory and vision. Hoffman points out that often a crucial part of counseling or therapy "consists in the lifting of amnesia of childhood," and healing occurs when a person again knows and lives his or her story.[50] It has even been suggested that reordering or transforming chaotic and traumatic events into a new story may be the essence of what takes place in psychotherapy.

Finally, it is worth noting that narratives engage us and involve us at different levels.[51] To begin with, each of us has our own personal life story, a unique blend of experience and activity that makes up our identity. In Christian terms, our personal life stories can serve as testimonials to God's grace, can communicate the faith to those outside it, and can inspire and renew those who are already believers. The latter is especially true of lives of the saints, biographies of outstanding Christians that have often been a mainstay in the practice of Christian formation and discipleship.

Personal life stories, however, are inseparable from community stories or tradition. For Christians, the history of the church is crucial here. Individual Christian believers are not only part of specific denominational traditions—which give rise to distinct patterns of worship, doctrine, and practice—but they are part of the church universal—the one, holy, catholic, apostolic community that began in the New Testament and continues its earthly pilgrimage until Christ's return.

It is within the context of this larger community story that the third level of narrative involvement becomes significant; namely, canonical story or scriptural story. The scriptures of the Old and New Testament are the authorized story of the Christian church, and its grand narrative of creation, fall, redemption, and consummation shapes the community's story as well as that of individual believers.

Conclusion

In this chapter we have observed the growing interest in the notion of story and have seen that narrative is a distinctive way of ordering and understanding human experience. In particular we have considered the key role that narrative plays in shaping personal as well as communal identity and morality. In so doing we confirmed the observations and conclusions of the previous chapter warning against an exclusively rationalist understanding of human experience in general and Christian experience and discipleship in particular.

At the same time, we need to issue a caveat. While it is true that narrative suggests a way of ordering experience in a different way than in the analytic approach, care must be taken not to make excessive claims for narrative or to use narrative categories in order to disparage and discount all abstraction and discursive reasoning. It is worth repeating that narrative is itself a conceptual framework. It is possible to analyze stories and to theorize about such narrative realities as plot and character. To be sure, a story is not an idea, and our response to stories is different from our response to an argument or a syllogism.

Stories do help us understand ourselves and our world better. Part of the reason for the popularity of narrative today is undoubtedly a response to a dominant rationalism in the Western world, a viewing of human experience though a very narrowly conceived notion of reason. Yet, to settle the ancient quarrel between philosophy and poetry by jettisoning philosophy altogether would be as serious an error as the philosophic attempt to eliminate stories. The rediscovery of narrative provides an enrichment of our understanding of human experience. It is also, we shall see in the next chapter, a constructive way of understanding the reason for and the goal of Christian education.

6

The Christian Story and the Christian School

Introduction

In Chapter Three we considered some tendencies in Christian education which reflect appropriate Christian convictions yet which through distortion or isolation from other beliefs and practices unwittingly undermine either the Christian or the education component of Christian education. Indoctrination, for example, is a threat to the school's task of nurturing an examined, mature Christian faith and worldview. Although the school is not a church, it does have a responsibility, in its own distinctive way, to nurture Christian discipleship. A broad narrative understanding of the school can, as we shall see, help us here.

We encounter a similar issue in thinking about the school's evangelistic task. Although the school plays a legitimate evangelical role in the Christian community, evangelism is not the defining characteristic of the school. Reformed Christians consider their children as members of God's covenant family, and that schools prepare students for kingdom citizenship. Once again, a narrative approach will help us see how the school can play a legitimate evangelical role as school.

The final threats discussed in Chapter Three were prophecy and excellence. In the former, the dilemma facing us is how to preserve a valid, biblically based, socially critical task for the school and encourage social justice as an integral part of Christian discipleship without the destructive politicizing and polarization that often take place. In addition, prophecy tends to subvert the distinctive educational identity of the school. And, with respect to excellence, while Christian schools should not apologize for maintaining high academic standards and insisting upon excellence, they need to avoid intellectual elitism and to define *excellence* in a way that acknowledges the demands of Christian discipleship and service to Christ's kingdom.

In Chapter Four, we considered developing the Christian mind as a necessary but finally insufficient way of describing the task of the Christian school. While not wanting to join the chorus of anti-intellectualism still found in some evangelical and Reformed Christian communities, or even to make the smallest concession to it, we acknowledged that the cognitivist assumption does need to be challenged. Furthermore, some cautions need to be observed with respect to grandiose and global claims about Christian perspective in every part of the school curriculum. Alternate pedagogical strategies such as modeling and selection enrich our awareness of what is possible and useful in Christian education. We also need to be aware that our perspective, vision, or worldview is not only shaped by ideas but also by personal and communal stories. This has significant implications for education in general but especially for Christian education since the Christian faith is itself so deeply rooted in a story.

The Story of God and His People

The Christian faith is, first and foremost, a story—the

true story of the triune God and his people. Christian testimony usually takes the form of a story: "This is how the Lord has changed my life." Sinful past, redeemed present, and anticipated glory become a single narrative plot, our spiritual autobiography. In the words of John Newton's beloved hymn: "I once was lost but now am found, was blind but now I see. . . . Through many dangers, toils and snares I have already come; 'tis grace hath brought me safe thus far, and grace will lead me home." The fundamental Christian experience of grace and conversion that cannot be told but by a story. As theologian Michael Novak has observed, "'Story' articulates a change in experience. It is a particularly apt method for expressing the sort of experience that alters one's fundamental 'standpoint' or 'horizon.'"[1] It is thus inevitable that, as Amos Wilder claims, "when the Christian in any time or place confesses his faith, his confession turns into a narrative."[2]

Communal confession in worship and liturgy, as well as personal testimony, is also fundamentally narrative. The most universal Christian articulation of faith, the Apostles' Creed, is a narrative on two levels. The overall trinitarian structure covers the entire narrative history of the universe from creation to consummation. The heart of the creed, the second article about Jesus the Savior, is a simple summary narrative about the life of the God-man from conception by the Spirit to rule at the Father's right hand and return in glory. The Old Testament communal confessions of faith are also narrative in nature, summaries of salvation history. One classic example, tied to the offering of firstfruits, is the credo of Deuteronomy 26:5-9:

> My father was a wandering Aramean, and he went down into Egypt with a few people and lived there and became a great nation, powerful and numerous. But the Egyptians mistreated us and made us suffer, putting us to hard labor. Then we

cried out to the Lord, the God of our fathers, and the Lord heard our voice and saw our misery, toil and oppression. So the Lord brought us out of Egypt with a mighty hand and an outstretched arm, with great terror and with miraculous signs and wonders. He brought us to this place and gave us this land, a land flowing with milk and honey.

In the previous chapter we noted John Shea's observation that "God not only loves to hear our stories, he loves to tell his own. And, quite simply, *we* are the story God tells."[3] There is a profound truth here. The Christian story is not simply about God's acts, and it is most assuredly not merely our story, our narrative of discovery and imagination in which we give account of our experience of God. The Christian story is the story of God and his people. From creation through redemption unto consummation, the Christian story is a covenantal narrative, a narrative about a relationship between the triune God and his people. John Calvin begins his *Institutes of the Christian Religion* by underscoring this inseparable covenantal duality: "Nearly all the wisdom we possess, that is to say, true and sound wisdom, consists of two parts: the knowledge of God and of ourselves."[4]

To be sure, no matter how inseparable God and his people are in our thoughts, this covenantal relationship does not involve equal partners. God is the sovereign who initiates and governs the relationship. He created the world for his glory and breathed life into human beings. His call to Abraham and his promises created and sustained the covenantal people of Israel. The virgin birth of Jesus reminds us that our salvation is not from us but from above. We are children of God, not by human will or decision. Rather, we are "born of God" (John 1:13). Today it is the Holy Spirit, the gift of the ascended Lord, who graciously initiates, endows, and preserves the community of faith, the church. God's people respond to his initiative, and their story is a recital of what God has done for them, in them, and through them.

And yet we must not lose sight of the fact that the story of what God has done, is doing, and will do, cannot be told apart from the community of faith. This is underscored by such New Testament metaphors as the body of Christ and the temple of the Spirit. Both remind us that the visible locus of God's presence, the manifest sign of Christ's kingly rule in the world, is the people of God. The apostle Paul's use of plurals underscores this: "You are the body of Christ" (1 Cor. 12:27); "You yourselves are God's temple" (1 Cor. 3:16).

Since in a real sense we are the story God is telling, it is important that we know the context of God's story today. We need to be aware of the influence of the ideologies of modernity and the other "isms" of our day, including post-modernism, secularism, and paganism (described in Chapter Two). We need to be aware of the pervasive influence of the media. All of these affect and shape the story of God and his people today. More important for our purposes here, we must have our eyes open to the grand, divine narrative within which our present story is a small segment. Our context today is a world that is at the same time created, fallen, and redeemed by Christ, as well as on the way to God's final, glorious destiny for it. The apostle Paul summarizes this for us when he tells us that God's purpose is "to bring all things in heaven and on earth together under one head, even Christ" (Eph. 1:10). Thus, one of the better summary definitions of the essence of Christianity is this one from the great Dutch Reformed theologian Herman Bavinck: "The essence of the Christian religion consists therein, that the creation of the Father, destroyed by sin, is again restored in the death of the Son of God, and recreated by the grace of the Spirit to a Kingdom of God."[5]

Putting this grand narrative up front means that we must have our eyes open to God's redemptive purpose for humanity and creation. To state it in different terms, we must be aware of God's mission and our role in that mission. The story of God and his people is fundamentally a mission story, a narrative of God's redeeming, restoring work and the community created by it. This community, it must be noted, is itself then called to be sent out as a missionary body, an instrument of God's redemptive mission to the world.[6]

Thinking about Christian education in narrative terms thus means that the question, How does the Christian school fit into the story of God and his people? really becomes, How does the Christian school serve the mission of God? The story of God and his people is the story of the triune God's mission—commissioned by the Father, accomplished by Christ, applied by the Holy Spirit, and still in process until the end comes and God is "all in all" (1 Cor. 15:28).

The Christian School: A Visionary Community of Memory

We have seen how the Christian faith in general must be understood narratively in terms of God's redemptive mission. We must now consider more precisely how the Christian school serves that mission in a distinctive way. We shall do that by thinking of the Christian school as a visionary community of memory. This is simply another formulation of a narrative framework, since all narratives are temporal in nature, joining characters and events in a plot over time. A narrative joins past to present in memory and then joins both to the future in anticipation or hope. A narrative understanding of the school, therefore, situates it between memory and vision.

To speak of the school as a community of memory still leaves many questions unanswered. It is, of course, true that all communities have memories, usually called traditions. The church at worship also remembers what God has done for his people in Christ when it recites the Apostles' Creed and celebrates holy communion Yet while the church is indeed a community that remembers, its memory is a memory of divine forgiveness and reconciliation, which leads it to be a forgiving and reconciling community (2 Cor. 5:18-20). In contrast, the school's very nature as an educational institution qualifies it and defines it by the special task of remembering. The school is the place where the broader community seeks to pass on to the next generation its civilizational memory, its cultural wisdom.

Put this way, we are clearly affirming the case, sketched in Chapter One, for cultural literacy as the characteristic task of the school. The school's task is to prepare its students for citizenship in a specific community, to mold character, and to encourage virtues consonant with the historic values and traditions of that community. Teachers are thus custodians of a civilization and students its heirs. The school is a specialized community in which the larger community preserves and passes on its cultural memory. Education is a matter of passing on and of nurturing students in a shared memory, incorporating them into a shared story. E. D. Hirsch in *Cultural Literacy* makes a similar point. Especially critical of educational theories that are preoccupied with process and thus tend to marginalize content, he observes, "All human communities are based upon specific shared information. . . . In an anthropological perspective, the basic goal of education in a human community is acculturation, the transmission to children of the specific

information shared by the adults of the group or polis."
And further, "Only by accumulating shared symbols, and
the shared information that the symbols represent, can we
learn to communicate effectively with one another in our
national community."[7] The Christian school is concerned
not only with the story and symbols of the national community but more broadly with the story and symbols of
God's kingdom and mission in the world.

It should be noted that the same point can be made by
focusing on the biblical idea of wisdom as a way thinking
about the task of education. Wisdom is rooted in memory
and tradition. In noting that wisdom can be learned as it is
passed on from generation to generation, the wisdom literature of the Old Testament underscores the importance of
tradition and memory. This biblical approach to wisdom is
not unlike classical Greek civilizing ideals of *paideia*, which
see the purpose of education to prepare for citizenship, to
produce virtue, to mold character, to tame the passions,
and to restrain unbridled desire.[8] To educate a person is to
civilize him or her, to make him or her wise. We are wise to
the degree we share traditional memories and live by traditional wisdom. We are educated to the degree that we know
and begin to participate in the community's story.

That suggests that seeing the Christian school as a community of memory is a plausible way of describing its distinct character and task. A good Christian school curriculum draws significantly from the wisdom of the ages, good
teachers drink deeply from the wells of tradition, and students are incorporated into a story of the past, present, and
future of God and his people. Incorporated into this story,
students are given a memory, a vision, and, in this way, a
mission.

Teaching As Storytelling[9]

Thinking of the school and teaching in narrative terms has implications for the identity of the teacher, the shape of the curriculum, and even the structure of specific lessons. We shall consider each of these briefly, recognizing that much more could and should be said about each one.

To begin with, we are led to think of the teacher as the community's storyteller or, to use a potentially misleading but nevertheless functionally accurate term, "the teller of our myths."[10] The term *myth* is misleading when understood in its popular sense as false story or fantasy. For Christians the term is particularly problematic because it has become a codeword used by critical scholars to devalue the historical, factual reality of such biblical miracles as the incarnation and the resurrection.[11] Yet as an anthropological term, *myth* points to that collection of stories and images which shape a community, which give a people an identity. It is true that these stories could be fictional, but they are not necessarily so. Powerful, historically factual stories can also serve as myths. It is in this latter sense—and only in this sense—that it would be correct to speak of the mythology of the Holocaust, for example. Mythology used in this sense does not play into the hands of anti-Semites who deny its ever having happened but to the power of Holocaust images and stories to shape the identity of post-World War II Jews. One lives by myths and some are historically based while others are fiction. Similarly, American mythology, for example, includes stories about George Washington's and Abraham Lincoln's honesty and Martin Luther King Jr.'s courage. Some are clearly based in history; others have the aura of legend. Thus, while the word *myth* can be and often is used popularly in order to discredit historical events, the more precise significance of the term points to the affective and symbolic significance of a story.

Myths are stories—factual or fictional—that have power. Myths shape and govern the way people live.

And now we are suggesting that the Christian school teacher ought to think of herself or himself as the community's storyteller.[12] In the light of what has been said earlier in this chapter, the Christian school teacher's identity must be self-consciously rooted in the grand narrative of God's redemptive mission. The story of the triune God's acts in creation, redemption, and renewal and our covenantal participation in God's mission must always be kept front and center. Keeping this story before us also has consequences for the Christian school curriculum.

Education professor Kieran Egan in *Teaching As Story Telling* contends that his suggestions "lead to an elementary curriculum which might be labeled a Great True Stories of the World curriculum."[13] What a great title for a Christian school curriculum! In such a curriculum, "designed to introduce children to the great stories by which we can make sense of our world and experience . . . teachers can be seen as the story-tellers of our tribe. . . . As teachers are our professional story-tellers, so the curriculum is the story they are to tell."[14] Recognizing that stories are the pre-eminent means by which we make sense out of our experience, and realizing that thanks to divine revelation Christians have access to the story by which all stories are judged, a Christian school curriculum that tells the Great True Story and all true derivative and supporting stories is the only way for Christian education to help students make sense of their experience.

At this point some concreteness and specificity is needed. Obviously the narrative of Scripture itself will play a foundational role in the Christian school. A good Bible curriculum that introduces students to the grand narrative plot of Scripture and explores its vast and rich imagery is the cornerstone of a solid Christian education.[15] Such basic biblical literacy is important, in the first place, to shape the Christian identity and character of students. Beyond this primary goal, it also has the benefit of providing students with an essential cultural vocabulary for understanding Western civilization. But the reverse is also true. Exposing students to the stories and images of Scripture for the deliberately restricted purpose of providing them with the cultural vocabulary necessary to understand Shakespeare, Milton, Blake, Tolstoy, Abraham Lincoln, or Martin Luther King Jr., is a dangerous activity. The story and the images have power. It is not surprising, therefore, that secularists go to great lengths to eliminate even non-devotional reading of the Bible and to remove paintings of Jesus from public school classrooms. It is also not surprising that vigorous opponents of the Christian religion also want to dismantle the traditional canon of Western literature, often in the name of multiculturalism. Even a secondary exposure to biblical story and image in the great stories of the West is dangerous because they have a power to convict and convert.

This leads us directly to the second building block of a "Great True Stories of the World Curriculum"—church history. To be taught effectively, church history must not be seen as so much data and information to be learned but as the ongoing story of God and his people. If students in the Christian school are going to become the kind of Christians who have the courage needed to resist the encroachments of a pagan world, they need to hear the stories of their brothers and sisters, the courageous and faithful, from Daniel to Stephen to Polycarp and Blandina to John Huss to the Huguenots to Dietrich Bonhoefer and Laszlo Tokes to the "house" Christians of China today. Can Christian students today be equipped with the requisite armor to resist the seductions of affluence and power without examples and alternative models such as those provided by the great Medieval monastic orders, Saint Francis of Assisi, Anabaptist and Pietist communities such as the Hutterites and the Moravians, and even the contemporary example of Mother Teresa? Can Christian students truly learn the meaning of Christian compassion and become committed to social justice if they don't know anything about the early church's example, about John Calvin's Geneva, about Abraham Kuyper's Netherlands, about William Wilberforce, about the role of Christians in the abolition movement, or about the German Confessing Church's resistance to Hitler while protecting Jews and caring for the handicapped destined for the death camps? These examples could be multiplied almost endlessly, but the point should be clear. Without the knowledge of such people and movements and the awareness that they are part of our story, can our children ever be inspired to devote themselves selflessly to God's redemptive mission in the world, to the righteousness, justice, and shalom of his kingdom? This means that a Christian school curriculum must provide students with a good measure of Christian biography so that students learn the story of God and his people, identify with it, and develop the habits and character that are consistent with the mission of God's people in his world.

Beyond the Bible and church history, a narrative focus has a direct and obvious bearing on literature and the broad rubric of schoolwork known as social studies. Students not only learn from the example of actual saints, they also benefit from John Bunyan's fictional heroic pilgrim. In Chapter Five, we considered Plato's concern about the role of stories in a child's education. Plato judged that some form of censorship was necessary to ensure that the proper civic virtues were communicated to children: "we must do everything to insure that what they hear first, with respect to virtue, be the finest told tales for them to hear."[16] This power of literature has been recently reaffirmed by William Kilpatrick. The argument of *Why Johnny Can't Tell Right from Wrong* is simply that the shift in moral education from art and story to moral reasoning approaches has resulted in overwhelming and catastrophic moral illiteracy among today's youth: "In recent decades educators have turned a deaf ear and a blind eye to the crucial role of music, art, and story in moral formation. The result has been that these powerful influences have been left almost entirely in the hands of the entertainment industry, which has, in effect, become the real moral educator of the young."[17] Kilpatrick observes the following about character education and the crucial role of stories in it:

> Philosophers, psychologists, and educators, working separately and pursuing different lines of inquiry, have been arriving at similar conclusions about the need for stories and models in moral formation. In addition, new curriculums are already under development: sex education and drug education programs that encourage abstinence and self-control rather than multiple-choice life styles; character education programs that use stories to teach virtues.[18]

The key role of stories in moral formation arises from the basic human need to provide meaning and purpose for one's life, a meaning frame that is narrative in nature. If we are to become responsible moral agents, each one of us needs, in some sense, to become "the hero of my own life."[19] It has been customary, going back to Homer, to model the good life on a heroic story. In Kilpatrick's words, "The desire to be a hero, so common to children and adults, is part of a larger wish: the hope that one's life can be like a story." This wish is basic to our very humanity, so basic "that we hardly reflect on it. For the most part we simply assume that our lives will make sense. And the kind of 'making sense' we intuitively have in mind is not the sense of a mathematical equation or of a scientific theorem but the kind of sense a story makes."[20]

Kilpatrick concludes *Why Johnny Can't Tell Right from Wrong* with an annotated bibliography of "Great Books for Children and Teens." A similar listing would be useful for Christian parents and Christian school teachers—an extensive list of books and stories that inspire readers heroically to identify with and participate in the larger story of God and his people. The battle in Christian education in the next decades will, I suspect, be less about abstract philosophies and psychologies of education than about who tells what stories to our children. This is already the case in much public education, where the control of stories about family life, gender roles, sexual identity, and ethnicity has become the battlefield of the current culture war. The chief defining characteristic of the Christian school in the next few decades may be its literary canon.

If it is the case that narrative is the way we make sense of our world of experience, then helping children make sense of their social world—the communities in which they live, the history of which they are the legatees as well as active participants—must also be done by story. Kieran Egan discusses the subject of history in elementary schools.

> History, then, need not remain untouched in the primary school, its absence at present being justified on the grounds that children lack the abstract concepts that are necessary to make history meaningful: chronological time, causality and so on. From observing how children make sense of fantasy stories, we can see that they do have available conceptual tools that can make history meaningful. They may lack a logical conception of causality, but they clearly have available the sense of causality that holds stories together and moves them along: the conceptual tools that can make sense of *Cin-*

derella and *Lord of the Rings* can be used to make sense of the Athenians' struggle for freedom against the tyrannous Persian Empire, or the monks' struggle to preserve civilized learning against the ravages of the Vikings. Nor need such understanding of history be trivial. Young children have the conceptual tools to learn the most profound things about our past; as a struggle for freedom against arbitrary violence, for security against fear, for knowledge against ignorance, and so on. *They do not learn these concepts; they already have them when they arrive at school. They use those concepts to learn about the world and experience.*[21]

History is an obvious candidate for a narrative approach. The very content of social studies, concerned as it is with "events, values, places, intentions, individual people and groups . . . already comes partly story shaped."[22] The challenge for the Christian school teacher is to frame these stories in the larger context of the story of God and his people.

Here the biblical stories of creation, the Tower of Babel, Israel among the nations, Pentecost, and the missionary expansion of the Christian church become essential for telling the stories of other cultures and for exploring the rich diversity of the earth's geography and cultures. Precisely because God is the creator of all, because the Christian story is inclusive and the Christian church universal, the Christian school can provide a truly multicultural education without the politicized indoctrination that characterizes so much of multiculturalism today. Children who discover that they have brothers and sisters in Latin America, Africa, and Asia, as well as Europe and North America, will appreciate hearing and reading the stories of other cultures. Learning such stories will also open them to the possibilities and challenges of God's redemptive mission to the nations.

Beyond the obvious candidates for a narrative approach

to teaching—Bible, literature, and social studies—it may be possible to extend the idea of teaching as storytelling to other parts of the curriculum as well. In fact, Egan's argument in *Teaching As Story Telling* is that the narrative model helps a teacher "to use the power of the story form in order to teach any content more engagingly and meaningfully."[23] He sees this narrative approach as a deliberate alternative to lesson planning that concentrates on objectives. The narrative alternative "is a model for planning teaching that encourages us to see lessons or units as good stories to be told rather than sets of objectives to be attained." The latter approach, he contends, focuses far too narrowly on a very "limited range of children's logical thinking skills" and virtually ignores children's imagination. The story approach focuses on the whole rather than the part; it is concerned with meaning. "It is an organic approach that puts *meaning* center stage. . . . [It is] a model primarily concerned with providing children with access to and engagement with rich meaning."[24] Kieran's point is that "we need, for the educational benefit of children, to reconstruct our curricula and teaching methods in light of a richer image of the child as an imaginative as well as a logico-mathematical thinker. What we call imagination is also a tool of learning—in the early years perhaps the most energetic and powerful one."[25] The concentration on story makes possible a more coherent and meaningful curriculum; it makes connections between otherwise disparate and fragmented units. Egan argues that the story model is appropriate in the elementary school even for mathematics and science. The use of stories in science would focus on the human discovery and mastery of the world.

> The science curriculum would be made up of what we know about the stories of life on earth, of our place in the universe, and the human ingenuity which discovered the material for

these stories. That ingenuity would be seen also in the stories of technological accomplishments, such as the story of our building machines to fly, from Daedulus to space-ships, of making and manipulating symbols, from the beginnings of alphabets, syllabaries, and numbers to the book and the computer, and so on.[26]

Thus, across the entire spectrum the school curriculum can be seen as a story and the school teacher as a storyteller.

A Note on Imagination

Repeatedly in the preceding section of this chapter, we have encountered the notion of imagination. A narrative approach to education is celebrated by many people precisely because of its capacity to capture students' imagination. We need to pause at this point to address the question of imagination—and its cousin, fantasy—because it has become a matter of controversy in North American evangelical Christianity. In some Christian school communities, concerted efforts have been undertaken to remove from libraries and reading lists all fantasy literature, including C.S. Lewis's Narnia Chronicles and the writings of Madeleine L'Engle. Why? The answer is relatively simple— fear of occultism and New Age religious practices. A growing number of evangelical writers in North America have set their critical sights on what they allege is "the seduction of Christianity" by dogmas and techniques of New Age pagan "sorcery." Books that purport to document this seduction have proliferated.[27]

In the process numerous Christian leaders, from James Dobson to Robert Schuller, as well as organizations such as Bread for the World and World Vision have been targeted as being in collusion with the New Age movement. The furor within evangelicalism has been so intense and the accusations and counter-accusations so vehement that two writers have, with some justification, spoken of a "witch hunt" within the evangelical community.[28]

What exactly is the fuss about? What is this new Age "sorcery" that is alleged to be seducing so many Christians? According to Dave Hunt and T. A. McMahon, the authors of the most popular volume in this genre, "One word that is often used to encompass all pagan/occult practices is 'sorcery.'" They follow this with what is admittedly a very broad definition: "[a]ny attempt to manipulate reality (internal, external, past, present, or future) by various mind-over-matter techniques that run the gamut from alchemy and astrology to positive/possibility thinking."[29] Hunt and McMahon cite as an example the most prominent current spokesman for positive mental attitude principles, Robert Schuller. "You don't know what power you have within you! . . . You make the world into anything you choose. Yes, you can make your world into whatever you want it to be."[30] The way the world is remade is through the imagination, and the technique is visualization. The power of the imagination is considered to be godlike, the creative force of the universe and humanity. In fact, Hunt and McMahon claim that "Korean pastor Paul Yoonggi Cho declares that it was through the power of the 'imagination' that God created the world, and that because man is a 'fourth-dimension' spirit-being like God, he too, whether occultist or Christian, can create his own world through the power of his imagination."[31]

It is far beyond the scope of our present concern to do a thorough analysis of this rather unedifying controversy within evangelicalism. Nor, in spite of my serious reservations about the irresponsible way so many of these accusations are made, do I wish to defend such advocates of positive mental attitude as Norman Vincent Peale and Robert Schuller. However, we must examine the broadsided attack on imagination and fantasy, particularly the consequences of this attack for Christian education. Let us begin by briefly considering exactly how imaginative visualization techniques are utilized by self-acknowledged practitioners of New Age spirituality.[32]

The basic New Age claim is that since we are the creators of our own reality, "we can bring into existence whatever we visualize." The root idea here is that visualization "is a kind of magic, a way of manipulating reality through mind power."[33] The technique of visualization or "forming visual images of a desirable situation or condition" is particularly popular for therapeutic purposes—one visualizes the healing of a wound or loss of weight, for example, in order to bring it about.[34] Insofar as the technique of visualization is linked with magical notions of power, it is clearly contrary to a Christian worldview. The gulf is great between the New Age conviction that we are gods with unlimited potential to create what we wish and the Christian understanding of the world and humanity as created, finite, and dependent. Caution against a careless and indiscriminate use of such New Age terminology is also called for. On all these points, the critics of positive mental attitude ideology have valid concerns. Christians have a sacred duty to distance themselves from magic and occultism.

And yet, Douglas Groothuis, a serious student and Christian critic of New Age thinking, contends that "Christians have erred in two directions concerning visualization and imagination. One group has uncritically accepted much of the New Age teaching, viewing the imagination as almost unfallen and unlimited. In not taking the New Age poisons seriously, they fall into the chameleon mentality." Thus the critics have a valid point. However, "the other group is so critical of New Age and Christian abuses of the imagination that it rules out the imagination entirely, declaring it to be the devil's playground, thus falling into the quarantine or taboo mentalities."[35]

There is a better way, according to Groothuis. While the imagination is a human faculty that is not intrinsically evil, it is, like all our mental faculties, affected by the Fall. In other words, the imagination—like reason, feeling, or the will—can be obedient or disobedient, sanctified or sinful. The imagination can be used for good or ill, to serve God or to create an idol. The problem is not with the imagination as such but with the object of one's imagination. A mental preoccupation with the increased material possessions one could accumulate "if only I won the lottery" is sinful covetousness; sexual fantasies outside of marriage are adulterous. However, an architect creatively imagining the details of his dream house or a husband contemplating the joy of a romantic weekend getaway with his spouse is altogether different. It is the content of the imagination—not the form—that creates problems with sin. There is no doubt that the imagination can be the devil's playground. However, the history of the church makes it abundantly clear that human reason and human will are no less usable vehicles for Satan. Why should we isolate the imagination as the problem area? The foolishness of this approach becomes even more clear when we consider exactly what the imagination is.

At its most basic level, imagination is the human capacity to make present to our consciousness that which is either spatially, temporally, or logically absent.[36] This can be illustrated with some simple examples. As I write, I sit in my office on a cold March day in Grand Rapids, Michigan. There is a heavy blanket of snow on the ground, and a few icicles hang from the roof outside my office. It is a beautiful scene, highlighted by occasional visits of a gorgeous scarlet cardinal. And yet, I would rather be in my hometown area of Vancouver, British Columbia, right now, where I know the temperature is higher and I suspect the crocuses are already in bloom. I don't detest winter, but I'm ready for spring. With the help of childhood memories and a calendar photo of the Vancouver skyline on my office door, I imagine what it would be like right now to be on the balmy West Coast rather than in the frigid Midwest. I bring to my present awareness that which is, in fact, spatially absent.

Aside from a possible offense against the Pauline injunction to be content in whatsoever state I find myself, the simple human act of imagining what it would be like to be in Vancouver or anywhere else is hardly sinful. In fact, without this human ability it would be impossible to teach children geography or have them try to understand cultures different from their own. Children need to imagine what it is like to live in a Philippine barrio, the sub-Sahara desert, or a Tibetan mountain village. Similarly, making present what is temporally distant—imagining what it was like living as a feudal lord or a peasant in the Middle Ages, for example—is essential for teaching history. And finally, the very ability to use language—so foundational to human experience—requires us to make present what is logically absent. All figures of speech imaginatively join together what in fact is logically separate. A comparison is made that is not automatic or obvious; it arises from human creative imagination and requires an act of imagination to be understood. When the poet says "My love is like a red red rose" or our Lord asks us to "consider the lilies of the field," we are being asked to join together aspects of our experience that are ordinarily quite separate. Linking botany and human emotions of love and dependence are not automatic; they are human creations. But, and this is the beauty and joy of language, when such creative joining takes place, our awareness of ourselves and our delight in God's

world is increased. Without imagination, language, literature, and art would be impossible and our lives would be
impoverished.

Imagination is thus such a fundamental human capacity
that some have even suggested that it is the image of God
in us.[37] Clearly, imagination is crucial for understanding
God's revelation in Scripture. Our Lord himself regularly
used imaginative figures of speech to explain the gospel of
the kingdom. One could justifiably paraphrase the opening
of many parables in this way: "Imagine the kingdom of
heaven to be like . . . mustard seeds, pearls, a sower, a measure of yeast," and so on. The books of Daniel, Ezekiel, and
Revelation cannot be understood without an imaginative
capacity to visualize strange creatures and conditions quite
different from our world. In fact, it can be argued that
God's people cannot receive and believe the scriptural
prophetic messages of promise and hope—New Jerusalem,
lion and lamb living in peace, swords beaten into plow-
shares—without a biblically informed and Spirit-endowed
imagination.[38]

From this it is clear that a general broadside against
imagination as evil per se is absurd and is an attack on one
of God's good gifts to humanity, a gift that in many
respects defines our very humanity as image-bearers of
God. What about fantasy and fantasy literature? On the
face of it, there seems to be no good reason why using the
human imagination to create literary worlds where rabbits,
mice, or lions speak or worlds populated by obviously unreal creatures such as hobbits, orcs, or marsh-wiggles should
be any more troubling for Christians than the realistic but
still fictional worlds of Tom Sawyer and Huckleberry Finn.
Once again, a wholesale condemnation of the genre seems
excessive, particularly since so many Christian writers—
from Dante to John Milton to John Bunyan to C. S. Lewis

to George MacDonald to J. R. R. Tolkien—have used it.[39] To think of *Paradise Lost* or *Pilgrim's Progress* as somehow occultist or New Age seems patently ridiculous. The judgment of Tolkien on this matter is more balanced. "Fantasy can, of course, be carried to excess. It can be ill done. It can be put to evil uses. It may even delude the minds out of which it came."[40] But since people have corrupted all of God's good gifts, "The entire fantasy genre itself need not be committed to the flames, but should rather be committed to the discerning mind of the mature believer."[41]

It is clear that the fantasy genre seems to have become a particularly favorite one for the dissemination of occult and New Age ideas. As Douglas Groothuis observes, "The premier fantasy role-playing game, Dungeons and Dragons (not to mention spinoffs), is incorrigibly occult, incorporating actual occult spell-casting (which is spoken), occult symbolism (the magic circle, pentagram and thaumaturgic triangle), hideous violence and a basic amoral, animistic/polytheistic world view." Furthermore, "Various movies such as the *Star Wars* trilogy, *The Karate Kid I* and *II*, and numerous other films either subtly or blatantly sound New Age themes. And even children's cartoons and toys, such as the immensely popular 'Masters of the Universe,' use occult symbolism and concepts to draw children into their world of error."[42] All of this demands careful discernment on the part of Christian parents and teachers. "Yet why should fantasy—when recognized as fantasy—be silenced from speaking God's truth. Why should human beings made in God's creative image not exercise that creativity through fantasy literature. As J. R. R. Tolkien put it, 'Fantasy remains a human right: we make in our measure and in our derivative mode, because we are made: and not only made, but made in the image and likeness of a Maker.'"[43] As in other areas of Christian experience, what is called for is spiritual discernment rather than the overkill of blanket condemnation. This is particularly important to emphasize since a narrative understanding of the Christian faith and Christian education makes such profound use of imagination.

It is helpful at this point to make some further distinctions about the different ways in which the imagination can be put to use, to suggest appropriate uses and to distance ourselves from some inappropriate uses.[44] The issue is not whether one intentionally makes use of the imagination in teaching—it is impossible to teach without it—but on the "what" of imagination. Which stories, even which fantasies, will be used to inspire children's imagination? William Kilpatrick claims that "Different kinds of stories can inspire different kinds of imagination, and the imagination, in turn, shapes our will and our character. It makes a difference, morally speaking, whether a youngster reads *To Kill a Mockingbird* or the latest book in the *Baby-Sitters Club* series. A regular diet of the latter makes it more difficult to acquire a taste for the former."[45]

In reflecting on the possibilities available to educators as they actively pursue the "path of imagination," William Kilpatrick suggests that there are two basic paths available—the easy path of "idyllic imagination," and the difficult path of "moral imagination." The difference between the two is that the latter respects the limits of reality while the former "is concerned with things as they can never be." He claims, "The moral imagination holds up an ideal that is attainable, although only through hard work; the idyllic imagination holds up an ideal that can never be attained in reality, but can easily be attained in fantasy or in feeling."[46] The idyllic or utopian imagination, supremely exemplified by the Romantic philosopher Rousseau, tends toward escapist daydreaming about the world as we would like it to be. Idyllic imagination, according to Kilpatrick, is wishful and self-centered. It resents the constraints placed on selfish pleasure by all external realities, including God, natural law, tradition, or social convention. The idyllic imagination is iconoclastic and bohemian; it considers itself progressive and avant garde.

By contrast, the moral imagination is relentlessly realistic. It "recognizes that appetites need to be restrained. . . . that reality does not conform itself to our wishes but often thwarts them. Far from being omnipotent, the self is often at the mercy of forces beyond its control. The moral imagination recognizes the sometimes tragic nature of life."[47] It should be noted at this point that the moral imagination can be expressed in literature that strictly speaking is not realistic. As Bruno Bettelheim has shown in his study of fairy tales, it is the realistic structure of stories with a clear sense of moral right and wrong, with an awareness of limits and the threat of evil, with the possibility of identification with heroic action that overcomes evil and circumstance, that is critical in children's moral formation. By identifying with a hero who overcomes evil, "the child imagines that he suffers with the hero his trials and tribulations, and triumphs with him as virtue is victorious. The child makes such identifications all on his own, and the inner and outer struggles of the hero imprint morally on him." Bettelheim recognizes that the sharp polarities of fairly tales are not fully true to life "with all the complexities that characterize real people." There is, however, a good reason for this: "Ambiguities must wait until a relatively firm personality has been established on the basis of positive identification."[48] The endings of fairy tales, according to Bettelheim, do not represent "unrealistic wish-fulfillment" but are a necessary means for children to deal with separation anxieties and achieve mature independence:

Today children no longer grow up within the security of an extended family, or of a well-integrated community. Therefore, even more than at the times fairy tales were invented, it is important to provide the modern child with images of heroes who have to go out into the world all by themselves and who, although originally ignorant of the ultimate things, find secure places in the world by following the right way with deep inner confidence.[49]

The moral imagination, also in fairy tales, thus "recognizes the sometimes tragic nature of life." Because the idyllic imagination lacks this tragic sense, because it is "essentially naive about evil," it is also often incapable of resisting evil.[50] In the twentieth century, we have seen the most destructive and horrendous evils performed by those who were captive to revolutionary and totalitarian idyllic or utopian imaginations. In fact, "T. S. Eliot and Russell Kirk suggest that the idyllic imagination, if not tempered by the moral imagination, often becomes 'the diabolic imagination.'"[51]

According to Kilpatrick, one of the prime examples of the idyllic imagination, "which flourishes particularly among the educated classes," is found among educators openly committed to New Age thinking. "One of the most influential of the New Age educators is Jack Canfield, the author of 'The Inner Classroom: Teaching with Guided Imagery' and other articles." Canfield emphasizes visualization techniques called "guided fantasy" or "guided imagery." Kilpatrick's comments on this technique are balanced and helpful:

> I wouldn't want to issue a blanket condemnation of visualization techniques. Visualization is an important way of rehearsing for or shaping a performance, whether it be imagining a football play, a painting, or the design of a house. But this is a little different. Anyone who has come to the point of actually executing a play on the playing field or an architectural design on the drawing board has already learned a great deal

about how these things are traditionally done. But guided imagery is meant to guide the child back to himself, not to any traditional body of wisdom. Canfield describes one girl in his class who asked her wise old woman [the product of a visualization technique—"a wise old woman inside our minds"], "What is the meaning of life?" The wise old woman "didn't say anything but held up a mirror to her"—an answer that Canfield calls an "amazingly sophisticated insight." "To me," writes Canfield, "the most interesting use of guided imagery is the evocation of the wisdom that lies deep with each of us."[52]

The assumptions here are that the real god is the god within each of us and the romantic, Rousseaunian notion, that children are essentially innocent and free, corrupted only by their evil environment. To become real gods, they must get in touch with the god within. Kilpatrick is absolutely correct in his assessment: "It is Values Clarification with a mystical twist."[53]

I have spent considerable time on this matter of imagination and fantasy because it is so essential to a narrative understanding of Christian education. It is crucial for parents and teachers to be alerted to harmful and potentially destructive uses of imagination without the kind of blanket condemnations and calls for censorship that are now taking place. It should also be mentioned here that there are Christian versions of the "idyllic imagination," forms of Christian utopianism that use the biblical language of shalom in such a way as to preempt the final consummation.[54] Such visions need to be tempered with a healthy biblical realism about what can and what cannot be achieved this side of the final eschaton. At the same time it is crucial that a defense be made of the validity and importance of imagination and Christian fantasy in Christian education. On this issue, Christian schools in the Reformed tradition must be very careful not to get drawn into the debate as it has been framed by North American evangelicalism. To repeat, neither outright approval nor blanket condemnation of the imagination is called for but, rather, careful spiritual discernment.

The Narrative Payoff

How does narrative now provide us with solutions to some of the problems we have raised earlier in this volume? I will suggest a few concluding observations about the benefits of a narrative approach to Christian education.

Simply telling the Christian story and telling it well is an invitation to students to join the mission of God and his people. Stories draw us in by calling us to identify with their characters and drawing us in as participants in the plot. Without indoctrinating and without treating the school as a place for evangelism, a compellingly told account of the Christian story as actually practiced in history by real individuals and groups will invite and convict students about the demands of Christian discipleship. Stories of such discipleship in action are necessary spurs and models to committed Christian discipleship in the world. Included will be stories of Christians at work, making their world a better place to live. Students will be inspired by such examples to make social justice concerns part of their own walk of discipleship while the school avoids the destructive kind of politicizing and polarization so characteristic of critical literacy curricula. In short, a focus on narrative does not simply pass on information about Christian involvement in culture and society; it models and invites participation in God's redemptive mission for the world. A narrative approach avoids the cognitivist mistake of assuming that knowing automatically leads to doing but at the same time avoids the activist error of doing without thoughtful reflection. Above all, the narrative frame of God's redemptive mission to the world provides the ultimate context for both reflection and action. In this way the Christian school provides a counter-cultural alternative to the influential story told by modern mass media.

What a narrative approach does is to permit the school to remain school without intellectualist isolation from the demands of Christian discipleship in the world. By passing on the memory of Christian reflection and action, the Christian school provides a vision for Christian living. It is also worth underscoring that passing on that memory is a public service. The Christian school is a place where the civilizational significance of the Christian religion is narrated, studied, and practiced. In an age where paganism is on the increase, this is truly a civic good. Simply by being there and by keeping the memory of the Christian faith and its civilizational significance alive, Christian schools provide an essential service to society. It also needs to be said once again that it is only within the story of the universal, catholic Christian church that a genuine multicultural education can take place. Here, too, the Christian school performs a public good.

Finally, while narrative is indeed a fashionable topic today in educational circles, I think it would be a mistake to dismiss it as just another one of the numerous fads that have plagued North American education in the twentieth century. By focusing on narrative, educators are on to something important. Not only is storytelling a universal phenomenon—a way that all peoples attempt to give order and meaning to their experience—it is also at the very heart of the Christian faith. The Christian story—the story of God and his people—is the only foundation, content, and goal of the Christian school.

Notes

Chapter 1. Critical Questions About Contemporary Education

1. Steven Vryhof, "Christian Schools: Ripe for Change (I)," *The Banner* (September 9, 1991), 6-7.

2. Susan D. Rose, *Keeping Them Out of the Hands of Satan: Evangelical Schooling in America* (New York and London: Routledge, 1988).

3. For a scathing critique of education faculties and teachers colleges, see Reginald C. Damerall, *Education's Smoking Gun: How Teachers Colleges Have Destroyed Education in America* (New York: Freundlich Books, n.d.). Also see Rita Kramer, *Ed School Follies: The Miseducation of America's Teachers* (New York: Free Press, 1991).

4. Daniel E. Griffiths, "The Crisis in American Education," *The Education Digest*, 48 (May 1983), 10.

5. The article by Paul Woodring "School Criticism in the 1950s and 1970s" appeared initially in *Phi Beta Kappan*, #59 (April 1978), 515-17. I have cited it from a condensed version in *The Education Digest*, 51 (November 1985), 160.

6. Diane Ravitch, "The Continuing Crisis: Fashions in Education," *American Scholar*, 53 (Spring 1984), 183-93.

7. Woodring, "School Criticism," p. 160.

8. Diane Ravitch, "Forgetting the Questions: The Problems of Educational Reform (1981)," in *The Schools We Deserve*: *Reflections on the Educational Crises of Our Time* (New York: Basic Books, 1985), p. 27.

9. Ibid., pp. 28-29.

10. For much of the following section, particularly details about reform movements, I am indebted to Diane Ravitch's summary essay "American Education: Has the Pendulum Swung Once Too Often? (1982)," in *The Schools We Deserve*, pp. 80-89.

11. Ravitch, *The Schools We Deserve*, p. 45.

12. Ibid., pp. 80-81.

13. Ibid., p. 84.

14. Ibid., p. 89.

15. Beatrice and Ronald Gross, eds. *The Great School Debate: Which Way for American Education* (New York: Simon & Schuster, 1985).

16. John E. Chubb and Terry M. Moe, *Politics, Markets, and America's Schools* (Washington, D.C.: The Brookings Institution, 1990).

17. Ibid., "Foreward," by Bruce MacLaury, p. ix.

18. Ibid., p. 12

19. Ibid., pp. 12-13.

20. Ibid., "Foreward," p. ix.

21. "Tough Choice," *Time* (September 16, 1991), 60.

22. Ibid., p. 56.

23. Ibid, pp. 57-60.

24. Ibid., p. 58.

25. See the collection of Machen's essays edited by John W. Robbins, *Education, Christianity and the State* (Jefferson, Md.: The Trinity Foundation, 1987).

26. See, for example, Blair Adams with Joel Stern and Howard Wheeler, *Who Owns the Children? Public Compulsion, Private Responsibility and the Dilemma of Ultimate Authority.* Book V in the Series, *Education as Religious War*, fifth edition (Waco, Tex.: Truth Forum, 1991).

27. See Rockne McCarthy, et.al., *Society, State, & Schools: A Case for Structural and Confessional Pluralism* (Grand Rapids: Eerdmans, 1981). This volume was produced by the fellows of the Calvin Center for Christian Scholarship, Calvin College during the 1978-1979 school year. Also, see Rockne McCarthy et.al., *Disestablishment a Second Time: Genuine Pluralism for American Schools* (Grand Rapids: Eerdmans, 1982).

28. Chubb and Moe, *Politics, Markets and America's Schools*, p. 51.

29. Stanley Oronowitz and Henry Giroux, *Education under Siege: The Conservative, Liberal, and Radical Debate over Schooling* (South Hadley, Mass.: Begen & Garvey, 1985), p. xi.

30. Cited in *The Great School Debate*, p. 23.

31. George Radwanski, "Ontario Study of the Relevance of Edu-

cation and the Issue of Dropouts," Ontario, Canada, Ministry of Education report, Feb. 15, 1988, p. 11.

32. Arnold De Graaf, "Return to Basics: Temptation and Challenge," *Christian Educators Journal*, 17, No. 4 (March/April 1978), 23.

33. John Van Dyk, *The Beginning of Wisdom: The Nature and Task of the Christian School*, (Grand Rapids: Christian Schools International, 1985).

34. Ronald H. Nash, *The Closing of the American Heart: What's Really Wrong with America's Schools* (Dallas, Tex.: Probe Books, 1990).

35. Aronowitz and Giroux, *Education under Siege*, pp. 200-1.

36. Ibid., p. 204.

37. "Md. Panel Backs New Graduation Rule," *The Washington Post*, August 1, 1991.

38. The former term is from a representative "radical" tract, Aronowitz and Giroux's *Education Under Siege*; the latter characterizes the project of E. D. Hirsch, Jr., which he first articulated in *Cultural Literacy: What Every American Needs to Know* (Boston: Houghton Mifflin, 1987) and is presently applying to the various grade levels of the school. "Cultural literacy" is also a useful shorthand designation for the revitalization of the humanities, particularly history and literature, proposed by Diane Ravitch and Chester Finn, *What Do Our 17-Year-Olds Know: A Report on the First National Assessment of History and Literature* (New York: Harper & Row, 1987).

39. Neil Postman and Charles Weingartner, *Teaching As a Subversive Activity* (New York: Delacorte, 1969), p. 2. Postman's change of heart on this question is interesting and significant. See *Teaching As a Conserving Activity* (New York: Dell, 1979).

40. Aronowitz and Giroux, *Education under Siege*, p. 206. The authors summarize their discussion of the "crisis" in public philosophy rather cautiously. What is remarkable is their demand that federal government money and policy be used for such revolutionary ideals:

> If the crisis in schooling is to be addressed adequately, we will need to construct a public philosophy that points to new approaches for the education of existing and future teachers. At the core of such an approach would be a commitment to developing forms of knowledge, pedagogy, evaluation, and research that promote critical literacy and civic courage. From this start-

ing point federal education policy would use its financial and political resources to promote absolute commitment to public schools as sites of learning, of social interaction, and of human emancipation. Within this theoretical context can be developed policy recommendations that encourage research and education that view teachers as intellectuals and moral leaders rather than mere technicians; students as critical thinkers and active citizens rather than simply future participants in the industrial-military order; and schools as centers of critical literacy and civic courage rather than merely training sites for occupational positions in the corporate order.

The concluding chapter of the book is worth noting because it acknowledges the risk of an open-ended, futuristic vision for emancipation.

> What we have suggested in this concluding chapter points to the need to infuse educational theory and practice with a vision of the future, one that is matched, hopefully, by the willingness of educators, parents, and others to struggle and take risks. The nature of such a task may seem impossible at times, but the stakes are too high to ignore such a challenge. Underlying such a struggle is a ringing call to take seriously the lives of our children. In this sense, what we have advocated is a political and pedagogical movement that speaks to life, to future generations; it is a call that chooses life and takes as its first principle the value and possibilities inherent in human struggles.

41. Diane Ravitch, *The Revisionists Revised: A Critique of the Radical Attack on the Schools* (New York: Basic Books, 1978), p. 57.

42. For critical assessments of 1980s peace curricula in American schools, see Joseph Adelson and Chester E. Finn, Jr., "Terrorizing Children," *Commentary* (April 1985), 29-36; Keith B. Payne and Jill Coleman, "Nuclear Age Education," *Policy Review* (Fall 1987), 59-63; Andri Ryerson, "The Scandal of 'Peace Education,'" *Commentary* (June 1986), 37-46.

43. Cited in Ryerson, "The Scandal of 'Peace Education,'" p. 37.

44. Sidney Hook, "Education in Defense of a Free Society," *Commentary* (July 1984), 22.

45. Hirsch, *Cultural Literacy*, p. 24.

46. Ibid., p. 11.

47. Postman, *Teaching As a Conserving Activity*, pp. 26-27.

48. James Davison Hunter, *Culture Wars: The Struggle to Define America* (New York: Basic Books, 1991). Page references which follow in the text are to this work. See also Richard John Neuhaus, *America Against Itself: Moral Vision and the Public Order* (Notre Dame and London: University of Notre Dame Press, 1992) and William J. Bennett, *The Devaluing of America: The Fight for Our Culture and Our Children* (New York: Summit Books, 1992).

49. Richard A. Baer, "American Public Education and the Myth of Value Neutrality," in *Democracy and the Renewal of Public Education*, edited by Richard John Neuhaus, Encounter Series #4 (Grand Rapids: Eerdmans, 1987), p. 24. In Canada, separate Roman Catholic Schools in Ontario and Quebec were established and protected by law in the original British North America Act of 1857.

50. The point here is that Christians should not be too sanguine about the nineteenth-century "common school" ideal in the United States and Canada represented by such vigorous advocates as Horace Mann in Massachusetts and Egerton Ryerson in Ontario. As Charles L. Glenn has observed ("'Molding' Citizens," in *Democracy and the Renewal of Public Education*, p. 43):

> The normal school, then, played an important part in the efforts of Mann and other 'liberal Christians' to promote a form of "common school religion" that was said to have no sectarian character but that was in fact consistent with their own beliefs and profoundly subversive of that of their Orthodox opponents. It was in the normal school, with its strong emphasis on the teaching of morality and on an atmosphere of liberal piety, that the teachers were formed upon whom the hopes of the education reformers rested. Training teachers was an effective way of avoiding the problems that a direct assault on local control of schools would have caused; it made it possible to argue, in all sincerity, that the common schools were under the direct oversight of local school committees elected by the parents and frequently chaired by an orthodox clergyman. The real content of public education would be determined by the emerging profession of teachers, shaped by state normal schools under control of the education reformers and not by the parents through their local representatives.

For a critical, historical overview of the common-school ideal in Ontario from the perspective of an advocate for distinct and autonomous Christian schools see John Vriend, "Independent Schools, Government Funding," and "A Contemporary Common

School Ideal: A Proposal from Ontario," Unpublished Ph.D. dissertation, State University of New York at Buffalo, 1988.

51. See Paul C. Vitz, *Censorship: Evidence of Bias in Our Children's Textbooks* (Ann Arbor: Servant, 1986). For a summary of Vitz's argument, see "A Study of Religion and Traditional Values in Public School Textbooks," *Democracy and the Renewal of Public Education*, (Grand Rapids: Eerdmans, 1987), pp. 116-40.

52. Ibid., p. 121.

53. Ibid., p. 140.

54. E. D. Hirsch, Jr., Joseph F. Kett, and James Trefil, *The Dictionary of Cultural Literacy: What Every American Needs to Know.* (Boston: Houghton Mifflin, 1988).

55. *Time*, (September 30, 1991), p. 77.

56. Christopher Dawson, *The Crisis of Western Education* (New York: Sheed & Ward, 1961), p. 204.

Chapter 2. Critical Questions About Our Culture

1. Lesslie Newbigin, *Foolishness to the Greeks: The Gospel and Western Culture* (Grand Rapids: Eerdmans, 1986), p. 31.

2. Alexander Solzhenitsyn, *Warning to the Western World* (London: the Bodley Head and the British Broadcasting Corporation, 1976). Also see Solzhenitsyn's Harvard University Commencement Address of June 8, 1978, *A World Split Apart* (New York: Harper & Row, 1978).

3. James Burnham, *Suicide of the West* (Chicago: Regnery Books, 1985).

4. Cited by Peter Kreeft, "'Darkness at Noon': The Eclipse of 'The Permanent Things,'" *Faith and Reason*, 17 (1991), 56.

5. Cited by Bernard Williams, "René Descartes," in *The Encyclopedia of Philosophy*, ed. Paul Edwards (New York and London: MacMillan, 1967), Vol. II, p. 345.

6. Ibid., p. 347.

7. Allan Bloom, *The Closing of the American Mind* (New York: Simon & Schuster, 1987), p. 196.

8. Hirsch, *Cultural Literacy*, p. xvii.

9. Stanley Hauerwas, *A Community of Character* (Notre Dame, Ind.: University of Notre Dame Press, 1980), p. 12.

10 Newbigin, *Foolishness to the Greeks*, p. 19.

11. Bloom, *Closing*, p. 196. This point has been argued with brilliance by Alasdair MacIntyre, *After Virtue*, 2nd ed. (Notre Dame, Ind.: University of Notre Dame Press, 1984). See especially Chapter 5: "Why the Enlightenment Project of Justifying Morality Had to Fail."

12. Andrew Ross, ed., *Universal Abandon: The Politics of Post-Modernism* (Winnipeg, Man.: University of Manitoba Press, 1988), p. xiii.

13. Ibid., p. 37.

14. Ibid., p. 35. The citation is from an unpublished paper by Carole Pateman, "Removing Obstacles to Democracy," presented to the International Political Science Association meeting, Ottawa, Canada, October 1986.

15. Ibid., p. 36.

16. See Nicholas Wolterstorff, *Reason within the Bounds of Religion Alone*, 2nd ed., (Grand Rapids: Eerdmans, 1984).

17. See Gordon J. Spykman, "The Principled Pluralist Position," in *God and Politics,* edited by Gary Scott Smith,(Philipsburg, N.J.: Presbyterian and Reformed, 1989), pp. 78-99.

18. For a passionate critique of the kind of pluralism envisioned by postmodernism, applied to Canadian life, see Reginald Bibby, *Mosaic Madness: The Poverty and Potential of Life in Canada* (Toronto: Stoddard, 1990). Also see responses to the essay by Gordon Spykman in Gary Scott Smith, *God and Politics.*

19. See the sections "Theonomy," "Christian America," and "National Confessionalism" in Smith, *God and Politics.*

20. See John W. Cooper, "Reformed Apologetics and the Challenge of Post-Modern Relativism," *Calvin Theological Journal*, 28 (1993), 108-20.

21. For what follows in analysis and critique of modernity, I am especially indebted to three authors: Peter Berger, Lesslie Newbigin, and Alasdair MacIntyre. See Peter Berger, *Facing Up to Modernity* (New York: Basic Books, 1977) and, with Brigette Berger and Hansfield Keller, *The Homeless Mind* (New York: Random House, 1973); Newbigin, *Foolishness to the Greeks;* and MacIntyre, *After Virtue.*

22. Jacques Ellul, *The Technological Society*, translated by John Wilkinson (New York: Vintage, 1964).

23. Newbigin, *Foolishness to the Greeks*, p. 31.

24. Ibid., p. 32.

25. Ibid., p. 33.

26. Berger, *Facing Up to Modernity*, p. 71.

27. Peter Berger has referred to this as "the heretical imperative." See *The Heretical Imperative: Contemporary Possibilities of Religious Affirmations* (Garden City, N.J.: Anchor Press, 1979).

28. MacIntyre, *After Virtue*, pp. 33-34.

29. David Reisman with Reuel Denney and Nathan Glazer, *The Lonely Crowd: A Study of the Changing American Character* (New Haven, Conn.: Yale University Press, 1950).

30. Newbigin, *Foolishness to the Greeks*, p. 32.

31. MacIntyre, *After Virtue*, p. 34.

32. For a description of the romantic youth-movements of the sixties and seventies as a revolution in consciousness, see Charles Reich, *The Greening of America* (New York: Random House, 1970).

33. Berger, *Facing up to Modernity*, p. 76.

34. Ibid., p. 77.

35. Ibid.

36. A classic work that describes the chaos of modern ethics with exceptional brilliance is Alasdair MacIntyre's *After Virtue*. MacIntyre begins his volume with a fascinating analogy. Imagine, he suggests, a world in which the practice of natural science as a coherent activity has ceased and all that is left are partial fragments of experiments and theories. Disorder abounds; arbitrariness and subjectivism seem to reign. He then summarizes the heart of his argument: "The hypothesis which I wish to advance is that in the actual world which we inhabit the language of morality is in the same state of grave disorder as the language of natural science in the imaginary world which I described. What we possess, if this view is true, are the fragments of a conceptual scheme, parts which now lack those context from which their significance derived. We possess indeed simulcra of morality, we continue to use many of the key expressions. But we have—very largely, if not entirely—lost our comprehension, both theoretical and practical, [of] morality." (p. 2). The reason for this is largely that "the nature of moral community and moral judgment in distinctively modern societies was such that it was no longer possible to appeal to moral criteria in a way that had been possible in other times and places." (p. ix) Thus, MacIntyre gives his fifth chapter the title: "Why the Enlightenment Project of Justifying Morality Had to Fail."

37. Robert Bellah, et al. *Habits of the Heart: Individualism and Commitment in American Life* (New York: Harper & Row, 1986). Page references that follow in the text will be to this work.

38. See MacIntyre, *After Virtue*, for a lucid critique of emotivism.

39. Ibid., p. 23.

40. Ibid., p. 33.

41. Solzhenitsyn, *A World Split Apart*, pp. 15-19.

42. See "Do We Have Too Many Lawyers?" *Time*, August 26, 1991, pp. 54-55.

43. Bellah, *Habits of the Heart*, p. 152.

44. Reginald Bibby, *Mosaic Madness: The Poverty and Potential of Life in Canada* (Toronto: Stoddart, 1990), p. vi.

45. Bibby, *Mosaic Madness*, p. 3. Page references that follow in the text will be to this work. "Faced with the problem of creating a society in which people of varied linguistic and cultural backgrounds can live together, Canadians have decided to convert a demographic reality into a national virtue. We have decreed that what is descriptively obvious should be prescriptively valued. Canada, we have concluded, will be a multinational society, a multicultural mosaic of people from varied backgrounds who will have the freedom to live as they see fit" (p.7). The notion of Canada as a "mosaic" dates back at least to an important sociological analysis by John Porter, *Vertical Mosaic: An Analysis of Social Class and Power in Canada* (Toronto: University of Toronto Press, 1965).

46. The following quotation from former Canadian Prime Minister Pierre Elliot Trudeau illustrates this point well: "[Canada's multicultural composition] and the moderation which it includes and encourages, makes Canada a very special place, and a stronger place as well. Each of the many fibers contributes its own qualities and Canada gains strength from the combination. We become less like others; we become less susceptible to cultural, social or political envelopment by others. We become less inclined—certainly less obliged—to think in terms of national grandeur; inclined not at all to assume a posture of aggressiveness, or ostentation, or might. Our image is of a land of people with many differences—but many contributions, many variations in view—but a single desire to live in harmony. . . .On a planet of finite size, the most desirable of all characteristics is the ability and desire to cohabit with persons of differing backgrounds, and to benefit from the opportunities which this offers." (Cited by Bibby, *Mosaic Madness*, pp. 49-50).

47. Cited by Bibby, ibid., p. 10.

48. Bellah, *Habits of the Heart*, p. 285.

49. A recent extensive and illuminating exploration of these differences can be found in Seymour Martin Lipset, *Continental Divide: The Values and Institutions of the United States and Canada* (New York and London: Routledge, 1990).

50. See "Whose America?" *Time*, July 8, 1991.

51. Arthur M. Schlesinger, Jr., *The Disuniting of America: Reflections on a Multicultural Society* (Knoxville, Tenn.: Whittle Books, 1991).

52. Bloom, *The Closing of the American Mind*, p. 1.

53. Harvey Cox, *The Secular City*, rev. ed. (New York: MacMillan, 1966).

54. Donald G. Bloesch, *Crumbling Foundations: Death and Rebirth in an Age of Upheaval* (Grand Rapids: Zondervan, 1984), p. 37.

55. Richard John Neuhaus, *The Naked Public Square: Religion and Democracy in America* (Grand Rapids: Eerdmans, 1984), p. vii.

56. See the defense of Christian theocracy by Dutch Reformed theologian Arnold Van Ruler in his essays, "Church and State," "Theocracy and Toleration," in *Calvinist Trinitarianism and Theocentric Politics: Essays Toward a Public Theology*, trans. by John Bolt (Lewiston, N.Y.: Edwin Mellen Press, 1989), pp. 149-88.

57. The expression "two swords," representing the spiritual authority of the church through the pope and the temporal authority of the ruler-king, dates back to the Middle Ages and was articulated with particular force by Pope Boniface VIII in his *Bull Unam Sanctam* of 1302. The Reformation notion of the "two kingdoms," understood and articulated with some significant different nuances by Calvin and Luther, is also a variant of this theme.

58. See Leonard Verduin, *The Anatomy of a Hybrid: A Study in Church-State Relationships* (Grand Rapids: Eerdmans, 1976).

59. Glenn Tinder, "Can We Be Good without God?" *The Atlantic Monthly*, December, 1989, pp. 68-85. The excerpt was from Glenn Tinder, *The Political Meaning of Christianity* (San Francisco: HarperCollins, 1991).

60. "One Nation, Under God: Has the Separation of Church and State Gone Too Far?" *Time* (December 9, 1991), 62.

61. Ibid.

62. Ibid., p. 68.

63. See Harvey Cox, *Religion in the Secular City: Toward a Postmodern Theology* (New York: Simon & Schuster, 1984).

64. What is truly remarkable in the post-glasnost era is the appeal from Russian leaders to religious leaders from the West to help put the country back together again. One such appeal included the following: "In the...often agonizing transitional period our country is experiencing in moving from a totalitarian system to parliamentarianism, a market economy, and an open society, spiritual and moral values acquire a great, if not paramount significance." Cited by Dr. Joel Nederhood, Director of Ministries, The Back to God Hour, in his December, 1991 letter to the Christian Reformed Church.

65. Michael Harrington, *The Politics at God's Funeral: The Spiritual Crisis of Western Civilization* (New York: Holt, Rinehart and Winston, 1983).

66. Neuhaus, *The Naked Public Square*, p. 86.

67. Ibid., p. 82.

68. *Time*, December 9, 1991, p. 65.

69. Donald Bloesch, *Crumbling Foundations*, (p. 77), and Charles Colson, with Ellen Santilli Vaughan, *Against the Night: Living in the New Dark Ages* (Ann Arbor: Servant, 1989).

70. Donald Bloesch, *Crumbling Foundations*, p. 77.

71. Ibid., p. 78.

72. Ibid., p. 38. Bloesch spells out this conclusion further in a paragraph relating the new gods to the old gods of the Graeco-Roman pantheon:

> This brings us again to the startling and chilling fact that the dominant issue facing the church today is idolatry. When the living God of the Bible is dethroned, other gods, what Ellul calls "the new demons," will seek to take his place. The ancient gods of the Graeco-Roman pantheon are reappearing in new guises: Mars, the god of war; Gaia, the Earth Mother; Apollo, the god of light, symmetry and artistry (the perfection of technique?); Hermes, the god of commerce and theft (the spiritual father of capitalism?); Dionysus, the god of vitalistic intoxication; Pan, the god of the forests and pastures; Moira or Fate; Prometheus, the defiant Titan; Hermaphroditus, the personification of the mythical vision of androgyny; Venus, the goddess of love and beauty; Priapus, the god of sex and fertility; and Fortuna (Chance).

73. Ibid., pp. 79-80.

74. Feminist Naomi Goldenberg claims that because "Jesus Christ cannot symbolize the liberation of women," the "feminist movement in Western culture is engaged in the slow execution of Christ and Yahweh." Her heading says it all: "Feminists are Cooking up Götterdämmerung." What will be the end result of this? "Surely new gods will be born. Since 'gods' always reflect the styles of behavior we see as possible, as our range of the possible expands so must our pantheon." *Changing of the Gods: Feminism and the End of Traditional Religions* (Boston: Beacon Press, 1979), pp. 4, 8, 22.

75. The *New York Times*, in an editorial on May 12, 1991, entitled "The Ultimate Mother," tells us that "goddess worship resonates with environmentalism, and in particular with the Gaia hypotheses—the theory, named for the earth goddess of the ancient Greeks, that the earth and its biosphere behave like a single living organism." Cited by Richard J. Neuhaus, "The Public Square," *First Things*, August/September 1991, p. 58.

76. Lawrence E. Adams, "The WCC at Canberra: Which Spirit?" *First Things*, June/July, 1991, p. 30.

77. The only qualification to this categorical claim is the fact that because idols make absolute a relative creaturely good (sex, power, money), we must not conclude that these relative goods are themselves evil. Idolatry is thus always an absolutization and corruption of good.

78. Herbert Schlossberg, *Idols for Destruction: Christian Faith and Its Confrontation with American Society* (Nashville: Thomas Nelson, 1983). Page references that follow in the text are to this work.

79. See C.S. Lewis *The Abolition of Man (New York: Collier Macmillan, 1978).*

80. Colson, *Against the Night*, pp. 23-24.

81. Peter Kreeft, "'Darkness at Noon': The Eclipse of 'The Permanent Things,'" p. 75.

82. This positive approach to the West as a mission field characterizes the writings of Lesslie Newbigin. See *Foolishness to the Greeks* and *The Gospel in a Pluralistic Society*. Newbigin's point of view can be summed up as follows: "Ours is a pagan society and its paganism having been born out of the rejection of Christianity, is far more resistant to the gospel than the pre-Christian paganism with which cross-cultural missions have been familiar. Here, surely, is the most challenging missionary frontier of our time." (*Foolishness to the*

Greeks, p. 20).

83. "She Wants Her T.V.! He Wants His Book! A Dinner Conversation between Neil Postman and Camille Paglia," *Harper's Magazine* (March, 1991), p. 55. See also Neil Postman, "Teaching as Amusing Activity," *Amusing Ourselves to Death: Public Discourse in the Age of Show Business* (New York: Penguin, 1985), pp. 142-54.

84. Postman, *Amusing Ourselves to Death*, p. 143. Postman's observations that follow this comment are worth citing in full:

> Which is to say, we now know that "Sesame Street" undermines what the traditional idea of schooling represents. Whereas a classroom is a place of social interaction, the space in front of a television set is a private preserve. Whereas in a classroom, one may ask a teacher questions, one can ask nothing of a television screen. Whereas school is centered on the development of language, television demands attention to images. Whereas attending school is a legal requirement, watching television is an act of choice. Whereas in school, one fails to attend to the teacher at the risk of punishment, no penalties exist for failing to attend to the television screen. Whereas to behave oneself in school means to observe rules of public decorum, television watching requires no such observances, has no concept of public decorum. Whereas in a classroom, fun is never more than a means to an end, on television it is the end itself.

85. Hunter, *Culture Wars*, p. 225.

86. Carol Tavris, "America is Still Shockable—Barely," *Los Angeles Times*, August 9, 1991. Cited by Michael Medved, *Hollywood Vs. America: Popular Culture and the War on Traditional Values* (New York: HarperCollins, 1992), p. 263.

87. Hunter, *Culture Wars*, p. 226.

88. Helle Bering-Jensen, "A Hell-Bent Crusade Against Pornography," *Insight*, 2 July 1990, p. 12. Cited by James Davison Hunter, *Culture Wars*, p. 227.

89. Hunter, *Culture Wars*, p. 227. Hunter cites, among others, the study of Lichter, et al., *The Media Elite* (Bethesda, Md.: Adler & Adler, 1986). See also S. Robert Lichter, et al. *Watching America: What Television Tells Us about Our Lives* (New York: Prentice Hall, 1991). See also Michael Medved, *Hollywood Vs. America*.

90. Quentin J. Schultze, *Redeeming Television* (Downer's Grove, Ill.: Inter Varsity Press, 1992), p. 59.

91. Ibid., p. 43. See pp. 44-5 for concrete examples.

92. Postman, *Amusing Ourselves to Death*, p. 145.

93. Ibid., p. 145.

94. This is the subtitle of Quentin Schultze's second chapter in *Redeeming Television*.

95. William K. Kilpatrick, *Why Johnny Can't Tell Right from Wrong: Moral Illiteracy and the Case for Character Education* (New York: Simon & Schuster, 1992), p. 187. The Pittman citation is from Ron Powers, "The Cool Dark Telegenious of Robert Pittman," in *The Beast, the Eunuch and the Glass-Eyed Child* (San Diego: Harcourt Brace Jovanovich, 1990), p. 24.

96. Ibid, pp. 187-88.

97. In addition to Neil Postman, perhaps the most thoughtful and controversial Christian analysis of the difference between word and image is Jacques Ellul, *The Humiliation of the Word*, trans. by Joyce Main Hanks (Grand Rapids: Eerdmans, 1985). For a rebuttal of this critique, which he judges to be "gnostic," see Quentin Schultze, *Redeeming Television*, pp. 23-28.

98. Malcolm Muggeridge, *Christ and the Media* (Grand Rapids: Eerdmans, 1978), p. 30.

99. Ibid., p. 15.

100. Ibid, p. 12.

101. "She Wants Her T.V.! He Wants His Book!" Page references that follow in the text will be to this article.

102. For a fuller statement of Paglia's celebration of this pagan revival in popular culture see her *Sex, Art and American Culture: Essays* (New York: Vintage Books, 1992).

103. Dawson, *The Crisis of Western Education*, p. 204.

104. MacIntyre, *After Virtue*, p. 263. These lines are taken from the closing paragraph. The entire paragraph reads as follows:

It is always dangerous to draw too precise parallels between one historical period and another; and among the most misleading of such parallels are those which have been drawn between our own age in Europe and North America and the epoch in which the Roman empire declined into the Dark Ages. Nonetheless certain parallels there are. A crucial turning point in that earlier history occurred when men and women of good will turned aside from the task of shoring up the Roman *imperium* and ceased to identify the continuation of civility and moral community with the maintenance of that *imperium*. What they set themselves to achieve instead—often not recognizing fully what they were doing—was the construction of new forms of community within which the moral life could be sustained so that both morality and civility might survive the coming ages of barbarism and darkness. If my account of our moral condition is correct, we ought also to conclude that for some time now we too have reached that turning point. What matters at this stage is the construction of local forms of community within which civility and the intellectual and moral life can be sustained through the new dark ages which are already upon us. And if the tradition of the virtues was able to survive the horrors of the last dark ages, we are not entirely without grounds for hope. This time however the barbarians are not waiting beyond the frontiers; they have already been governing us for quite some time. And it is our lack of consciousness of this that constitutes part of our predicament. We are waiting not for a Godot, but for another—doubtless very different—St. Benedict.

105. Jeffrey R. Holland, "A 'Notion' at Risk: The Greater Crisis in American Education," *American Educator*, 20 (June, 1984), 19. Quotation from C. Woodward, *The Effect of Historical Change on University Purpose* (Charlottesville, Va.: University of Virginia, Office of the Dean of Students, 1976), p. 7. What's really at risk in American education, according to Holland, are civic and moral values in our schools, a conclusion shared and explored in detail by William Kilpatrick in *Why Johnny Can't Tell Right from Wrong*.

Chapter 3. "Christian" Threats to Christian Education

1. Henry Zylstra, *Testament of Vision* (Grand Rapids: Eerdmans, 1958), pp. 95-96.

2. See Douglas Wilson, *Recovering the Lost Tools of Learning: An Approach to Distinctively Christian Education* (Wheaton, Ill.: Crossway, 1991). While Wilson is careful not to say that the classical approach is necessarily or the only Christ-centered approach, and acknowledges that the Logos School of Moscow, Idaho, which he helped found and operates on this model, is not finished in formulating a Christian approach to education, the impression given is indeed that classical and Christian are ideals to be integrated.

3. See John Van Dyk, "The Practice of Teaching Christianly," in

Christian Schooling: Education for Freedom, Edited by Stuart Fowler (Potchefstroom: Potchefstroom University for Christian Higher Education, 1990), pp. 155-68. For a critique of such identification, see Leo Van Arragon, "Intelligent Servants: Intellectual Service," in *OCSTA News* (Publication of the Ontario Christian School Teacher's Association), vol. 11, No. 2 (Dec 1989).

4.   See Alan Peshkin, *God's Choice: The Total World of a Fundamentalist School* (Chicago and London: University of Chicago Press, 1986).

5.   I have spelled out my own trinitarian understanding of Reformed Christian education in the sixth chapter of *Christian and Reformed Today* (Jordan Station, Ont.: Paideia Press, 1984).

6.   About a decade ago when my wife and I inquired about enrolling our second child in the preschool program of the Roman Catholic separate school system in Hamilton, Ontario, an administrator told us that this would be possible only if we agreed to have our child brought up as a Roman Catholic. This is the parochial understanding of the school as a branch of the church.

7.   Jaroslav Pelikan, *The Emergence of the Catholic Tradition,* Vol. 1 of *The Christian Tradition* (Chicago and London: University of Chicago Press, 1971), p. 9.

8.   Donald E. Sloat, *The Dangers of Growing Up in a Christian Home* (Nashville, Tenn.: Thomas Nelson, 1986), pp. 26-27.

9.   Ibid., p. 27.

10. Ibid., pp. 34-35.

11. Richard Mitchell, *The Leaning Tower of Babel* (Boston: Little, Brown, 1984) p. 215. Cited by Douglas Wilson, *Recovering the Lost Tools of Learning,* p. 61.

12. Douglas Wilson, *Recovering the Lost Tools of Learning,* pp. 60-61.

13. Steven Vryhof, et al, *12 Affirmations: Reformed Christian Schooling for the 21st Century* (Grand Rapids: Baker, 1989), p. 31.

14. Wilson, *Recovering the Lost Tools of Learning,* p. 61.

15. Ibid., p. 115.

16. Ibid., pp. 120-21.

17. Ronald Nash, *The Closing of the American Heart: What's Really Wrong with America's Schools,* (Dallas, Tex.: Probe Books, 1990), pp. 137-38.

18. Rose, *Keeping Them Out of the Hands of Satan,* p. 209.

19. Ibid., p. 212. Cited by Nash, *The Closing of the American Heart*, p. 133.

20. Nash, *The Closing of the American Heart*, p. 132.

21. Rose herself speaks of the unintended "socialization" of students in Christian schools. Rather than preparing students for a life of Christian discipleship, they are unconsciously and unthinkingly socializing children to adapt to specific class roles. This, too, is a form of indoctrination.

22. Rose, *Keeping Them Out of the Hands of Satan*, pp. 205-6. Rose understands this difference primarily in terms of class differences rather than theological differences.

23. Ibid., p. 5.

24. John Calvin, *Institutes of the Christian Religion*, Edited by John T. MacNeil, Translated by Ford L. Battles, Library of Christian Classic, Vol. XX (Philadelphia: Westminster, 1960), II. ii. 16, 15.

25. John Bolt, *Christian and Reformed Today* (Jordan Station, Ont.: Paideia Press, 1984), p. 69.

26. Zylstra, *Testament of Vision*, p. 90.

27. Bolt, *Christian and Reformed Today*, p. 69.

28. Ibid., p. 121.

29. Zylstra, *Testament of Vision*, p. 95.

30. I am therefore not in agreement with, among others, Protestant Reformed pastor David Engelsma who [in *Reformed Education* (South Holland, Ill.: The Federation of Protestant Reformed School Societies, 1977), p. 22,] argues the following from the covenant basis of Christian education: "From the covenant-basis, it also follows that the school is for covenant children. Children outside the covenant are not to be accepted, i.e., children of unbelieving parents. In my judgment, we should accept children from outside the Protestant Reformed churches, and even from outside the Reformed denominations, but only on the condition that the parents evidence true faith in Christ and are motivated by the desire that their child get a Christian education."

31. See "Form for the Baptism of Children," *Psalter Hymnal* (Grand Rapids: CRC Publications, 1987), p. 961.

32. Abraham Kuyper, *Lectures on Calvinism* (Grand Rapids: Eerdmans, 1931), p. 79.

33. Zylstra, *Testament of Vision*, pp. 93-94.

34. Postman, *Teaching as a Conserving Activity*, pp. 106-8.

35. See Stanley Hauerwas and William Willimon, *Resident Aliens* (Nashville: Abingdon, 1989).

36. Schlossberg, *Idols For Destruction*, pp. 6-7.

37. Ibid., p. 6.

38. S. Fowler, H. W. Van Brummelen, and J. Van Dyk, *Christian Schooling: Education for Freedom*, (Potchefstroom: Institute for Reformational Studies, 1990), p. 57. Fowler is the author of the chapter from which the citation is taken.

39. Postman and Weingarten, *Teaching As a Subversive Activity*, p. 2.

40. In what follows I am citing a printed but unpublished version of this speech, "Beyond 1984 in Philosophy of Christian Education." See also "The Mission of the Christian College at the end of the 20th Century," *Reformed Journal* (June 1983), 17-8; "Christian Education—What Direction: An Interview with Nicholas Wolterstorff," *Dialogue* (April, 1984), 4-7; and "Teaching for Justice," Joel A. Carpenter and Kenneth W. Shipps, eds., *Making Higher Education Christian* (Grand Rapids: Eerdmans, 1987), pp. 201-30.

41. Wolterstorff develops the notion of "tendency learning" at some length in his *Educating for Responsible Action* (Grand Rapids: CSI Publications and Eerdmans, 1980).

42. Engelsma, *Reformed Education*, p. 17.

43. See particularly the conclusion of his *Dialogue* interview, p. 7.

44. "The Mission of the Christian College," p. 17.

45. See Schlossberg, *Idols for Destruction*, chapter 2, "Idols of Humanity."

46. William Stringfellow, *Dissenter in a Great Society: A Christian View of America in Crisis* (New York: Holt, Rinehart and Winston, 1966), p. 162.

47. Herbert London, *Why Are They Lying to Our Children?* (New York: Stein and Day, 1987).

48. Wolterstorff, "The Mission of the Christian College," p. 17.

49. Daniel J. Singal, "The Other Crisis in Education," *The Atlantic Monthly* (November 1991), pp. 59-74.

50. I have borrowed this expression from a document developed by an ad hoc CSI committee wrestling with the question of Reformed and Christian identity in CSI schools. Discussions over

more than a year's time with fellow committee members Sheri Haan, Glen Walstra, Mark Hiskes, Sheryl Wiers, Ray VanderLaan, and Steven Vryhof have been very stimulating and helpful to me in my writing of this manuscript. I gladly acknowledge my debt to them here.

    51. See Bolt, *Christian and Reformed Today*, pp. 120-21.

Chapter 4. The Christian Mind: Necessary But Not Sufficient

    1. See Paul F. Persons, *Inside America's Christian Schools* (Macon, Ga.: Mercer University Press, 1987). Parsons raises and partly answers the conventional objection: "This growing popularity of Christian schools inevitably raises the question of racism. Indisputably, racial prejudice served as a motive in the establishment of many 'Christian' schools, especially in the South where the courts first began the process of dismantling a dual public school system. Yet it is simplistic to conclude that all Christian schools today are racially motivated." (p. xii-xiii).

    2. The section that follows is adapted from John Bolt, "Christian Education: A Beacon for Life," a speech given to the annual convention of Christian Schools International, in Victoria, British Columbia, August 11, 1985. An excerpt appeared in *Christian Home and School*, October 1985, pp. 9-11.

    3. Henry Zwaanstra, *Reformed Thought and Experience in a New World* (Kampen: J. H. Kok, 1973), p. 64.

    4. John De Jager, "The Christian School and American Society," *Christian Educators Journal* (March 1973), 5. The article originally appeared in *Religion and Culture*, Vol. 1, No. 3, 1919.

    5. Ibid., pp. 7-9.

    6. Ibid., p. 7.

    7. The objection has in recent years surfaced with full vigor in the Canadian Province of Ontario in opposition to the extension of government funding to separate Roman Catholic high schools, and one still hears complaints about the "isolation" of Christian schools, especially in Canada.

    8. See James Edward Hakes, "A Comparison of Freshmen at Calvin College from Protestant Day School and Public School Backgrounds Relative to Bible Knowledge, Value-orientation and Dogmatism," Ed.D. Dissertation, University of Pittsburgh, 1967. A key

conclusion of Hake's study: "There is no statistically significant difference, at the .05 level of confidence, between the male [and female] student from the church-related schools and the male [female] students from public schools in value orientation as measured by the *Differential Values Inventory.*"

9. Arnold De Graaf, "Return to Basics: Temptation and Challenge," *Christian Educators Journal*, 17, #4 (March/April 1978), 23.

10. Steven Vryhof, "Christian Schools: Ripe for Change (I)," *The Banner* (September 9, 1991), 7. These categories may be borrowed from Harro Van Brummelen, *Telling The Next Generation: Educational Development in North American Calvinist Christian Schools* (Lanham, Md.: University Press of America, 1986), chapter 10, "Isolation, Conformation, or Transformation."

11. For our purposes in this study it is not necessary to define "worldview" with any great precision or to distinguish it carefully from "philosophy" or "theology." I simply have in mind a *thoughtful* (therefore primarily but not exclusively *cognitive*), comprehensive view of human life in relation to God, the world and other humans. There is a significant and growing body of literature on worldview both from a Christian and non-Christian perspective. See Ninian Smart, *Worldviews: Crosscultural Explorations of Human Beliefs* (New York: Scribners, 1983); Harry Blamires, *The Christian Mind: How Should a Christian Think?* (Ann Arbor: Servant Books, 1978; Arthur F. Holmes, *Contours of a Worldview* (Grand Rapids: Eerdmans, 1983); Brian J. Walsh and J. Richard Middleton, *The Transforming Vision: Shaping a Christian WorldView* (Downers Grove: IVP, 1984); Nicholas Wolterstorff, *Reason within the Bounds of Religion*, 2nd ed. (Grand Rapids: Eerdmans, 1984); and Albert M. Wolters, *Creation Regained: Biblical Basis for a Reformational Worldview* (Grand Rapids: Eerdmans, 1985). A classic in the Reformed tradition is, of course, Abraham Kuyper's famous Stone Lectures of 1898, *Lectures on Calvinism* (Grand Rapids: Eerdmans, 1931). An interesting attempt to articulate the worldview of the Bible itself primarily through its symbols is James B. Jordon, *Through New Eyes: Developing a Biblical View of the World* (Brentwood, Tenn: Wolgemuth & Hyatt, 1988).

12. The text is John 8:32. Most often overlooked by secular educators who cite the proverb is Jesus' qualifying contention, "If you hold to my teaching, you are really my disciples. Then you will know the truth, and the truth shall set you free." In the Gospel of John it is, of course, Jesus himself who is the truth.

13. Arthur F. Holmes, *All Truth Is God's Truth* (Grand Rapids: Eerdmans, 1977), pp. 8, 11.

14. There is a growing body of literature on these topics. General studies include Harold Heie and David L. Wolfe, eds., *The Reality of Christian Learning: Strategies for Faith-Discipline Integration* (Grand Rapids: Christian University Press, 1987); Joel Carpenter and Kenneth Shipps, eds., *Making Higher Education Christian* (Grand Rapids: Christian University Press, 1987); and Arthur F. Holmes, *Faith Seeks Understanding* (Grand Rapids: Eerdmans, 1971). More specific studies can be found in the Christian College Coalition Series of books published by Harper & Row: *Biology through the Eyes of Faith*, by Richard T. Wright (1989); *History through the Eyes of Faith*, by Ronald A. Wells (1989); *Literature through the Eyes of Faith*, by Susan V. Gallagher and Roger Lundin (1989); *Psychology through the Eyes of Faith*, by David G. Myers and Malcolm A. Jeeves (1987); *Business through the Eyes of Faith*, by Richard C. Chewning, John Eby, and Shirley Roels (1990); and *Sociology through the Eyes of Faith*, by David A. Fraser and Tony Campolo (1991). Another series of books sponsored by the Institute for Advanced Christian Studies (IFACS), edited by Carl F. H. Henry and published by William B. Eerdmans Publishing Company (Grand Rapids) includes the following: *Contours of a World View*, by Arthur F. Holmes (1983); *Christianity and Philosophy*, by Keith E. Yandell (1984); *The Person in Psychology*, by Mary Stewart Van Leeuwen (1985). Mention should also be made here of the Turning Point Christian Worldview Series, edited by Marvin Olasky and published by Crossway Books, Wheaton, Il. including *Turning Point: A Christian Worldview Declaration* by Herbert Schlossberg and Marvin Olasky (1987); *Prodigal Press: The Anti-Christian Bias of the American News Media*, by Marvin Olasky (1988); *Freedom, Justice, and Hope: Toward a Strategy for the Poor and the Oppressed*, by Marvin Olasky, Herbert Schlossberg, Pierre Berthoud, and Clark H. Pinnock (1988); *Beyond Good Intentions: A Biblical View of Politics*, by Doug Bandow (1988); *Prosperity and Poverty: The Compassionate Use of Resources in a World of Scarcity*, by E. Calvin Beisner (1988); *The Seductive Image: A Christian Critique of the World of Film*, by K. L. Billingsley (1989); *All God's Children and Blue Suede Shoes: Christians and Popular Culture*, by Kenneth A. Myers (1989); *A World without Tyranny: Christian Faith and International Politics*, by Dean C. Curry (1990); *Prospects for Growth: A Biblical View of Population, Resources and the Future*, by E. Calvin Beisner (1990); *More Than Kindness: A Compassionate Approach to Crisis Childbearing*, by Susan Olasky and Marvin Olsasky (1990); *Reading between the Lines: A Christian Guide*

to Literature, by Gene Edward Veith, Jr., (1990); State of the Arts: From Bezalel to Mapplethorpe, by Gene Edward Veith, Jr. (1991); Recovering the Lost Tools of Learning: An Approach to Distinctively Christian Education, by Douglas Wilson (1991).

15. Blamires, The Christian Mind, pp. 3, 4, 13, 16.

16. See, for example, the illuminating debate between Ronald H. Nash and Eric H. Beversluis, Economic Justice and the State, Christian College Coalition Study Guides, Vol. 1, Edited by John A. Bernbaum, (Grand Rapids and Washington, D.C.: Baker and Christian College Coalition, 1986).

17. See, for example, Robert Schoone-Jongen, "Censorship in Christian Schools," Christian Educators Journal 26/3 (February-March, 1987), 16-17.

18. Bloom, The Closing of the American Mind, p. 196.

19. Interestingly, Dr. Hilda Neatby made a similar point about Canadian education some forty years ago in her devastating critique So Little for the Mind (Toronto: Clarke Irwin, 1953).

20. Bloom, The Closing of the American Mind, p. 59.

21. Dawson, The Crisis of Western Education, pp. 99, 150.

22. Holmes, All Truth Is God's Truth, p. 4.

23. Ibid., pp. 4-8.

24. Ibid., p. 10.

25. Edward E. Ericson Jr., "Full schools, empty heads?" Reformed Journal 37, #9 (September, 1987), p. 30.

26. Blamires, The Christian Mind, p. 71.

27. Richard M. Weaver, Ideas Have Consequences (Chicago and London: University of Chicago Press, 1948).

28. William Harry Jellema, "Calvinism and Higher Education," God-Centered Living (Grand Rapids: Baker, 1951), p. 125. I am indebted to Professor Nicholas Wolterstorff's speech to the Ontario Christian School Teacher's Convention in October 1984, "Beyond 1984, in Philosophy of Christian Education" (unpublished), for this quotation from Jellema and for the stimulation to develop the argument in this section of the chapter.

29. Kuyper, Lectures on Calvinism, pp. 11-12.

30. Wolterstorff, "Beyond 1984, in Philosophy of Christian Education," p. 4.

31. John Van Dyk, The Beginning of Wisdom, Section 3. (Grand

Rapids: Christian Schools International, 1965).

32. H. Richard Niebuhr, *Christ and Culture* (New York: Harper & Row, 1951).

33. *From Vision to Action: The Basis and Purpose of Christian Schools* (Grand Rapids: Christian Schools International, 1993), pp. 5-9. It will be noted that this statement tends to be more a theological type of statement than a philosophical one. In response to this objection, if it is that, it should be remembered that worldviews are not the same as well-articulated philosophies, they tend to be more general expressions of belief. Furthermore, Reformed Christians in particular tend not to create as large a gulf between philosophy and theology as do Roman Catholic thinkers, for example. The statement given here, it must be noted, is hardly exhaustive; it is only a first word. Much more can be and needs to be said.

34. Wolterstorff, *Educating for Responsible Action*, pp. 13-14.

35. Wolterstorff, "Beyond 1984," p. 21.

36. Ibid., p. 19.

37. Ibid., p. 22.

38. Ibid., pp. 24-25. A fuller discussion of these strategies can be found in Wolterstorff's, *Educating for Responsible Action*, especially Part Two: "Strategies for Tendency Learning."

39. Ibid., p. 22. Wolterstorff himself makes use of an extensive analysis of the structures of wealth and poverty in a volume which has as its final goal the praxis of justice. See *Until Justice and Peace Embrace* (Grand Rapids: Eerdmans, 1983), Chapter II, "The Modern World-Systems?" What is noteworthy here is that Wolterstorff even contends that while praxis-oriented theory is necessary, purely theoretical knowledge also has its *intrinsic* worth. "Not every legitimate *logos* is the *logos* of a praxis. Understanding, comprehension, knowledge—these too constitute a fulfillment of our created nature. The grasp that the theorist can provide of ourselves and of the reality in the midst of which we live—of its unifying structure and its explanatory principles—is a component of the shalom that God meant for us. Where such knowledge is absent life is withered" (p. 171).

40. Ibid., p. 19. See also *Until Justice and Peace Embrace*, Chapter VI, "A City of Delight," and Chapter VII, "Justice and Worship: The Tragedy of Liturgy in Reformed Worship." I have made a similar point in *Christian and Reformed Today*, pp. 119-20, in a section on "Joy in Learning": "It is the task of the Christian School and the

Christian teacher to assist students in the joy of discovering that this world is God's world. This means concretely that teachers must delight (take joy in) their subject matter and radiate the joy of the Lord in their own walk of life. Not only knowledge of subject matter but joy in it and enthusiasm for it are essential. It also means that we must not consider subjects whose primary purpose is to cultivate delight (art, music, literature) as secondary luxuries but every bit as crucial as writing, arithmetic and computer science. Christian schools may, in the next few years, especially in the face of a sluggish economy, face a real temptation to go the way of the world and to focus programs and curricula on useful courses, i.e. those that give students employable, marketable skills. In the crunch, the art, drama, and music courses and teachers might be the first ones considered expendable. This would be a serious mistake. Christian schools must not be tyrannized by what the world considers *economically* useful, at least not if there is to be joy in our learning. Christian students need to learn that there is a life-long joy in studying the humanities that cannot be measured by how much will it pay me? On this score too, Christians must resist that spirit of our age."

41. See Theodore Plantinga, *Public Knowledge and Christian Education* (Lewiston, N.Y., and Queenston, Ont.: Edwin Mellen Press, 1988). Citations that follow in the text will be to this work.

42. It should also be noted that Christian thinkers ought to be wary about jettisoning the goal for universal truth. In our relativistic culture Christians need to be vigorous defenders of some universal claims. Universality is not the prerogative of Enlightenment modernists alone.

43. It should also be noted that worldviews are not exclusively cognitive in nature. Ninian Smart (*Worldviews*) points out that worldviews have experiential, mythic, ethical, cultural, and social as well as doctrinal dimensions.

Chapter 5. The Rediscovery of Narrative

1. Hauerwas, *A Community of Character*, p. 12.

2. Bellah, *Habits of the Heart*, p. 153.

3. George F. Will, commencement address at Duke University, quoted in *Reader's Digest*, January 1992, p. 172.

4. Arthur Lerner and Ursula Malendorf, *Life Guidance through*

Literature (Chicago and London: America Library Association, 1992).

5. Elie Wiesel, *The Gates of the Forest* (New York: Holt, Rinehart and Winston, 1966). For this citation and the Hasidic story it concludes, see John Shea, *Stories of God* (Chicago: The Thomas More Press, 1978), p. 7.

6. Shea, *Stories of God*, pp. 7-9.

7. William Kilpatrick, *Why Johnny Can't Tell Right from Wrong: Moral Illiteracy and the Case for Character Education* (New York: Simon & Schuster, 1992), p. 26.

8. William G. Doty, "The Stories of Our Times," in James B. Wiggins, ed. *Religion As Story* (Lanham, Md.: University Press of America, 1975), p. 94.

9. Novak, "'Story' and Experience," in *Religion As Story*, p. 175.

10. Ibid., pp. 175-76.

11. My citations, which will be indicated in the text using the standard notation, are from *The Republic of Plato*, translated by Allan Bloom (New York: Basic Books, 1968).

12. Robin Barrow, *Plato and Education* (London, Henley and Boston: Routledge & Kegan Paul, 1976), pp. 65-66.

13. Ibid., p. 61.

14. Ibid, p. 62.

15. Ibid.

16. Ibid.

17. Ibid., p. 63.

18. For what follows in this section, I am deeply indebted to Craig Dykstra, *Vision and Character: A Christian Educator's Alternative to Kohlberg* (New York/Ramsey, N.J.: Paulist Press, 1981); Nicholas P. Wolterstorff, *Educating for Responsible Action* (Grand Rapids: Eerdmans, CSI Publications, 1980); and Stanley Hauerwas's writings, particularly *Vision and Virtue: Essays in Christian Ethical Reflection* (Notre Dame, In.: University of Notre Dame Press, 1981 [1974] and *A Community of Character* (Notre Dame & London: University of Notre Dame Press, 1981).

19. Wolterstorff, *Educating for Responsible Action*, p. 26.

20. We are not concerned at this point to examine the validity of the Kohlberg/Piaget claim about the stages themselves. For a clear and, in my judgment, fundamentally correct critique, see the Dykstra and Wolterstorff volumes referred to above. William Kil-

patrick's *Why Johnny Can't Tell Right from Wrong* is a sustained critique of the Piaget/Kohlberg model as applied to education.

21. Wolterstorff, p. 81.

22. Dykstra, *Vision and Character*, p. 2.

23. Ibid., p. 7.

24. Ibid., p. 9.

25. Wolterstorff, *Educating for Responsible Action*, p. 27.

26. Ibid., pp. 84-90.

27. Dykstra, *Vision and Character*, p. 19.

28. Ibid., p. 45.

29. Hauerwas, *Vision and Virtue*, p. 69.

30. Dykstra, *Vision and Character*, p. 59.

31. Ibid., pp. 19, 23.

32. Ibid., p. 80.

33. Ibid., p. 28.

34. Hauerwas's comments on the inadequacy of this last point are worth noting: "Our cognitive capacities as moral agents are dependent on our being timeful beings who are able to form our intentions in efficacious ways. But the very efficacy of our intentions is dependent on the content of our beliefs about ourselves, others, and our environment. In other words, our beliefs, desires, and intentions cannot be isolated as the 'motives' of our moral action where motive is understood to be independent of the description of the action as a moral action. The motive certainly cannot be thus isolated if the agent's intention is taken seriously as part of his moral activity since intentionality cannot be reduced to psychological-causal accounts of motivations." (*Vision and Virtue*, p. 78.)

35. Hauerwas, *Vision and Virtue*, p. 74.

36. Kilpatrick, *Why Johnny Can't Tell Right from Wrong*, p. 17.

37. Published by Houghton Mifflin, Boston, 1989. References that follow in the text are to this work.

38. See Gabriel Fackre, "Narrative Theology: An Overview," *Interpretation*, 37 (1983), 340: "We begin our inquiry sobered by Johann Batist Metz's comment on the damage done to narrative when it is 'pinned and classified like a butterfly in a collector's case.' After all, is not the rediscovery of story bound up with well-founded doubts about the inordinate claims of discursive thought? Yet the art of

theological storytelling today is recommended and expounded in tracts and tomes of intricate analysis. And irony upon irony, a systematic theologian is doing this introduction. But with the same author who warns us about the risks of pinning butterflies, we believe that 'there is a time for storytelling and a time for argument.'" The reference in this citation is to Johann B. Metz, *Faith in History and Society*, trans. David Smith (New York: The Seabury Press, 1980), pp. 216 and 209.

39. Ibid., p. 341.

40. Donald Polkinghorne, *Narrative Knowing and the Human Sciences* (Albany, N.Y.: SUNY Press, 1988), pp. 17-18.

41. Ibid., p. 17. Polkinghorne cites cognitive psychologist Jerome Bruner, who suggests that "narrative understood is itself one of two basic intelligences or modes of cognitive functioning. There are two modes of cognitive functioning, two modes of thought, each providing distinctive ways of ordering experience, of constructing reality. The two (though complementary) are irreducible to one another. . . . Each of the ways of knowing, moreover, has operating principles of its own and its own criteria of well-formedness. They differ radically in their procedures for verification." Citation is from Jerome Bruner, *Actual Minds: Possible Worlds* (Cambridge, Mass.: Harvard University Press, 1986), p. 11.

42. The notion of scripts in counseling has been used extensively by the founder of transactional analysis, Eric Berne, who claims, "Script theory is based on the belief that people make conscious life plans in childhood or early adolescence which influence and make predictable the rest of their lives." In Claude M. Steiner, *Scripts People Live* (New York: Grove Press, 1974), p. 23, cited by John C. Hoffman, *Law, Freedom, and Story: The Role of Narrative in Therapy, Society and Faith* (Waterloo, Ont.: Wilfred Laurier University Press, 1986), p. 43.

43. Polkinghorne, *Narrative Knowing*, p. 11.

44. Hauerwas, "Story and Theology," *Religion in Life*, XLV, 3 (1976), 344.

45. Hoffmann, *Law, Freedom, and Story*, pp. 66-67.

46. A classic essay arguing this point is Stephen Crites, "The Narrative Quality of Experience," *Journal of the American Academy of Religion*, 39 (1971), 291-311, and reprinted in S. Hauerwas and L. G. Jones, *Why Narrative: Readings in Narrative Theology* (Grand Rapids: Eerdmans, 1989), pp. 65-88.

47. Hoffman, *Law, Freedom and Story*, p. 68.

48. Sallie TeSelle, "The Experience of Coming to Belief," *Theology Today*, XXXII, 2 (July 1975), 159-60. Cited by S. Hauerwas, "Story and Theology," 339-40.

49. Hoffman, *Law, Freedom and Story*, p. 35.

50. Ibid., p. 41.

51. For what follows, I am indebted to Gabriel Fackre, "Narrative Theology: An Overview," 343-52.

Chapter 6. The Christian Story and the Christian School

1. Michael Novak, "'Story' and Experience," *Religion As Story*, Edited by James B. Wiggins, p. 175.

2. Amos N. Wilder, *The Language of the Gospel: Early Christian Rhetoric* (New York: Harper & Row, 1964), p. 67. Cited by George Stroup, *The Promise of Narrative Theology* (Atlanta: John Knox, 1981), p. 80.

3. Shea, *Stories of God*, p. 8.

4. Calvin, *Institutes of the Christian Religion*, I.i.1.

5. Herman Bavinck, *The Sacrifice of Praise*, Translated by John Dolfin (Grand Rapids: Louis Kregel, 1922), p. 71.

6. For a helpful introduction to the idea of the *Missio Dei,* see George F. Vicedom, *The Mission of God*, Translated by Gilbert A. Thiele and Dennis Hilgendorf (St. Louis: Concordia, 1965), especially chapter I.

7. Hirsch, *Cultural Literacy*, pp. xv-xvi; xvii.

8. The classic study of this is Werner Jaeger, *Paideia*, 3 vols., Translated by Gilbert Highet (Oxford: Basil Blackwell, 1939-63).

9. See Kieran Egan, *Teaching As Story Telling* (Chicago: University of Chicago Press, 1989 [1986]).

10. Ibid., p. 113.

11. For an example, see *The Myth of God Incarnate*, edited by John Hick (Philadelphia: Westminster, 1977). For an example of one evangelical theologian who does use the word <u>myth</u> while insisting upon the factual, historical reality of such events as the incarnation and resurrection, see Clark Pinnock, *Tracking the Maze* (San Francisco: Harper & Row, 1990). Pinnock leans on such British fantasy writers as Tolkien and C.S. Lewis to affirm that the gospel is a

"myth made fact," "the quintessential fairy tale" (p. 163). His concern is that the gospel not be reduced to "brute facts" but bear the full symbolic and existential weight of myths. The mythic dimension is that which affects us, changes us, orients us.

12. I shall use the term *story* rather than *myth* in what follows, but it must be recognized that *story* has many of the same potential pitfalls. Think, for example, how often suspicions of falsehood are formulated in this fashion: "Are you telling me the truth or a 'story'?"

13. Egan, *Teaching As Story Telling*, p. 108.

14. Ibid., pp. 108-9.

15. See The Story of God and His People (Grand Rapids: CSI, 1989).

16. Plato, *Republic*, 378 D.

17. Kilpatrick, *Why Johnny Can't Tell Right from Wrong*, p. 24.

18. Ibid., p. 26.

19. Kilpatrick begins his eleventh chapter, "Life Is a Story," with the opening line from Charles Dickens' *David Copperfield*: "Whether I shall turn out to be the hero of my own life, or whether that station will be held by anybody else, these pages must show."

20. Ibid., p. 191.

21. Egan, *Teaching As Story Telling*, p. 14.

22. Ibid., p. 65.

23. Ibid., p. 2.

24. Ibid., p. 2.

25. Ibid., p. 17. The chief culprit here, according to Egan, is Piaget. Ironically, Egan concludes that "most of the inferences one sees in education from his [Piaget's] learning/development theory concern what children cannot do." (p. 22)

26. Ibid., p. 108.

27. Perhaps the most successful example of this genre is Dave Hunt and T. A. McMahon's *The Seduction of Christianity: Spiritual Discernment in the Last Days* (Eugene, Oreg.: Harvest, 1985). Other significant volumes include Constance Cumbey's *The Hidden Dangers of the Rainbow* (Shreveport, La..: Huntington House, 1983) and Tex Marrs' *Dark Secrets of the New Age* (Westchester, Ill.: Crossway, 1987).

28. Bob and Gretchen Passantino, *Witch Hunt* (Nashville:

Thomas Nelson, 1990). The Passantinos' analysis and calls for proper balanced spiritual discernment are a necessary and welcome antidote to some of the careless hysteria that is all too evident elsewhere in this controversy.

29. Hunt and McMahon, *The Seduction of Christianity*, p. 12. The Passantinos rightly note that "This definition is so broad that Christians and even the Lord himself could be sorcerers! God is Spirit (John 4:24) and his mind certainly has mastery over the material world. Is he a sorcerer? Scripture commands Christians to pray, using their minds and spirits to participate in God's intervention in the world. Is prayer sorcery?" (*Witch Hunt*, p. 92).

30. Ibid., p. 25.

31. Ibid., p. 33.

32. Two succinct and reliable accounts can be found in Ruth A. Tucker, *Another Gospel: Alternative Religions and the New Age Movement* (Grand Rapids: Zondervan, 1989), pp. 330—331; and Douglas R. Groothuis, *Confronting the New Age* (Downers Grove, Ill.: 1988), pp. 180-87.

33. Groothuis, *Confronting the New Age*, p. 180.

34. Tucker, *Another Gospel*, pp. 330-31.

35. Groothuis, *Confronting the New Age*, pp. 180-81.

36. I have loosely borrowed this understanding of imagination from the German idealist philosopher Immanuel Kant's definition: "*Imagination* is the faculty of representing in intuition an object that is *not itself present.*" Immanuel Kant, *Critique of Pure Reason*, Translated by Norman Kemp Smith (New York: St. Martin's Press, 1968), B 151; cited by Garrett Green, *Imagining God: Theology and the Religious Imagination* (New York: Harper & Row, 1989), p. 62.

37. For example, Cheryl Forbes, *Imagination: Embracing a Theology of Wonder* (Portland, Oreg.: Multnomah, 1986), pp. 18-19: "Imagination is the *imago Dei* in us. It marks us as God's creatures. It helps us know God, receive his grace, worship him, and see life through his eyes. That means, imagination is a way of seeing life— or ways of seeing life. . . . As C.S. Lewis put it, imagination is 'the organ of meaning.' All the information we receive about God, our responsibility as his stewards, our roles as husbands, wives, sons, daughters, siblings, employers, or employees are so much dust without imagination to help us act on the information." See also Garrett Green, *Imagining God: Theology and the Religious Imagination* (San Francisco: Harper San Francisco, 1989), Ch. 5, "The Image of God:

The Meaning of Revelation."

38. One biblical scholar's interpretation of Israel's exile prophecies is appropriately entitled "hopeful imagination." See Walter Brueggemann, *Hopeful Imagination: Prophetic Voices in Exile* (Philadelphia: Fortress, 1986).

39. For a thorough overview of Christian fantasy, see Colin Marlowe, *Christian Fantasy from 1200 to the Present* (Notre Dame, Ind.: University of Notre Dame Press, 1992).

40. Cited by Douglas Groothuis, *Confronting the New Age*, p. 186.

41. Ibid.

42. Ibid., p. 185.

43. Ibid., p. 186.

44. For what follows, I am indebted to William Kilpatrick, *Why Johnny Can't Tell Right from Wrong*, ch. 12, "Myth Wars."

45. Ibid., p. 207.

46. Ibid., p. 208. The duality of these two visions, as applied to the political realm, is explored with characteristic brilliance by Thomas Sowell in *A Conflict of Visions* (New York: W. Morrow, 1987). Sowell distinguishes between what he calls the constrained vision (Kilpatrick's moral imagination) from the unconstrained vision (idyllic or utopian imagination).

47. Ibid., p. 209.

48. Bruno Bettelheim, *The Uses of Enchantment: The Meaning and Importance of Fairy Tales* (New York: Vintage Books, 1977, p. 9.

49. Ibid., p. 11.

50. Kilpatrick, *Why Johnny Can't Tell Right from Wrong*, pp. 209-10.

51. Ibid., p. 210.

52. Ibid, p. 216.

53. Ibid., p. 217.

54. See discussion on the "threat" of "prophecy," pp. 111-19.

Bibliography

Adams, Lawrence E. "The SCC at Canberra: Which Spirit?" *First Things* (June/July 1991): 30.

Baer, Richard A. "American Public Education and the Myth of Value Neutrality." *Democracy and the Renewal of Public Eduction.* Encounter Series #4. Grand Rapids: Eerdmans, 1987.

Barrow, Robin. *Plato and Education.* London, Henley and Boston: Routledge & Kegan Paul, 1976.

Bavinck, Herman. *The Sacrifice of Praise.* Translated by John Dolfin. Grand Rapids: Louis Kregel, 1922.

Bellah, Robert, et al. *Habits of the Heart: Individualism and Commitment in American Life.* New York: Harper & Row, 1986.

Berger, Peter. *Facing Up to Modernity.* New York: Basic Books, 1977.

Bering-Jensen, Helle. "A Hell-Bent Crusade Against Pornography." *Insight,* 2 (July 1990): 12.

Bettelheim, Bruno. *The Uses of Enchantment: The Meaning and Importance of Fairy Tales.* New York: Vintage Books, 1977.

Bibby, Reginald. *Mosaic Madness: The Poverty and Potential of Life in Canada.* Toronto: Stoddart, 1990.

Blamires, Harry. *The Christian Mind: How Should a Christian Think?* Ann Arbor: Servant Books: 1978.

Bloesch, Donald G. *Crumbling Foundations: Death and Rebirth in an Age of Upheaval.* Grand Rapids: Zondervan, 1984.

Bloom, Allan. *The Closing of the American Mind.* New York: Simon & Schuster, 1987.

Bolt, John. *Christian and Reformed Today.* Jordan Station, Ont.: Paideia Press, 1984.

Burnham, James. *Suicide of the West.* Chicago: Regnery Books, 1985.

Calvin, John. *Institutes of the Christian Religion.* Edited by John T. MacNeil. Translated by Ford L. Battles. Volume 2 of Library of Christian Classics. Philadelphia: Westminster, 1960.

Chubb, John E., and Terry M. Moe. *Politics, Markets, and Americaís Schools.* Washington, D. C.: The Brookings Institution, 1990.

Coles, Robert. *The Call of Stories: Teaching and the Moral Imagination.* Boston: Houghton Mifflin, 1989.

Colson, Charles, with Ellen Santilli Vaughan. *Against the Night: Living in the New Dark Ages.* Ann Arbor: Servant, 1989.

Cox, Harvey. *The Secular City.* Rev. ed. New York: MacMillan, 1966.

Dawson, Christopher. *The Crisis of Western Education.* New York: Sheed & Ward, 1961.

DeGraaf, Arnold. "Return to Basics: Temptation and Challenge." *Christian Educators Journal* No. 17, 4 (March/April 1978): 7, 23-5.

Doty, William G. "The Stories of Our Times." In *Religion As Story.* Edited by James B. Wiggins. Lanham, Md.: University Press of America, 1975.

Dykstra, Craig. *Vision and Character: A Christian Educator's Alternative to Kohlberg.* New York and Ramsey, N.J.: Paulist Press, 1981.

Egan, Kieran. *Teaching As Story Telling.* Chicago: University of Chicago Press, 1989.

Ellul, Jacques. *The Technological Society.* Translated by John Wilkinson. New York: Vintage, 1964.

Engelsma, David. *Reformed Education.* South Holland, Ill.: The Federation of Protestant Reformed School Societies, 1977.

Ericson, Ed. Review of *The Closing of the American Mind,* by Allan Bloom. In *Reformed Journal* (September 1987): 35.

Fackre, Gabriel. "Narrative Theology: An Overview." In *Interpretation 37* (1983): 340-52.

Fowler, S.; H. W. VanBrummelen; and J. VanDyk. *Christian Schooling: Education for Freedom.* Potchefstroom: Institute for Reformational Studies, 1990.

Griffiths, Daniel E. "The Crisis in American Education." *The Education Digest* 48 (May 1983): 10.

Gross, Beatrice, and Ronald Gross, eds. *The Great School Debate: Which Way for American Education.* New York: Simon & Schuster, 1985.

Groothuis, Douglas R. *Confronting the New Age.* Downers Grove, Ill.: Intervarsity, 1988.

Harrinton, Michael. *The Politics at God's Funeral: The Spiritual Crisis of Western Civilization.* New York: Holt, Rinehart and Winston, 1983.

Hauerwas, Stanley. *A Community of Character*. Notre Dame, Ind.: University of Notre Dame Press, 1980.

Hauerwas, Stanley, and William Willimon. *Resident Aliens*. Nashville: Abingdon, 1989.

Hauerwas, Stanley. *Vision and Virtue: Essays in Christian Ethical Reflection*. Notre Dame, Inc.: University of Notre Dame Press, 1981.

Hauerwas, Stanley. "Story and Theology." *Religion in Life* 45, 3 (1976): 339-50.

Hirsch, E. D., Jr. *Cultural Literacy: What Every American Needs to Know*. Boston: Houghton Mifflin, 1987.

Hirsch, E. D., Jr.; Joseph F. Kett; and James Trefil. *The Dictionary of Cultural Literacy: What Every American Needs to Know*. Boston: Houghton Mifflin, 1988.

Hoffman, John C. *Law, Freedom, and Story: The Role of Narrative in Therapy, Society and Faith*. Waterloo, Ont.: Wilfred Laurier University Press, 1986.

Holland, Jeffrey R. "A Nation at Risk: The Greater Crisis in American Education." *American Educator* 20 (June, 1984): 19.

Holmes, Arthur F. *All Truth Is God's Truth*. Grand Rapids: Eerdmans, 1977.

Hooks, Sidney. "Education in Defense of a Free Society." *Commentary* (July 1984): 17-22.

Hunt, Dave, and T. A. McMahon. *The Seduction of Christianity: Spiritual Discernment in the Last Days*. Eugene, Oreg.: Harvest, 1985.

Hunter, James Davison. *Culture Wars: The Struggle to Define America*. New York: Basic Books, 1991.

Jellema, William Harry. "Calvinism and Higher Education." In *God-Centered Living*. Grand Rapids: Baker, 1951.

Kilpatrick, William K. *Why Johnny Can't Tell Right from Wrong: Moral Illiteracy and the Case for Character Education*. New York: Simon & Schuster, 1992.

Kreeft, Peter. "'Darkness at Noon': The Eclipse of 'The Permanent Things,'" *Faith and Reason* 17 (1991): 51-85.

Kuyper, Abraham. *Lectures on Calvinism*. Grand Rapids: Eerdmans, 1931.

Lerner, Arthur, and Ursula Malendorf. *Life Guidance through Literature*. Chicago and London: America Library Association, 1992.

London, Herbert. *Why Are They Lying to Our Children?* New York: Stein and Day, 1987.

MacIntyre, Alasdair. After Virtue: *A Study in Moral Virtue.* 2nd ed. Notre Dame, Ind.: University of Notre Dame Press, 1984.

Mitchell, Richard. *The Leaning Tower of Babel.* Boston: Little, Brown, 1984.

Muggeridge, Malcolm. *Christ and the Media.* Grand Rapids: Eerdmans, 1978.

Nash, Ronald H. *The Closing of the American Heart: What's Really Wrong with America's Schools.* Dallas, Tex.: Probe Books, 1990.

Neuhaus, Richard John. *The Naked Public Square: Religion and Democracy in America.* Grand Rapids: Eerdmans, 1984.

Newbigin, Lesslie. *Foolishness to the Greeks: The Gospel and Western Culture.* Grand Rapids: Eerdmans, 1986.

Niebuhr, Richard. *Christ and Culture.* New York: Harper & Row, 1951.

Novak, Michael. "'Story' and Experience." In *Religion As Story.* Edited by James B. Wiggins. Lanham, Md.: University Press of America, 1975.

Oronowitz, Stanley, and Henry Giroux. *Education under Siege: The Conservative, Liberal, and Radical Debate over Schooling.* South Hadley, Mass.: Begen & Garvey, 1985.

"One Nation, Under God: Has the Separation of Church and State Gone Too Far?" *Time* (December 9, 1991): 60-68.

Passantino, Bob, and Gretchen Passantino. *Witch Hunt.* Nashville: Thomas Nelson, 1990.

Pelikan, Jaroslav. *The Emergence of the Catholic Tradition.* Volume 1 of *The Christian Tradition.* Chicago and London: University of Chicago Press, 1971.

Plantinga, Theodore. *Public Knowledge and Christian Education.* Lewiston, N. Y. and Queenston, Ont.: Edwin Mellen Press, 1988.

Polkinghorne, Donald. *Narrative Knowing and the Human Sciences.* Albany, N. Y.: SUNY Press, 1988.

Postman, Neil, and Charles Weingartner. *Teaching As a Subversive Activity.* New York: Delacorte, 1969.

Postman, Neil. *Teaching As a Conserving Activity.* New York: Dell, 1979.

Postman, Neil, and Camille Paglia. "She Wants Her T.V.! He Wants

His Book!" A dinner conversation between Neil Postman and Camille Paglia. *Harper's Magazine* (March, 1991): 44-55.

Postman, Neil. *Amusing Ourselves to Death: Public Discourse in the Age of Show Business.* New York: Penguin, 1985.

Powers, Ron. "The Cool Dark Telegenuis of Robert Pittman." In *The Beast, the Eunuch and the Glass-Eyed Child.* San Diego: Harcourt Brace Jovanovich, 1990.

Radwanski, George, "Ontario Study of the Relevance of Education and the Issue of Dropouts." Ontario, Canada, Ministry of Education report. February 15, 1988.

Ravitch, Diane. "The Continuing Crisis: Fashions in Education." *American Scholar* 53 (Spring 1984): 183-93.

Ravitch, Diane. "Forgetting the Questions: The Problems of Educational Reform." In *The Schools We Deserve: Reflections on the Educational Crises of Our Time.* New York: Basic Books, 1985.

Ravitch, Diane. *The Revisionists Revised: A Critique of the Radical Attack on the Schools.* New York: Basic Books, 1978.

Reisman, David, with Reuel Denney and Nathan Glazer. *The Lonely Crowd: A Study of the Changing Americn Character.* New Haven, Conn.: Yale University Press, 1950.

Rose, Susan D. *Keeping Them Out of the Hands of Satan: Evangelical Schooling in America.* New York and London: Routledge, 1988.

Ross, Andrew. *Universal Abandon: The Politics of Post-Modernism.* Winnipeg, Man.: University of Manitoba Press, 1988.

Schlesinger, Arthur M., Jr. *The Disuniting of America: Reflections on a Multicultural Society.* Knoxville, Tenn.: Whittle Books, 1991.

Schlossberg, Herbert. *Idols for Destruction: Christian Faith and Its Confrontation with American Society.* Nashville, Tenn.: Thomas Nelson, 1983.

Schultze, Quentin J. *Redeeming Television.* Downer's Grove, Ill.: Inter Varsity Press, 1992.

Shea, John. *Stories of God.* Chicago: The Thomas More Press, 1978.

Singal, Daniel J. "The Other Crisis in Education." *The Atlantic Monthly* Vol. 286, No. 5 (November 1991): 59-74.

Sloat, Donald E. *The Dangers of Growing Up in a Christian Home.* Nashville, Tenn.: Thomas Nelson, 1986.

Solzhenitsyn, Alexander. *Warning to the Western World.* London: The Bodley Head and the British Broadcasting Corporation, 1976.

Solzhenitsyn, Alexander. *A World Split Apart*. Commencement address delivered at Harvard University, June 8, 1978. New York: Harper & Row, 1978.

Stringfellow, William. *Dissenter in a Great Society: A Christian View of America in Crisis*. New York: Holt, Rinehart and Winston, 1966.

TeSelle, Sallie. "The Experience of Coming to Belief." *Theology Today* 32, 2 (July 1975): 159-66.

"The Christian School and American Society." In *Christian Educators Journal* (March 1973): 5.

"Tough Choice." In *Time* (September 16, 1991): 54-61.

Tucker, Ruth A. *Another Gospel: Alternative Religions and the New Age Movement*. Grand Rapids: Zondervan, 1989.

VanDyk, John. *The Beginning of Wisdom: The Nature and Task of the Christian School*. Grand Rapids: Christian Schools International, 1985.

Vryhof, Steven. "Christian Schools: Ripe for Change (I)." *The Banner* (September 9, 1991): 6-7.

Vryhof, Steven, et al. *12 Affirmations: Reformed Christian Schooling for the 21st Century*. Grand Rapids: Baker, 1989.

Weaver, Richard M. *Ideas Have Consequences*. Chicago and London: University of Chicago Press, 1948.

Wiesel, Elie. *The Gates of the Forest*. New York: Holt, Rinehart and Winston, 1966.

Wilder, Amos N. *The Language of the Gospel: Early Christian Rhetoric*. New York: Harper & Row, 1964.

Wilson, Douglas. *Recovering the Lost Tools of Learning: An Approach to Distinctively Christian Education*. Wheaton, Ill.: Crossway, 1991.

Wolterstorff, Nicholas. "Christian Education—What Direction: An Interview with Nicholas Wolterstorff." *Dialogue* (April, 1984): 4-7.

Wolterstorff, Nicholas. *Educating for Responsible Action*. Grand Rapids: CSI Publications and Eerdmans, 1980.

Woodring, Paul. "School Criticism in the 1950s and 1970s." *The Education Digest* 51 (November 1985): 160.

Zwaanstra, Henry. *Reformed Thought and Experience in a New World*. Kampen: J. H. Kok, 1973.

Zylstra, Henry. *Testament of Vision*. Grand Rapids: Eerdmans, 1958.